KIN

Politics in Britain and the United States

Politics

in Britain and the United States

Comparative Perspectives

Edited by Richard Hodder-Williams and James Ceaser

Duke University Press   Durham 1986

© 1986, Duke University Press
All rights reserved
Printed in the United States of America
on acid-free paper ∞
Library of Congress Cataloging in Publication Data
Politics in Britain and the United States.
Bibliography: p.
Includes index.
1. Great Britain—Politics and government—Addresses,
essays, lectures.   2. United States—Politics and
government—Addresses, essays, lectures.   I. Hodder-
Williams, Richard.   II. Ceaser, James W.
JN125.P65   1986   320.941   86-2121
ISBN 0-8223-0525-9 (alk. paper)

IN MEMORY OF PHILIP WILLIAMS

Contents

Introduction

For many years, political analysts in the United Kingdom and the United States have been fascinated with the political institutions and practices of the "other" land, and some of the most perceptive writings on these nations' politics has been done by non-natives. Hence, in the summer of 1984, four hundred years after the first settlers from Britain landed on what is now Roanoke Island in North Carolina, the British and American contributors to this volume welcomed the opportunity offered by Duke University and the North Carolina Department of Cultural Resources to address the issues as part of a jointly sponsored British-American Festival. At a conference on the political systems of Great Britain and the United States sixteen scholars from both sides of the Atlantic met at Duke for an intensive series of seminars held over a two-day period. This book presents the papers that were delivered at that conference, revised in light of the lively and stimulating discussion that took place in Durham.

The point of departure of such comparative analysis as this volume represents has normally been the awareness of differences. Outsiders naturally see the contrasts and in this way each country enlightens the other as to the peculiarities of what it may take for granted. Although it has been commonly acknowledged that the two nations share a commitment to the fundamental values of popular government, the rule of law, and the protection of individual rights, the focus of scholarship has traditionally been on the ways in which we differ. In describing the political institutions of the two nations, a contrasting picture is usually drawn between the United Kingdom, with its parliamentary sovereignty, fusion of the executive and the legislature, centralized authority, disciplined and ideologically cohesive political parties, and an apolitical judiciary, on the one hand, and the United States, with its divided sovereignty, separation of the executive and the legislature, federalism, loose and ideologically inchoate political parties, and a politically active judiciary, on the other. The contrasts depicted between the political cultures of the two countries are equally great. In the United Kingdom, it is said, citizens accept a wide-ranging role for the state, are generally deferential to those in authority, structure their political activity through enduring parties, and divide along class lines; in the United States, however, it is said that citizens are generally opposed to much state involvement in economic and social matters, are suspicious of government power, structure their input into politics through group action, and divide along ethnic, regional, and religious lines which cut across class divisions.

However, there were in 1984 some specific considerations which made a comparative review of the two countries' political systems especially apposite. It seemed that on both sides of the Atlantic there were certain developments which suggested a growing similarity between the two countries: parallels in the economic strategies of President Ronald Reagan and Prime Minister Margaret Thatcher, a loosening of attachments to the parties, and the nationalizing and personalizing of politics through the ubiquitous reach of television, to mention but three. To some analysts, these and other developments offered the possibility that, despite manifest institutional and cultural differences, there was a genuine process of what might be considered a convergence of the two political systems. Indeed, some have argued that the very nature of modern industrial economies and the environment in which democratic politics takes place may almost ineluctably be driving these states along similar paths of development, making the differences between them merely decorative variations on a central theme. The essays assembled in this volume, with each focusing on one particular aspect of the political systems, implicitly address this more general thesis.

In several of the chapters there is corroborative evidence for this view and illustrations of the way in which the two nations are growing more alike than different. The most explicit expression of such a perspective is found in Jorgen Rasmussen's essay, where he writes that "by the 1980s grounds existed for thinking that the American and British systems were converging in practice . . . the powers and roles [of President and Prime Minister] have more in common than in contrast . . . the similarities do seem more striking than the differences." But there are echoes in Gary Marks's concern to contrast the broadly similar Anglo-American political economies with their European variants, in Dennis Kavanagh's initial presentation of the issues associated with the party systems, in Richard Hodder-Williams's concentration on showing the political nature of the British appeal courts, and in Anthony King's observation that "British and American politicians operate in pretty similar moral climates."

Yet, while these essays taken as a whole may challenge the starting assumption that has guided so much scholarship, it is important not to speak in simplistic terms as though an entirely new approach or paradigm was being offered. References to "similarities," if one is not careful, can prove to be highly misleading, for they are of two distinct kinds. The first kind embraces attitudes and behavior patterns which are, as a matter of observation, very nearly the same. The second focuses upon tendencies, upon the direction of change that brings one set of observed phenomena closer to another. It is in this latter sense that one may emphasize similarities between the United States and the United Kingdom in recent years. Identifying similar trends over time—say, dealignment or a growing readiness of interest groups to use litigation to advance their political programs—is quite different from asserting that the two political systems have reached a stage of functioning in broadly similar ways. Hence, the growing politicization of the judicial process and the developing presidentialism in Britain would be good examples of unmistakable trends but bad examples of contemporary similarities in actual performance.

These reflections lead to the observation that, if there is merit today in emphasizing the elements of convergence between the two political systems, it is as well still to keep in mind the often quite different baselines from which similar trends begin. Furthermore, there is the need to recognize those areas in which the two countries are obstinately different and in which one finds little or no trace of convergence. The essays in this volume, then, are not suggesting the radically novel view that the United States and the United Kingdom are converging in terms of their political systems, but they do provide a contemporary estimation of the extent to which there are growing similarities within systems retaining their distinct institutional forms and political cultures.

The book also addresses some of the most difficult and fascinating questions of comparative politics, illustrating how the comparative approach can illuminate our understanding of the politics of a single country. On the one hand, the difficulty of explaining political phenomena is highlighted by the continuous attention given to the relative significance of such factors as political and social institutions, economic and social changes, and political culture. The book points up the complexity of the interrelationships among these often tangled causes, sometimes stressing one, sometimes another. Those seeking simple explanations for recent developments in the two nations will not find them here. On the other hand, the focus on one country often throws into clear relief a distinguishing feature of the other, suggesting that explanation often depends on the absence of certain very fundamental elements that are present in the other system, such as confessional parties or widespread occupational and geographical mobility. These elements become much more observable in a comparative study.

It may be useful at this stage to abstract from the various essays the central themes of the conference to which the participants regularly returned, especially during the lengthy discussions which followed the brief presentation of each paper. Explanations for the tendency to converge alongside the enduring differences in the form and substance of political action could be categorized under three analytically separate heads. (Although they are analytically separable, in the real world of politics they interrelate in highly intricate and complicated ways.)

First, the environment in which political life took place in both the United States and the United Kingdom changed radically in the decades after the Second World War. The economic growth of the 1950s and 1960s did not continue at the same rate; social changes—educational expansion, the growth of leisure time, the decline of heavy industry, and the rise of service industries—metamorphosed the political maps of much of the electorate; technological changes, particularly those associated with the media, revolutionized the form and nature of political communication. From this perspective, the political systems of the two nations were pushed in similar directions as they responded to these major movements in the economy and society at large.

Second, the institutions and political cultures peculiar to each country largely determined the precise ways in which responses were made. It was just not sensible to explain the developments in the

United Kingdom and the United States—such as dealignment or attempted reforms in the bureaucracies—without a firm emphasis on the importance of federalism, or the separation of powers, or the sovereignty of Parliament. Nor, however, was it sensible to explain such developments without reference to the ideas and expectations held by political actors in the two countries. Precisely which factors were of crucial significance in any particular instance often depended not on some general theory of the relative importance of institutions and culture but on the details of that instance.

Third, therefore, the need to consider the details of individual political events was frequently stressed. The explanations for some actions and developments necessitated on occasion a particularist focus, not a general framework. Specific occurrences, indeed sometimes chance ones, profoundly affected the direction and timing of change as well as the style of political action and discourse.

It is important to keep these three themes separate and to avoid attributing some development to one rather than another through a failure to do so. For instance, the central importance of the Public Sector Borrowing Requirement, which became a major concern of Mrs. Thatcher's monetarist policies, originated, it should be remembered, under a Labour government. Perhaps we can best envisage the developing political systems of the United States and the United Kingdom as moving hesitantly in similar directions perpetually responding to three interlinked sources of pressure: social and technological change, the political institutions themselves together with their existing but not ossified political cultures, and the wild card of personality, chance, and accident. It would take a very complex equation indeed to provide a reliable predictive model involving these variables.

In many of the previous comparative studies of the United States and the United Kingdom, and indeed in many of the studies of one country by natives of the other, there has been a strong didactic tradition; the aim has seldom been just to explain, but rather to teach certain lessons and show how the weaknesses of one system might be alleviated by the importation of models from the other. This tendency has been particularly pronounced in the case of American students of British institutions, who, since at least the time of Woodrow Wilson, have made of the British system something of a model for American politics.[1] More recently, however, the problems encountered by successive British governments have led certain American writers to think of British approaches more in terms of measures to avoid than to emulate.[2] Learning from the "other" country has been a lesser concern to British observers.[3] The reason may have something to do with a well-known British complacency, but more likely it is a function of an intellectual tradition in Britain which divorces the academic study of politics from the offering of programmatic advice. Perhaps, too, the limited size of the political science profession in Britain when placed beside its American counterpart helps account for the difference. Yet a fascination for the United States remains. After all, the United States was torn from the British Empire, inherited many of the values and practices of the mother country, kept the English language—or, at least, a recognizable variant thereof—and became an ally of the United Kingdom and a partner in a shared alliance designed to help maintain Western Europe's security.

The essays in this volume, as well as the discussions, seem again to pose a challenge to those who believe in either the possibility or desirability of major institutional transfers between the two countries. This point was strongly made by Jorgen Rasmussen and Dennis Kavanagh, both of whom appeared to adopt the view that each political system, like the human body, had a rejection system for any implants not strictly congruent with its political blood. Yet, it is by no means clear that their position entailed an entirely defeatist position to the effect that nothing could be transplanted. To continue the analogy, hearts and lungs might create impossible difficulties; but less central organs could perhaps survive the move. Certainly the specialist committees in the House of Commons were partly modeled on the congressional committees and, although they are less powerful and less well regarded than their American counterparts, they are an important and far from irrelevant innovation in the British parliamentary system.

Some areas of a political system, it can be argued, are more autonomous than others. The greater the degree of autonomy, the greater the possibility of institutional transfer. Party systems, political career patterns, legislative links to constituents and executives, these are all highly dependent upon so many people—already deeply socialized into certain beliefs, expectations, habits of thought, and perceptions—that their form and practice must necessarily be a function of the wider evolving political universe. But the staff organization of the chief executive, the role of "inners and outers" in public administration, and the campaigning techniques of individuals may be sufficiently autonomous for change to be induced or adopted by an act of will. The Prime Minister's research unit is an obvious case in point; advertising techniques would be another; and staffing capacities of legislatures would be a third. The point is simple: one country can learn from another, but the practicality of introducing major changes into an enduring and evolving political system, whose roots are deeply embedded in the political culture of the land, is a limited one.

Traditionally, writers on either side of the Atlantic had seen virtues in the opposite system which compensated for what seemed to be shortcomings in their own; in 1984 none of the participants was so dewy-eyed as to believe that major improvements could be had by institutional transfer. Even the least revolutionary suggestions would likely have a choppy passage. "Outers," who might in theory improve the decision-making process in Whitehall and introduce there new perspectives and ideas, would have to face an ingrained suspicion of outsiders from most of the permanent civil service and many politicians; any attempt in Britain to limit the sovereignty of Parliament, through specialist committees with real power to override ministers or a Bill of Rights with the duty to rein in overexuberant legislatures, would in all probability find majorities for such changes lacking. Interestingly, there has been little recent borrowing by American idealists from the British offerings, apart from searches to make executives more accountable to the elected legislature, but that too fell foul of a deeply ingrained belief in the ultimate virtue of separated powers.

This volume, accordingly, can be read on three levels. On the first, it describes through broad interpretive essays the political systems of the two oldest English-speaking democracies as they functioned in the early 1980s. On the second level, it sheds some light on reasons both for convergence and for continuing differences between the United Kingdom and the United States. The essays point up the subtle balance that existed in both countries between a number of factors, some with deep historical roots, some embedded in cultural expectations, some reflecting immediate and pressing problems, some the whimsical effect of chance. Systems which have persisted without revolution yet without a hardening of the arteries (as have both the British and American political systems) are continually changing in rhetoric and substance as different factors in turn become especially significant. This perspective, with its emphasis on the integrated and organic nature of the two systems, is the prerequisite for any consideration of institutional transfer. On the third level, this volume addresses some very central questions in comparative politics by explaining the complex interrelationships among institutional, economic, and cultural forces in the context of two political systems with sufficient similarities to make such comparisons valuable and instructive. There is one final point to be made by way of introduction.

It is rare that scholars from two different countries have the chance to confer at leisure on so broad a topic, and some special thanks are in order to those who helped afford the opportunity. We are grateful to the British-American festival committee, and especially George Holt, Carolyn Conley, Joel Fleishman, and Richard Rowson, for their efforts in arranging so productive a seminar. Nelson Polsby kindly agreed to serve as moderator for the conference, injecting his own great wisdom and humor into the proceedings. Finally, the participants at the conference, including the large contingent of scholars from North Carolina, added greatly to the quality of the papers by their comments and suggestions. This volume is much more of a collaborative effort than most such emanations from academic conferences. We hope that the product is a fitting commemoration of the great collaborative enterprise begun on Roanoke Island four hundred years ago.

RICHARD HODDER-WILLIAMS

JAMES CEASER

1

Executive and Legislative Roles

JORGEN RASMUSSEN

In the first chapter, Jorgen Rasmussen considers one area in which
the political systems of the United States and Great Britain are sometimes thought to be converging: the growing dominance of the chief
executive. Focusing upon those concerns which interested scholars
of an earlier period who compared the two systems—preparation for
executive leadership, coordinated policy programs, and executive accountability—he argues that the similarities do seem more striking
than the differences. But the parallel is by no means simple. While
the British Prime Minister might give the appearance of dominance
within the executive and party solidarity in the legislature suggests
few difficulties from that quarter, the reality is actually a Prime Minister defeated on several issues and a legislature constantly to be
wooed. In the United States the President, too, has his failures and
must negotiate with the legislature. The institutional arrangements
and the informal conventions associated with the two systems do
vary, but the political realities have made Presidents more like Prime
Ministers and Prime Ministers more like Presidents. Even in the matter of accountability, where the British convention of ministerial responsibility was held to be qualitatively different from the divided
responsibility associated with Washington, recent events have rendered more similar the actual practice of accountability for these
chief executives. Viewed from one perspective, therefore, the operation of central government appears to be growing more similar. Yet

Rasmussen concludes, unlike other comparativists who have recommended transference of institutions from one country to the other, that successful changes in practice and institutional form must grow from internally generated forces. Although several developments in recent years happen to have drawn the two systems closer together, there is no certainty either that future developments will continue that process or that current trends will overcome the power of deeply ingrained political cultures to influence the form and style of systemic change.

The American "Innovation"

The last twenty years have seen considerable debate in both Britain and the United States about the scope of executive power. These debates have focused, however, on contrasting points in the political systems of the two countries. In the United States the concern for most of the period was whether an imperial presidency had come to dominate Congress and even threaten democracy.[1] Across the Atlantic the question was whether Britain had passed from cabinet government to prime ministerial government, that is, whether the Prime Minister had come to dominate the rest of the executive.[2] To be specific, in the United States the debate centered on legislative-executive relations, while in Britain it centered on intra-executive relations.

A primary reason for this contrast is the difference in political institutions between the two countries. Britain long has accepted the idea that the executive should dominate, or at least control, the legislature with the plural and collective nature of the executive relied upon to check arbitrary personal power. The United States, on the other hand, has accepted presidential domination of the executive and expected the separation of powers among distinct branches of government to check abuses of power. Briefly stated in historical perspective, the Prime Minister was more powerful than the President vis-à-vis the legislature, while the President was more powerful than the Prime Minister within the executive.

The common concern has been whether, despite the contrasting mechanisms relied upon, recent trends have tended in both countries to enervate the intrinsic checks on power. Interestingly, should such developments be occurring, the two systems would be converging. A growth in presidential power in relations with Congress would tend to produce legislative-executive relations more of the British type, while prime ministerial ascendency within the cabinet would move

British government in the direction of the U.S. type of intra-executive relations.

That any such convergence should have been delayed for nearly two centuries after the drafting of the U.S. Constitution is ironic because the political leaders who gathered in Philadelphia really had not sought to create an innovative political system de novo. They had revolted against the colonies' subservient status and the substance of British government policy of that time rather than against the political system as such. They looked for guidance to such theorists as Locke and Montesquieu, both of whom regarded English government as a separation of powers system. Even as late as eighty years after the Constitutional Convention Walter Bagehot felt compelled to correct the erroneous belief that the English Constitution embodied such a system.[3]

Furthermore, the practical political experience of most of the political leaders of the newly independent nation tended to reinforce such an interpretation of the English system. The political system which the early colonists had brought with them was the English system, but the English system modified for a colonial setting. It included a colonial governor—a separate executive—whose tenure in office did not depend, any more than did that of the British monarch, whose agent he was, on the preferences of the colonial legislature.

Thus in creating the American separation of powers system the Founding Fathers were seeking to retain what they regarded as one of the best features of the English system and to adapt it to American circumstances. Despite these relatively limited objectives, the American and English systems did diverge in the nineteenth century. And before that century was out three leading political theorists—one English (Walter Bagehot), one Irish (James Bryce), and one American (Woodrow Wilson)—all argued at length that the Founding Fathers had botched the job: American political institutions, especially in the matter of relations between the executive and the legislative structures, were inferior to English ones.

Space does not permit quoting their charges in detail. Suffice it to say that the perceived failings of the American system were all-encompassing. Separation of powers produced less able leaders and government policies that were not only substantively less satisfactory, but which were implemented less effectively. Furthermore, it vitiated democracy by blurring responsibility and failing to educate the people politically. Thus on leadership, policy, and accountability the English parliamentary system was better.[4]

The Course of Institutional Divergence

The publication dates of these three critiques—Bagehot, 1867; then Wilson, 1885, and Bryce, 1888—neatly bracket the formative period of the British parliamentary system as we have known it for the last century. A brief summary of the key events of the period will help to clarify how the English and American systems diverged in practice.

In 1867 the Second Reform Bill nearly doubled the electorate to 2.5 million. The same year the Conservatives founded a party organization outside Parliament. In 1872 secret ballots were instituted. In 1877 the Liberals followed the Conservative lead and created a mass party organization. Between 1877 and 1882 the procedures of the House of Commons were altered significantly—closure, guillotine motions, and limits on the ability of MPs to delay action through emergency debates were introduced—so that for the first time the government had the advantage over individual members of Parliament.[5] Bribing of electors was prohibited by the Corrupt Practices Act in 1883 and the following year the Third Reform Bill nearly doubled the electorate again to almost 6 million.

These changes eliminated the old style electoral management, which had survived the first installment of electoral reform in 1832. The huge growth of the electorate and the effective safeguards against corruption meant that voters no longer could be manipulated as individuals, but had to be appealed to as groups. The most effective appeal was one offering beneficial governmental action. Since individual MPs lacked the power to make good on such promises, like-minded ones needed to agree on programs having some elements in common to be offered to voters in constituencies throughout the country.

Parties had to agree not only on some form of electoral program, but also to remain sufficiently united in the Commons to have some hope of passing the necessary legislation. The growth during this period in disciplined partisan voting in the Commons was remarkable.[6]

Although the intervening one hundred years have seen both institutional and behavioral change in the British political system, its modern configuration was in place by 1885. Citing a specific similar date for the American political system is more difficult because not only were the key changes more scattered over time, but they also had opposed effects.

Procedural changes from 1877 to 1885 concerning appropriations bills contributed to the fractionalization of power in the House of

Representatives.[7] The results of Speaker Thomas B. Reed's efforts to give some focus and direction to the shambles Congress had become amply supported Bryce's assertion that the Speaker of the House had more influence over legislation than did the President. Twenty years passed before the reaction to the "tyranny" of "Czar" Reed and his successors was sufficiently strong to swing the locus of power back in the other direction. Then from 1909 to 1911 another set of procedural reforms sharply curtailed the Speaker's power.[8]

These reforms did not produce a return to the previous chaos, however, because partisan organization of the House of Representatives in the form of the Democratic Caucus was established at the same time. Once two-thirds of the Democrats voted in caucus for a measure, *all* Democratic congressmen were bound to support the measure in the House unless they had made contrary pledges to their constituents during their election campaign.[9] Woodrow Wilson, now President, doubtless was pleased with a development much in keeping with his prescription in *Congressional Government*. The American separation of powers system had come to function in practice much like the English parliamentary system.

These halcyon days were short-lived, however, as the Democratic party split over foreign policy. By 1918 "the binding party caucus had ceased to be an effective instrument in the hands of the leadership. The Republican minority, meanwhile, had all but abandoned use of the binding caucus in 1911 . . . by 1919, the House no longer was willing to accept the centralization of power that had developed" under previous Speakers and then had passed to the party caucus.[10] Thus the American and British political systems diverged and Wilson suffered in full measure the trials of separation of powers.

Ironically, at almost the same time the first step toward strengthening the President was taken when the Bureau of the Budget was created in 1921 and the President was required to submit an annual budget message to Congress. The founding of the Executive Office of the President in 1939 provided even greater institutional support for this role as policy formulator and coordinator. This initiative was developed further immediately after World War II with the addition to the Executive Office of the National Security Council and the Council of Economic Advisers, along with obligating the President to prepare an annual economic report.

Finally, the period from 1970 to 1976 saw another set of significant reforms in congressional procedures "deemed necessary . . . for stricter accountability of members and for re-establishment of Congress as an equal with the presidency."[11] These changes tended to cut both ways. As had been true of the reforms in the latter part of the nineteenth century and the early twentieth century, the power of committee chairmen and long-term members was curtailed and dispersed to subcommittees.[12] Although the Democratic Caucus was revitalized, it did not play as extensive a role as it had early in the century. Thus the impact of these changes did little to advance development of an integrated policy program in Congress.

On the other hand, the Congressional Budget and Impoundment Control Act of 1974, which created Budget Committees in both houses and a Congressional Budget Office, required Congress "to confront such fiscal policy issues as the effect of the budget on inflation, unemployment and economic growth. Congress also had to decide on budget priorities."[13] The aim was to give Congress an overall control of funding which it had hitherto lacked.

Perhaps even more directly relevant to legislative-executive relations was the War Powers Resolution of 1973, which prohibited the President from using or maintaining troops in a conflict situation for more than ninety days without express congressional approval. Congress clearly feared that power had shifted so decisively to the President that it was in danger, despite the Constitution's explicit conferral, of losing the power to declare war.

Thus, while in Britain executive-legislative relations have moved in an almost teleological process, a virtual linear progression toward increased executive dominance, in the United States the course of development has been more halting and uncertain. Within the Congress power has shifted back and forth, at one time moving toward greater concentration and at another toward diffusion, even fractionalization. These internal shifts obviously have played a significant part in determining whether the legislature or the executive is the dominant branch. Nonetheless, the long-term trend in the United States, despite short-term variations, has been in the same direction as in Britain. Whereas the nineteenth century critics saw a weak President and a dominant Congress, the relevant literature of the 1950s and 1960s "tended to glorify presidential power and to see it as intrinsically good."[14] And by the 1970s the concern was with excessive executive power and its abuse. Thus by the 1980s grounds existed for thinking that the American and British systems were converging in practice. The three primary concerns of Bagehot, Bryce, and Wilson—leadership, policy, and accountability—provide convenient focal points for assessing the extent to which such a belief is true and, should it be, what the implications are for an effective political process.

A Contemporary Comparison

Bryce regarded at least eight of the nineteen men elected President during the first century of the American political system as "personally insignificant," while he considered only six of the eighteen Prime Ministers during the same period to be so. Furthermore, while he judged seven or eight Prime Ministers to "belong to a front rank," he granted such accolade among Presidents only to Washington, Jefferson, Lincoln, and Grant[!].[15] Such an idiosyncratic and blinkered assessment indicates that ratings of this sort are too subjective to justify further discussion. More to the point are the implications of contrasts on some more objective personal characteristics between the leaders each system generates.

Prior legislative service differs significantly between the two systems. Ten of the eighteen men who have become President since 1885 had not served in Congress. The eight who had ranged from 6 to 26 years of service with the mean 13 years. (That the two with the longest periods of congressional service both were Vice-Presidents who became President by succession, rather than in their own right, indicates how little previous congressional service is valued.) Of the nineteen who first became Prime Minister from 1885 to the present, only one had not served in the Commons (but he *had* been in the House of Lords for 26 years). The period of service ranged from 14 to 38 years with the mean being a quarter of a century—twice as long as for even those minority of Presidents who had served in Congress. Thus the British system fuses the executive and the legislature not only in giving the former seats in the latter and in making the executive's term of office dependent upon legislative support, but also in generating chief executives with extensive personal knowledge of legislative practices and behavior. The constitutional separation of executive and legislature in the United States could be better bridged and thus, perhaps, made to operate more effectively simply by changing the patterns of presidential recruitment to select candidates who had spent a substantial portion of their political careers in Congress before becoming the chief executive.

A necessary result of extensive prior legislative service is Prime Ministers who tend to be older than Presidents at the time of first obtaining executive office. More than a third (seven of nineteen) of the Prime Ministers of the last one hundred years were older on first attaining office than was the oldest person to become President, excluding Reagan, whose age at inauguration was quite atypical for American Presidents. While older leaders could be regarded as providing a political system with more mature judgment, they are more likely to be troubled with the physical infirmities associated with aging. Although Churchill's eventual senility is atypical, still the typical Prime Minister cannot be expected to possess as much vigor as the typical President.

It might be thought that Presidents make up for a lack of congressional service by prior administrative or managerial experience that might be even more relevant to their executive duties. But here as well Prime Ministers have the edge. None of the Presidents of the last one hundred years served as secretary of state and no President ever has been secretary of the treasury. More than half of the last nineteen Prime Ministers (ten) had been either chancellor of the exchequer or foreign secretary before becoming Prime Minister and two (Macmillan and Callaghan) had held both offices. Nor can it be argued that American Presidents have gained executive experience at the sub-national level, since only a third of the last eighteen had been state governors.

While the presidency hardly is one of those positions for which one feels comfortable in arguing that on-the-job training can make up for lack of experience, nonetheless, Presidents do have more time to work themselves into the office than do Prime Ministers. Over the last century Prime Ministers have served on the average almost as long (five years) as have Presidents (five and a half years). But this is true only if *total* period of service is considered. If each period in office for Prime Ministers serving more than once is considered separately, then Prime Ministers have averaged terms of only three and a half years in office during the last century, nearly two years shorter than the average President. Furthermore, a quarter of all terms of service were one and a quarter years or *less*, while the lower quartile for Presidents is four years. The point is that Presidents have come closer than Prime Ministers to having the sustained period in office necessary for formulating and implementing an integrated policy program.

Of course, the ability of chief executives or parties to deliver coordinated policies is not just a matter of length of continuous time in office. The distribution of power within the executive branch and between the executive and the legislative branch is crucial. Bagehot,

Bryce, and Wilson all regarded the President as weak in both relations. Wilson, in a prescient comment in the preface for the 15th printing of his book in 1900, did recognize, however, that what he called "the plunge into international politics" initiated by the Spanish-American War enhanced the President's power and was likely to "have a very far reaching effect upon our whole method of government."[16]

So great was the impact of international crises and concerns during the next three-quarters of a century that Arthur Schlesinger, Jr., argued that they had grossly inflated presidential powers and encouraged their abusive use.[17] Reaction to any possible danger posed by this development was almost immediate, however. Only a decade later President Reagan and Secretary of State George Shultz were berating Congress for meddling in foreign affairs and thus undermining any hope of effective American international action. While this charge was political, it was more than merely partisan. Already at the start of the 1980s the most influential and insightful student of American executive power, Richard Neustadt, had pondered: "Is the Presidency possible?" In his view, "We currently have neither an 'Imperial Presidency' as popularly understood nor have we congressional government in Wilson's terms, rule by the chairmen of committees. Rather we have some of each and much of neither as we drift with the crowd."[18]

Policy programs are deemed to be more integrated in Britain because they are not diluted by legislative modification. The executive can govern in Britain in a way that it cannot in the United States because the cabinet dominates the Commons beyond presidential dreams of controlling Congress. Prime Ministers are regarded as having an easier task than Presidents because the British system would seem to guarantee that the same party controls both the executive and the legislature, a situation for which a President only can hope.

Presidents have not fared as badly, however, as might be thought. From 1913 to the present the United States has had coincident partisanship two-thirds (48 out of 72 years) of the time. It is only recently that the two branches have tended to be out of phase politically, with non-coincident partisanship for 20 of the last 38 years. Furthermore, the President's problem is thought to be compounded because even coincident partisanship is no guarantee of legislative support for his policies.

Nonetheless, despite both academic and journalistic recent comment suggesting that the pendulum has swung significantly against

Table 1.1   Congressional Approval of Presidential Policies

	Defense and foreign		Domestic	
	Average positions per year	% Approved	Average positions per year	% Approved
Eisenhower	60	57	132	42
Kennedy	60	58	280	36
Johnson	52	66	307	57
Nixon	42	43	116	30
Ford	41	47	123	35
Carter	94	82	148	73
Reagan (1981–82)	66	79	134	77

the President in American legislative-executive relations, the figures in table 1.1 make one wonder what all the shouting has been about. Contrary to the widespread belief that a recalcitrant Congress has been thwarting every step of the way the foreign policy of the last two Presidents, those supposedly embattled chief executives have been the most successful by far in the last generation in winning legislative support for their positions.[19] Both Carter and Reagan were able to gain the support of Congress for more than three-fourths of their foreign and defense stands, compared with a success rate of only about 55 percent for the five Presidents before them. Nor was this a matter of Congress giving way on foreign and defense policy and taking its hostility out on the President on domestic policy. While these figures suggest that in the past Congress had been much less supportive of the President in domestic matters than in defense and foreign policy, the differences in level of success between these two substantive areas have been slight for Carter and Reagan.[20]

Clearly Carter and Reagan did not enhance their success levels by exercising self-restraint and taking fewer positions on defense and foreign policy issues than their predecessors had. On domestic matters, while they were less activist than Kennedy and Johnson, they were not less so than Eisenhower, Nixon, and Ford. Thus any "law of anticipated reaction" according to which the President asks only for what he reasonably can hope to obtain can be no more than a partial explanation at best for the success which Carter and Reagan enjoyed on domestic policy.

Thus while Congress has been willing recently to pass various limitations on presidential power, such as the War Powers Resolution, which have suggested constant confrontation between the two branches, it has been reluctant to enforce these restraints.[21] Certainly, a number of developments can be cited to explain why a shift in power to Congress at this time is understandable, perhaps the most important being that body's establishing the staff and institutions to give it some policy capabilities of its own.[22] But "not even the most enthusiastic revisionist has suggested that Congress has become an innovator or initiator in foreign policy."[23]

Thus a balanced view would reject both portraits of an imperial presidency and of congressional government as jeremiads that have extrapolated trends beyond reality to logical extremes. The President is the policy-formulating leader, especially in foreign affairs but in domestic matters as well, while Congress influences substance, as well as detail, and, occasionally, thwarts even key presidential initiatives.

Even such a qualified statement, however, suggests greater constraints on the U.S. than on the British executive's ability to gain legislative approval for policy proposals. But the contrast with Britain in this regard tends to be overdrawn, the much stronger party discipline in the Commons notwithstanding. For losing a vote in the House of Commons is not the only way that a government can be beaten. Precisely because the executive lacks a fixed term, a greater incentive exists under the parliamentary system for a government to avoid defeat or reduced support by changing its proposals to meet the complaints of MPS, especially those of its own party. So while Mrs. Thatcher never was defeated during the first session of the 1979–83 Parliament, this does not mean that all her proposals were accepted as desired. She did not even enjoy a honeymoon period with the Commons. Hardly was she in office before she had to give way on the size of pay increases for MPS and on the establishment of specialist select committees in the Commons.

Nor were her reversals during the first session limited to internal House of Commons matters. She was forced to abandon a plan to charge £2 for eye examinations under the National Health Service and cuts she wanted in BBC foreign broadcasting. Under pressure from the United States the EEC foreign ministers had agreed to make a ban on trade contracts with Iran retroactive by some six months to the date at which the U.S. hostages were taken. The uproar among MPS was so great that only twenty-four hours after the foreign ministers meeting she had to reverse British acceptance of this action. She also was compelled to accept an amendment to the housing bill to prevent the sale of council housing suitable for the elderly. Ian Aitken commented in *The Guardian* that the "Government was forced into a humiliating surrender . . . to save a major part of its legislative programme."[24] And this was only the first session.

Before the Parliament was completed the following had occurred. The government was forced to withdraw proposals for increased council rents. Its proposed tax increase on diesel oil had to be cut in half. Its proposed cuts in BBC foreign broadcasting (if at first you don't succeed, fail again) were reduced by half. Its bill to provide for referenda on budgets in areas of high local government spending had to be withdrawn. By the end of 1981 *The Economist* noted that "parliamentary managers view with horror the prospect that next spring's budget will become the subject of horsetrading with truculent backbenchers. . . . The revolt has undermined the confidence of most ministers in the Cabinet."[25]

Late 1981 and early 1982 saw a drawn-out battle over "coloured" immigration into Britain. A curious coalition of right-wing Conservatives and Labour MPS combined to defeat the government on a vote in the Commons. Eventually the government did get most of its proposals accepted, but had to provide assurances on the administration of the policy without thereby further alienating Labour. And before the Parliament ended the government had to drop proposals to give police access to confidential files of medical and "caring" agencies.

Despite a nearly tripled majority in 1983, it was déjà vu for Mrs. Thatcher. Once again she was immediately forced to give way on the size of MPS' pay increase. Then the government had to withdraw administrative guidelines which would have made building in green belts easier for developers. In the continuing battle on local government spending, the government was forced to concede limits on the power it wanted to control the property taxes levied by local governments and to give up entirely on Mrs. Thatcher's pledge to reform the local property tax system.

The significant point about this list of defeats, retreats, and concessions is that it includes social policy, taxation, economic policy, and foreign affairs. These were not just little local difficulties. The fact that calculating a prime ministerial support score from divisions in the Commons is meaningless does not permit concluding that a Prime Minister can count on legislative acceptance of policy programs. The Commons, to a considerable extent like the Congress, can thwart, dilute, or modify executive proposals so that the final policy output may lack the coherence and integration necessary to be a program rather than a collection of disparate initiatives.

While low party cohesion in Congress means that the President can be less certain that members of Congress from his party will support him, it also means that gaining the votes of members of the other party is easier than would be the case in Britain. To say that legislative majorities in the United States are not one-party, as in Britain, is not to say that they are less common.

Even should one-party majorities be thought to be more conducive to policy coherence, the recent fashion in Britain has been to question their salubriousness. The essential charge of the adversary politics view is that each party has a contrasting program, which, on obtaining office, it proceeds to implement with little hindrance by means of its automatic legislative majority. The result is wide variation and sharp reversals in government outputs—long-term policy incoherence resulting not from the absence of a governing power able to implement integrated policies, but precisely because of the existence of such a power. Clearly, if one's first priority is broad consensus and long-term stability of policy, as opposed to decisive but unrestrained action, then the basic design of the American system is likely to be more appealing.

On the other hand, the characterization of British government as facilitating unconstrained, decisive action can be questioned. We already have seen how even a Prime Minister resolutely determined not to compromise has had to modify her program. But the portrait of prompt, decisive action unimpeded by institutional roadblocks is subject to even more serious challenge than this. Rose argues that powerful secular trends plus a consensual electorate have produced striking similarities of behavior regardless of which party controls the executive. He sees about three-fourths of all government legislative proposals as resulting from "the ongoing policy process in Whitehall," with another one-tenth being the reaction to unexpected events.[26] The fact that two-thirds of the legislative proposals a government derives from its election manifesto cause partisan division in the Commons has only a limited importance because such measures account for only a tenth of all government proposals. British politics is a moving consensus retarded by much inertia with civil servants serving as "the institutional spokesmen for the obstacles."[27]

The concern about the lack of policy coherence in the United States derives not just from the nature of legislative-executive relations, but also from the alleged debilitating impact of intra-executive relations. A recent survey of the cabinet throughout U.S. political history has argued that, although in the nineteenth century it often had a primary policy role, now its main concern is administration. Cabinet members are responsible for running their separate departments, not for formulating a coordinated program.[28] While the development of the Executive Office of the President provided him with needed help, it tended also to divorce him from the cabinet by creating an insulating layer of staff between the two of them. The result has been friction between the cabinet and presidential staff. George Shultz and Kenneth Dam, in a book written prior to their appointments to the State Department, described the result as "a balkanized executive branch" in which "policymakers are under the constraint that they are not permitted to view problems whole."[29]

The Reagan administration has sought to integrate both groups into the policy process by creating subject matter cabinet councils bringing together the relevant staff and cabinet members.[30] While these structures provide some focus for policy, they fail to solve the basic problem identified by Richard Rose as the absence of "a single collective authority to reconcile disparate political demands."[31] Governmental output remains more an aggregate of discrete actions dealing with various subject areas rather than a program of interrelated policies shaped by a few general themes or underlying objectives.

That Americans should look to the British system to find remedies for such a state of affairs is a bit curious, since a century ago the institutional structure of the executive was no better elaborated in Britain than in the United States. No agenda, minutes, or even record of decisions existed for cabinet meetings. The result was confusion, as can be seen from an 1882 note from one minister's secretary to Prime Minister Gladstone's secretary: "Harcourt and Chamberlain have both been here this morning, and at my chief about yesterday's Cabinet proceedings. They cannot agree about what occurred. There must have been some decision, as Bright's resignation shows. My Chief told me to ask you what the devil was decided for he be damned if he knows." World War I finally made this state of affairs intolerable.

The key characteristic of the secretariat created in 1916 was that it was a cabinet office, not, as occurred in the United States nearly a quarter of a century later, an executive office of the President; it was to serve the collective, not the chief individual, executive. Thus, while the entire executive support structure in Britain is small by American standards, that directly subject to the Prime Minister is minuscule compared to that of the President. Prime ministerial staff of all kinds down to the lowest level total only about one hundred and probably no more than a dozen of these are involved significantly in policy-making.[32]

Nonetheless, a number of students of British government have accepted the thesis offered by Richard Crossman and John Mackintosh that the Prime Minister has come to dominate British government by controlling the cabinet (through management of political careers and cabinet procedures), the civil service (managing appointments through the Treasury), and the party machine (through preeminence as party leader).

Rose argues a contrary view, stressing the limits on prime ministerial power.[33] He questions whether a Prime Minister can have a program of his or her own. Paradoxically, however, he maintains that the absence of a preeminent figure within the executive, such as the United States has, tends to produce the coherent set of policies lacking in the United States. While cabinet ministers argue their departmental briefs with vigor, the eventual decision—achieved without the need for long hours of discussion—reflects a collective view.[34] Each policy is constrained by global cabinet guidelines to create a coherent program.

The experience of the Thatcher governments has compounded the difficulty of judging which of these opposed views of the British system is more nearly accurate. Mrs. Thatcher's image has been the domineering ideologue, but the reality often has been the pragmatic compromiser. Within three months of each other Peter Jenkins of *The Guardian* could assert, "Cabinet government has all but been suspended," while *The Economist* maintained, "Cabinet government is alive and kicking."[35] Not three years later, however, *The Economist*'s view had become that the cabinet long since had ceased to be of sustained significance in the policy process and the Prime Minister's dominance had rolled on to crush the next level. "Full cabinet is regarded with little greater respect than parliament. Cabinet committees are withering on the bough. . . . A quite different hierarchy of influence is established from the classic one of the minister in cabinet responsible to parliament. The new hierarchy is responsible to Downing Street."[36]

Mrs. Thatcher's governing style has been highly personalized.[37] She has attempted to be informed on the details of everything that has caught her momentary interest, has been reluctant to delegate, and has intervened directly at lower levels in the administrative process more often than has been typical of past Prime Ministers. She has treated cabinet ministers as subordinates, rather than as colleagues—to be berated, hectored, and undercut in public as well as in private. She has sought advice by proclaiming the course of action that should be obvious to any fool and defying those "consulted" to point out any flaw.

Yet this supposedly dictatorial Prime Minister probably has lost more cabinet battles than any other Prime Minister in recent history. Hardly had she come into office before her ministers forced her to abandon the positions she had taken publicly on admitting boat people refugees to Britain and on Rhodesia. In the space of a single month in August 1980 she lost three times—on the teachers' pay increase, on the award of a major computer contract, and on returning three state-owned shipyards to private ownership—despite being supported by the Chancellor of the Exchequer on the first two. A cabinet overruling a Prime Minister supported by the Chancellor had been virtually unknown. Nonetheless, only a couple of months later it happened again on an attempt to cut back pension increases.

On the other hand, Mrs. Thatcher decided to spend £5 billion on Trident without having the matter discussed in cabinet. And when the budget was made public in 1981 the cabinet almost revolted, since most ministers strongly opposed the underlying strategy which she had approved.[38] Even this instance is somewhat ambiguous, however, because eventually she and the Chancellor were forced to accept higher public spending totals. And to avoid another such outcry, she adopted a new procedure in January 1982 of consulting the entire cabinet early in the budget process.

But the longer Mrs. Thatcher's time in office, the fewer seem to be the battles that she has lost. Bit by bit she has purged the cabinet of her most vigorous opponents. Thus in 1983 she and the Chancellor were able to get the cabinet to knuckle under on spending cuts.

Her relationship with her cabinet is a curious one because despite her abrasive, combative approach and her self-imposed isolation from her leading colleagues, she apparently entered office intending to involve the cabinet fully in policy-making. She cut back on the policy and political advisers in Downing Street and shifted the few appointed to party funds, rather than making them temporary civil servants: her political advisers were to be her cabinet colleagues. The Prime Minister's office retained only a small policy unit and it was concerned more with party policy (although not political tactics) than with long-term government strategy.

While she might well have abandoned this approach in any event, the Falkland Islands conflict ensured a shift. The Foreign and Commonwealth Office's failure to protect her from being caught off-guard by the Argentine invasion destroyed any confidence that she might have retained in the FCO. And the experience of directing operations through a war cabinet of four ministers (only one of whom was "difficult") encouraged a belief in the virtues of small, ad hoc policy groups. Thus she quickly added to her economics adviser both a foreign affairs and a defense adviser and was thought to be moving toward establishing a Prime Minister's Department. Following the 1983 election, the Management and Personnel Office, left over when the Civil Service Department was abolished in 1981, was moved to the Cabinet Office, rather than disappearing within the Treasury, and the Rayner unit (on governmental efficiency) was shifted from the MPO to Number 10. Furthermore, she abolished the Central Policy Review Staff, created by Edward Heath in 1970 to serve the entire cabinet. Finally, she cut back on the number of political advisers that cabinet members were permitted. While this restriction was motivated by her belief that ministers should not need advisers to keep them committed to party principles, it also was likely to have been encouraged by a desire to ensure that none of her colleagues was better informed than she was.

This shift from traditional collective policy-making to individual government reduced, rather than increased, policy coordination. Rose's criticism of policy-making in the United States is just as valid for Britain, despite the contrast in institutional structure.[39] Mrs. Thatcher's interventions are not coordinated because she lacks sufficient staff and because bilateral negotiations between particular departments and the Prime Minister are common.[40] The current practice is that she decides government strategy assisted by ad hoc handfuls of ministers and advisers. The job of the ministries then is to implement these decisions. This is how the decision was reached early in 1984 to ban trade unions at the intelligence gathering and communications headquarters in Cheltenham.[41] The damage done to the government's standing by this action is a good example of the potential dangers of this style of personal, segmented decision-making.

When such a segmented process is the reality of policy-making, the formal institutional rule of cabinet collective responsibility can do little to produce an integrated, coherent program. Thatcher is unwilling to concede that a rule requiring ministers to resign if they cannot accept a policy should entitle them to a voice in key decisions. As a result, they have little reason to abandon their efforts to reverse official policy and little incentive to defend it vigorously in public.

This development has interesting implications for the doctrine of collective responsibility. Since the end of World War II twenty-five ministers have resigned because of policy reasons, an average of three every four and one-half years.[42] While such resignations in the past, therefore, hardly could be called frequent, since Mrs. Thatcher became Prime Minister they have become nonexistent. Not a single minister has resigned for policy reasons; as Ian Aitken of *The Guardian* has observed, Mrs. Thatcher's opponents in the cabinet "have been shown to have qualities which even a limpet might envy."[43] Apparently, those in the minority in a cabinet increasingly believe that it is better to remain in to fight for their views and to try to prevent even more distasteful policies.

Furthermore, the steps which Mrs. Thatcher has taken to strengthen her vis-à-vis the cabinet have not so much achieved that as they have weakened the entire executive. Having been denied the resources of the Central Policy Review Staff (cprs) and of adequate political advisers, ministers are less well equipped to deal with a recalcitrant civil service concerned primarily to point out the obstacles involved in any departure from existing policy. Clearly, policy output shaped primarily by civil servants is going to be departmental oriented policy—segmented policy, rather than an integrated program. This truth may well eventually have been appreciated by Mrs. Thatcher, since at the start of her second administration the number of political advisers attached to ministers expanded considerably.

This development gains in significance because Mrs. Thatcher's personal advising structure has not been very successful. Speculation about whether she was intent on creating a Prime Minister's Department had no more than reached a peak when in rapid succession her defense adviser and her foreign affairs adviser resigned, both less than a year after they had accepted the position, and her economics adviser partially resigned to only a quarter time. None of them was replaced; talk of a Prime Minister's Department lapsed. The problem apparently is that Mrs. Thatcher's personality is such as to prevent her from making effective use of advisers. When the first of them went, *The Economist* observed, "None has found an effective role at Downing Street."[44] And Richard Norton-Taylor used virtually the same words a few months later in reporting the next resignation.[45]

Thus policy coordination and integration has left something to be desired in Britain in recent years as well. And the primary reason would appear to be a shift away from the collective nature of the cabinet system and a movement toward a presidential system. And such a shift is rather more the product of leader personality than of institutional change.

As for the other side of the Atlantic, the United States could move toward a considerable amount of the intra-executive unity which characterized Britain even before Mrs. Thatcher. And in fact some movement in this direction occurred under Eisenhower.[46] Maybe what is needed in the United States are Presidents with experience as chairmen of boards of large corporations or service as strategic (not field commanders like Patton) generals, especially when that role requires mediating among subordinates of differing nationality. In any event, the contrast in the nature of policy programs between Britain and the United States is overstressed and certainly derives little from constraints intrinsic to institutional arrangements.

Attempting to say whether the Prime Minister or the President, the British or the American executive, is the more powerful within their respective systems (ignoring American superiority due to greater military power and international status) tends to obscure the nature of the relationships. The Prime Minister must obtain intra-executive policy agreement, usually by persuasion (Mrs. Thatcher's attempts to do so by domination notwithstanding and perhaps demonstrating the validity of the general rule), and manage his or her party to prevent extensive dissension. The President also must seek intra-executive agreement. More so than the Prime Minister, he can do so by directive, although it is not clear that this is the most effective means of gaining policy integration within the executive and he may be better advised to choose a more collegial style not too dissimilar from that of the typical Prime Minister. Second, the President must manage not so much his party as the Congress across party lines. The tasks of the two executives, then, may focus on somewhat different points in their respective political systems and may involve somewhat different political styles. Both, however, require managing and negotiating and neither executive can be assured of success. To this extent the powers and roles have more in common than in contrast and the structural differences in the national systems make considerably less difference in governmental policy output than normally is thought.

Although Parliament doubtless has dealt setbacks to prime ministerial policies, clearly the intensity of legislative-executive conflict has not been as great as in the United States. Woodrow Wilson identified a key reason for this in arguing that Congress misconceived its main purpose: "The informing function of Congress should be preferred even to its legislative function . . . the only really self-governing people is that people which discusses and interrogates its administration."[47] Congress should not attempt to make policy, but should concentrate on calling the President to account. The model clearly was the British system, ideally structured to give the executive freedom to formulate an integrated program while being responsible to the legislature for its direction of public affairs.

Three recent events help to indicate the benefit anticipated from ensuring that the locus of responsibility is clear. The nature of the American system was not exaggerated too greatly by a cartoon appearing in the *Washington Post National Weekly Edition* after the investigation into the Beirut bomb attack killing 241 Marines. One man comments to another, "Boy, that Pentagon report really hits security measures in Beirut—several key military leaders could be in *deep trouble!*" The other responds, "Yeah, but President Reagan has just accepted *all* the blame . . . so now, nobody's in trouble!" From the perspective of the British system, Reagan's behavior was incredible. He embraced responsibility without the slightest suggestion that anything followed from this. The idea that his acceptance might entail resigning would have amazed him. He again accepted the blame when the U.S. Embassy in Beirut was bombed in September 1984 with further loss of life, thus demonstrating that in the United States responsibility and accountability do not go hand in hand. Yet for Lord Carrington and his two colleagues in the Foreign and Commonwealth Office not at least to have offered to resign when Argentina took the Falklands (without at that point any loss in lives) would have been equally unthinkable.

The concern with accountability in the British system has given rise to a supporting doctrine—individual responsibility—and a supporting procedure—question time. Both, however, have become of doubtful effectiveness.

From 1946 to the present only seventeen ministers have resigned because of individual responsibility, an average of well under one every other year, and more than a third of these have been matters of personal impropriety rather than administrative misconduct.[48] Recently the doctrine of individual ministerial responsibility has been weakened further. In September 1983 thirty-eight members of the IRA, in the Maze prison for various criminal activities, escaped. The report from the body set up to investigate the escape cited a wide range of failures at the prison and recommended seventy-three improvements in security. James Prior, the Northern Ireland Secretary, declined to resign. He argued that "the report shows that there was no policy decision which contributed to the escape. It is on those grounds that I believe there are no grounds for ministerial resignations. . . . I do not believe that in any policy decisions there was negligence by myself."[49]

This novel distinction comes close to abolishing individual responsibility; it totally ignores the fact that maladministration of sound policy traditionally had been regarded as grounds for resigning. The typical way to avoid doing so was to accept responsibility and then indicate that steps had been taken to revise procedures so that the same thing could not happen again. Prior specifically said, however, that he could not guarantee that arms would not be smuggled into the prison again. If his decision to remain in office and, more important, his rationale for doing so, become a precedent, then it will be difficult to see how the British situation will differ much from the American, whatever conclusions one may draw from the cases of James Watt and Earl Butz.

The best known, but beyond doubt the most vastly overrated, mechanism for calling leaders to account in Britain is question time. Whatever the procedure once may have been, it has acquired now all the seriousness and significance of bear-baiting. If you believe that political leaders benefit from occasionally being made to look foolish in public, then you may be able to claim some current purpose for question time. But as a means of control over policy-making or administration, it is useless. Sir Barnett Cocks, a Clerk of the House from 1962 to 1973 and editor of four editions of Erskine May, has protested: "There must surely be better methods of interrogating the Government."[50] He has decried the "time-wasting charades" and the immature "guessing games of the House of Commons which enable Ministers to pose as omniscient."

In the case of the Prime Minister the procedure has reached the height of ridiculousness. The Speaker of the Commons was driven to denounce an "outrageous" situation that was ruining question time. And The Guardian editorialized that the current practice made "the order paper a rather ludicrous object, festooned with questions to which no one really wanted to know the answer."[51] The cause is the growth of questions asking the Prime Minister to state her official engagements or whether she will visit a specific location. No one cares about this; the point is that such a question enables MPs then to ask the supplementary question, that does interest them, in hopes of catching the Prime Minister off-guard because she had no fore-warning. The object is not to acquire information or to call the executive to account, but to embarrass the Prime Minister. No doubt this is fun and games for the MPS, but it is of no interest or use to the public. In the space of just five parliamentary sessions in the 1970s such juvenile questions tripled in number and were bidding to become as frequent as those directed to the Prime Minister on general government, international, or economic matters.[52]

It is difficult to know why British procedures on questioning ministers have had such a high reputation when one considers the corresponding practice in the United States. Under the American system legislators are not limited to questioning a member of the cabinet for only a few minutes every two or three weeks. Congressional committees summon them to the Hill and grill them for hours on end. In fact a single member of Congress will have more time to question a member of the cabinet on a pressing topic than will the entire House of Commons. Granted that the development of the select committee system is enhancing the information available to MPS, yet this reform does not provide the Commons with the same powers of legislative oversight exercised by the Congress. Thus in an area in which it is supposed to excel, the British system in fact performs less well than does the American.

Accountability extends not just from the executive to the legislature, of course, but from there on back to the people. Legislative-executive relations do not take place in a vacuum. Neustadt's concern about presidential effectiveness results not just from complex problems and congressional assertiveness; the difficulties are compounded by a mood of public distrust.[53] And this mood is conditioned not only by current events, but also by legislative-executive relations.

For example, Franck and Weisband defend congressional activism in foreign policy-making by asserting that "the costs are not as high as had been feared and . . . there are some unanticipated benefits."[54] One that they cite is legitimation. They claim that compelling the executive to justify action has resulted in a U.S. foreign policy supported by a more wholehearted, rather than an unthinking, consensus. The point is that despite not feeling much personal impact on policy-making, citizens might willingly accept governmental outputs because of respect for decisionmakers and the processes through which they resolve public issues.

Therefore, it is worth inquiring whether the contrasting American and British structures are associated with different levels in public support. Has the impact of Vietnam and Watergate undermined public trust and confidence in a way not present in Britain? Examining patterns of presidential and prime ministerial approval is instructive in this regard. As table 1.2 shows, from January 1953 to August 1974—a period of 21.5 years—most of the people supported the President most of the time. Since Nixon's resignation they have done so little more than a third of the time. But the British portion of table 1.2 is the more striking—the period of majority approval of the Prime Minister is not nearly as long, stretching only from October 1951 to October 1963, a period of only 12 years. And since that period ended, a majority have supported the Prime Minister little more than a fifth of the time.

The United States is said to have undergone a crisis of confidence, of having presidential authority and credibility undermined by the malaise resulting from Vietnam and Watergate. Yet Britain, which experienced neither of these, has enjoyed a shorter period of sustained executive support and lower frequency of majority approval in the time since that period ended. Obviously, economic failures have to a considerable extent had an impact in Britain similar to that of Vietnam and Watergate in the United States.

Whether the shocks to the American system were intrinsically more or less severe than those to the British system is a matter of subjective judgment. There is no way of determining whether those of one type should have been handled more easily than those of another and thus should have been expected to produce more or less strain. The point is that the British system proved no better able— indeed was less able—to handle the particular shocks which it did encounter.

Conclusion: Don't Ever Take a Chance to Tinker

Returning, then, to the basic question initially posed—whether the two systems are converging, with what implications for their countries' policy processes—the similarities do seem more striking than the differences. The British system produces chief executives with greater previous legislative and executive/administrative experience. But it also produces older (thus, perhaps, less vigorous) chief executives and gives them less time to develop and implement a policy program, thereby losing much of the advantage it otherwise would have over the American system. The British executive does not dominate the legislature as much as is thought, while the President does

Table 1.2   Support for Chief Executives

United States ("Do you approve or disapprove of the way —— is handling his job as President?")

	Number of surveys 50% or more approve	Number of surveys less than 50% approve	% of surveys most approve
Truman	13	28	32
Eisenhower	106	2	98
Kennedy	40	0	100
Johnson	44	39	53
Nixon	56	37	60
Ford	9	27	25
Carter	39	54	42
Reagan (to May 1984)	27	41	40

Britain ("Are you satisfied or dissatisfied with —— as Prime Minister?")

	Number of surveys 50% or more satisfied	Number of surveys less than 50% satisfied	% of surveys most satisfied
Attlee	7	22	24
Churchill	7	2	78
Eden	14	3	82
Macmillan	36	31	54
Home	0	11	0
Wilson	25	42	37
Heath	0	42	0
Wilson	5	19	21
Callaghan	16	21	43
Thatcher (to May 1984)	6	54	10

Sources: The information has been compiled from (for the United States) *The Gallup Opinion Index*, no. 125 (November–December 1975), pp. 12, 16–18, 20–22, 24–25, 27–30, and 32–33; *The Gallup Opinion Index*, no. 182 (October–November 1980), pp. 13–14, 17; *The Gallup Report*, no. 219 (December 1983), p. 18; and *The Gallup Report*, no. 225 (June 1984), p. 11. (For Britain) Norman Webb and Robert Wybrow, eds., *The Gallup Report* (London: Sphere Books, 1981), pp. 168–85, and the monthly issues of *Gallup Political Index* for the period of January 1981 through May 1984. Interestingly, Thatcher's six positive

rather better in gaining support than commonly is supposed. The collective aspects of the executive in Britain have been diminished recently so that relations do not differ greatly from those in the United States. Thus Britain does little better than the United States in producing coherent, integrated policy programs. Personal governing style appears to be more significant than institutional arrangements in determining the extent of any contrasts that do exist between the two countries. Mechanisms for calling the executive to account prove to be little better in Britain than in the United States and the British system has done even less well than the American in sustaining popular confidence in the executive.

These developments in Britain and the United States are immensely significant, not only for legislative-executive relations, but also for public policy. While their effects should indeed be matters of concern, frustratingly, there is not much that can be done about them. Historically, American political reformers have looked to the supposedly superior British political system for imports that could improve the political process in the United States. When, after World War II, the flaws of the British system became increasingly clear, the traffic across the Atlantic became more of a two-way flow.[55] While this trade in ideas was not without some useful insights and provided the occasional attachment to the machinery of government, all too often it suffered from the fact that the reformers misperceived the nature and operation of the system they were recommending as a model to be copied.[56] Furthermore, political scientists have become aware increasingly that even minor constitutional tinkering is about as easy to accomplish as implanting an artificial heart.

Thus skepticism about the desirability of institutional reform has grown. Rose, after his damning critique of the American political system, eschews any recommendations for constitutional changes and instead urges parties to change their rules and exhorts the voters to exercise better judgment.[57] Theodore Sorensen, despite believing that the United States is on the brink of a governmental crisis, feels that the "problem is not primarily organizational. Certainly it is not constitutional. The problem is, to a large degree, attitudinal. . . . I am very wary of structural reforms because most of them turn out badly. They don't solve the problems they are intended to solve; they often

---

months were June and July 1982 (just as the Falklands conflict was ending) and May through September 1983 (immediately before and some time after the general election).

make them worse."[58] Even relatively minor proposals, such as giving cabinet members access to the floor of Congress, are greeted skeptically.[59] As for Britain, although I have proposed elsewhere a desirable package of institutional reforms—including a fixed term for the Commons, primary elections, and a reformed upper house based on the regions—I labeled these "more suggestive than requisite."[60]

Clearly, wholesale institutional change is not the appropriate response in either system. Unfortunately, in a democracy this leaves the Mr. Micawber solution—one hopes that something will turn up. And, indeed, something may well be turning up. The key issue is what one considers to be the dominant causal influence, even if one grants a reciprocal relation. For example, Hugh Berrington, analyzing the shift from legislative factionalism in nineteenth century Britain to highly cohesive parties in the twentieth century, argues that institutional change produced behavioral change.[61] The same belief motivates those reformers committed to strengthening the Commons' specialist select committees, the most recent example of institutional change imported from the United States.

This approach, however, tends to overlook the significant interrelated behavioral changes that are occurring in Britain at two levels— greater dissension in the Commons and partisan dealignment. These developments need to be seen in historical perspective. As Britain developed a mass democracy in the nineteenth century, the primary factor structuring partisan preference was religion. Kenneth Wald has explained how the influence of this factor disintegrated, leaving a vacuum which was filled by social class beginning around the time of World War I.[62] Now social class as a variable dividing the electorate into relatively cohesive opposed groups is waning.[63] What variable, if any, will replace social class remains to be seen.

In the meantime, however, the diversity of the United Kingdom— too seldom fully appreciated in the United States—is free to assert itself. The cement which formerly bound MPs into cohesive parties is crumbling. Any attempt to maintain the virtually perfect discipline of the past is likely to produce the Canadian result—a multi-party system. Only where diversity does not assert itself because of the overriding impact of a key social variable can a two-party system with highly cohesive parties be maintained. The combined impact of religion *and* regionalism in Britain shattered the party system toward the close of the nineteenth century. The Unionist split, however, proved to be the first step in a realignment, rather than a transformation of the two-party nature of the system. During the transitional period in which class replaced religion as the variable structuring partisan preference, Britain again experienced a multi-party system as part of a realignment rather than a transformation. Whether the current dealignment simply is a prelude to yet another realignment or the first step toward an unprecedented transformation cannot be foretold, but the result may well be influenced by changes in legislative-executive relations.

For the behavior of MPs, as well as of the electorate, has been in flux, as they have become much more willing to vote against their party in the Commons. This change in behavior is not just a matter of ego gratification, but of a new representational role and a responsiveness to local policy concerns increasingly able to flourish with the waning of class concerns.[64] Reinforcing these changes is the shift in MPs' social backgrounds. The new middle class, political professional has come to replace the working class and upper class "amateurs" who dominated the Commons in the past.[65] A British government that ignores these developments and tries to maintain strict cohesion is likely only to generate increased parliamentary dissension. And such assertiveness in Parliament might well come to be reflected in the alternatives presented to voters and thus move Britain toward transformation rather than realignment. A sensible government is likely to find that it needs to make policy concessions to the Commons about as frequently as does the President to the Congress.

American parties always have been fractionalized, of course. Currently, the American electorate appears to be realigning, a development not unlike what is occurring in Britain.[66] Such a transitional period can only reduce partisan cohesion in Congress even further. While this will compound the problem of effective executive leadership, it does not threaten to produce systemic change because only rarely have American leaders attempted to impose tight discipline on congressional parties. Therefore, counterproductive behavior contributing to party system transformation is less likely in the United States than in Britain.

Thus what is needed are effective leaders with highly developed negotiating and bargaining skills, who will work in accord with the behavioral changes that are occurring, rather than resist them by drawing up structural reforms that might have a superficial abstract attractiveness. Such an attitude toward political development always has been the hallmark of the British political genius. The question now is whether either the British or the American political system will manage to maintain this genius.

2

The Revival of Laissez-Faire

GARY MARKS

———

In this chapter, Gary Marks examines another aspect of national politics in which the United States and Great Britain seem to be following similar paths: the resort to a laissez-faire economic approach by governments in the 1980s. His argument falls into three main parts. First, the particular strength of the return to laissez-faire ideals in the 1970s was not merely a response to the special economic problems of the age but was more significantly shaped by certain distinctive features of the conservative parties in these countries. Second, political constraints on economic policy, deriving mainly from the special role of interest groups, reinforced the turn to laissez-faire ideals among conservatives. But Marks argues that the reasons for this are different in each case. Although the relations between interest groups and the government and between interest group leaders and their members are markedly different in each country, nevertheless the reality is that interest groups in both countries often have the political influence to frustrate government policies yet lack the consistent ties to government and a centralized organizational structure to allow effective coordination in a government economic plan. Third, the special characteristics of the conservative parties and interest group structure in Great Britain and the United States differentiate these countries from other western democracies (perhaps making them appear more similar than they really are) and help to explain the extraordinary attraction of laissez-faire policies to the administrations of Mr. Reagan *and Mrs. Thatcher. Only by situating the two countries in the wider context of industrialized democracies generally can some important and special characteristics of the two states be isolated and thus the attraction to laissez-faire policies in these countries be explained.*

———

Less than twenty years ago the growth of government, and of government intervention in the economy, were viewed by political scientists and economists as part of an inexorable process of political development in advanced industrialized society. Although the absolute level of state intervention varied among Western societies, the direction of change was the same. Today, however, it is clear that parties of the Right in several Western countries are challenging to reverse this trend. With the accession of the Right into government in Britain in 1979, and in the United States in 1980, the doctrine of laissez-faire, emphasizing the retrenchment of state intervention in the economy, has been revived as a guide to economic policy-making.

This chapter will explore why this revival has taken place. For our purposes, this broad question involves three specific ones: Why has the revival of laissez-faire been stronger in the United States and Britain than in other Western democracies? Why is it taking place at the present time? And what characteristics of the political systems of the United States and Britain have influenced the revival of laissez-faire in these countries?

The minimal defining element of laissez-faire is the separation of state and economy so that the state does not exercise authority over the allocation of scarce economic resources. However, in this form laissez-faire has never existed, even in its heyday in the United States and Britain in the third quarter of the nineteenth century. In fact, it is hard to see how laissez-faire could exist in pure form, for even "night-watchman" governments, operating in far simpler societies than our own, have exercised controls over the currency and have regulated the organization of markets.[1] In the context of contemporary Western society, the revival of laissez-faire has taken the form of "neo-laissez-faire," and is most usefully understood as a tendency rather than an absolute. In the programs of the present conservative governments of the United States and Britain, neo-laissez-faire emphasizes the following broad goals of economic policy: (1) the retrenchment of government ownership of industry and of public spending (with the exception of defense spending), in order to encourage private enterprise; (2) the avoidance of systematic govern-ment intervention in market decision-making (e.g., through incomes policy or industrial policy), so as to minimize political control over the allocation of private economic resources; and (3) the furtherance of competition, especially in the labor market, by constraining mo-nopoly power, especially of labor unions.[2]

These components of neo-laissez-faire were elaborated by econo-mists in response to deficiencies in economic policy that became in-creasingly apparent from the late 1960s. In both the United States and Britain, as well as in other Western democracies, a search for new approaches to economic policy was stimulated by the perceived failures of Keynesian economic policy to cope with a series of eco-nomic problems, most notably rising levels of inflation and unem-ployment and the worsening terms of trade-off between them, de-teriorating real economic growth, and the appearance of a sharper trade cycle with deeper and longer lasting troughs of recession. But if neo-laissez-faire was a response to the limitations of conventional economic policy, it was by no means a unique response. An idea of the range of doctrines that might have served to guide policy as ra-tional alternatives to neo-laissez-faire can be seen simply by looking at the experiences of other Western societies in this period, from at-tempts to guide the economy by concerting the demands of func-tional interest groups, as in Sweden or Norway, to more dirigist strat-egies of state planning, as in France.

In this chapter, I shall explore a path of explanation which is complementary to the economic approach, but which focuses ex-plicitly on two aspects of what might be described as the political dimension of an explanation of neo-laissez-faire. First, there is the question of how the economic problems of the period were inter-preted on the political Right. This is important because the simple recognition of a particular policy problem does not define the solu-tion that is adopted by a political group or party. A policy problem may be (and usually is) interpreted in several mutually exclusive ways, each suggesting a different solution. Second, there is the ques-tion of the political constraints on alternative solutions to the policy problem. Some conceivable approaches to a policy problem may be unworkable or ineffective within a particular political system, how-ever desirable they may be on other, even economic, grounds. In this sense, the political context of economic policy serves to constrain the policy options that are available to policymakers.

The political dimension of my explanation is, I believe, particularly important if we wish to explain why neo-laissez-faire has been stronger in the United States and Britain than in other Western societies. While it may be true that the degree of severity of the economic problems that the United States and Britain faced in the late 1960s and 1970s had some impact on the willingness of parties in these countries to adopt radical policy programs, the link between economic problems and party actions is very complex. Too many variables intervene between economic performance and policy formulation to postulate a straightforward relationship between the two. And, however it is measured, the level of state intervention in the economy, which is the target of neo-laissez-faire, is relatively low in the United States and only moderately high in Britain when compared to other Western societies where the demand for neo-laissez-faire has been weaker.[3]

Is it possible to find common political factors in the United States and Britain that influenced the revival of laissez-faire? The supposition of this chapter is that two broad political factors are indeed common to these societies and did influence the doctrines of the political Right in the same direction.

The first factor concerns the traditional orientation of the Republican and Conservative parties toward state intervention in the economy. Distrust of government economic controls was voiced by significant elements of each party well before the economic crises of the 1970s. Support for neo-laissez-faire, in both cases, was linked to the rising fortunes of political groupings that claimed to be returning the party to its traditional moorings of support for individual initiative and private enterprise. Within the Republican and Conservative parties, neo-laissez-faire, as a guide to interpreting the economic problems of the 1970s, was consistent with doctrines that were already well established.

In the next section of this chapter, I hypothesize that these doctrines were influenced by certain fundamental features of the political Right in the United States and Britain, in particular, the strength, unity, and religious heritage of the Republican and Conservative parties. The absence of party fractionalization within the Right has meant that conservative parties have not had to enter broad-based coalitions with agrarian or religious parties if they wish to govern. The major source of cleavage within the party systems of the United States and Britain is socioeconomic, emphasizing the question of state intervention in the economy, alongside welfare and equality issues. In addition, the absence of Catholic influence on the political

Right in the United States and Britain, with its traditional links to the ancien régime and emphasis on antiliberal and anticapitalist values, sets these countries apart from those of Central and Southern Europe, where the Right is dominated by Christian Democratic parties.

A second broad political factor that appears to have influenced the doctrines of the political Right in the United States and Britain in the same direction concerns the difficulties that face governments in pursuing economic policies that would serve as an alternative strategy to that of neo-laissez-faire. In both countries, governments have tried to find ways to control the course of the economy systematically by directly influencing the demands of economic interest groups in line with national priorities of price stability, low unemployment, and economic growth. But the principal avenues of such control—incomes policy and industrial policy—are extraordinarily difficult to implement in the United States and Britain. Economic policy in both societies has been described in terms of pluralist stagnation, where major interest groups are able to thwart the state's policy initiatives. The existence of severe political constraints on state intervention in the economy has contributed to the belief among many conservatives that the best government policy is one of disengagement, emphasizing monetary restraint and economic stability, without otherwise intervening in market decision-making.

Before discussing these political factors in more detail, I should make clear that I am concerned with neo-laissez-faire as a policy doctrine, as a guide to policy-making rather than as a set of policy outcomes. To what extent the doctrine is reflected in policy outcomes is a fascinating issue, but one about which—for the purposes of this article—we can afford to withhold judgment. Although neo-laissez-faire has been stressed in the programmatic pronouncements of the Republican and Conservative governments, the strength of neo-laissez-faire in the practice of policy is questionable. The pursuit of economic policy is constrained by numerous influences, domestic and international, over which an executive has little control, and the expectation of, say, domestic opposition or an international recession will, of course, influence the kind of policy selected. The pursuit of neo-laissez-faire is subject to a further, and perhaps unique, constraint, for it places a government in the paradoxical position of having to exert considerable effort to reduce its influence over certain forms of economic activity. This is particularly true in Britain, where the role of the state in the economy is more extensive than in the United States. Thus, the economic policies of the Thatcher government in the early 1980s are mixed if we categorize them simply in terms of the scope of government. On the one hand, the government has adopted unambiguous neo-laissez-faire policies of extensive denationalization and free collective bargaining in the private sector; on the other hand, it has extended the scope of central governmental control over local government finances, and has regulated the nationalized steel and coal industries more closely than any of its Labour predecessors. Neo-laissez-faire involves a radical restructuring of the role of the state in a society such as Britain, and, as Mrs. Thatcher has recognized, this demands the active use of state power to overcome bulwarks of resistance. Paradoxically, but also perhaps inevitably, the pursuit of neo-laissez-faire in a modern industrialized society may demand a strong and interventionist state.

The role, or "power," of the factors that I shall examine in the following pages is hard to gauge with precision because causation is very difficult to trace at the level of whole societies. While they only partially determine the relative strength of neo-laissez-faire, a careful examination of their causal influence should demonstrate that the revival of laissez-faire in these societies was no coincidence, but is rooted in underlying commonalities of the two political systems. However, the United States and Britain share many features, apart from the ones dealt with here, which might have influenced the doctrines of the Republican and Conservative parties in the same direction. That is why it is useful to compare these societies with others sharing some of each of their features, but differing in others. The societies I shall refer to are mainly the larger societies of Western Europe (excepting Spain and Portugal) and Australasia, all of which are roughly similar to the United States and Britain in the liberal democratic character of their party competition, their mixed economies, and in their level of economic development.

A comparison framed in this way may help to shed light on some Anglo-American similarities that would not be apparent in a straight United States-Britain comparison, in the same way that two members of a family, however different when viewed in isolation, share some basic features when compared among a larger population. The contrasts between the United States and Britain that will emerge in this chapter are seen against a background of impressive similarities rooted in shared political traditions and trajectories of political development, and which touch on their political cultures, their party and electoral systems, and, for our purposes perhaps most important of all, their interest group systems.

The Political Right and Neo-Laissez-Faire
in the United States and Britain

Parties of the Right in the United States and Britain share two fundamental characteristics that differentiate them from parties of the Right on the continent of Western Europe. First, the Republican and Conservative parties are unitary in their representation of the political Right. They operate within electoral systems based on the principle of plurality ("first past the post") which serves to punish fractional parties. Neither party has to compete or ally with other right-wing parties based on religious or rural constituencies. In the United States and Britain, the orientation of the parties of the Right is simplified because of the lack of major social cleavages that compete with the left/right dimension of party competition. Second, the Republican and Conservative parties are broadly secular. To the extent that they have been affected by religious values, these have been Protestant. In this they are to be contrasted with the Christian Democratic parties of the Right in Central and Southern Europe which have been deeply influenced by Catholic values, and share, to varying degrees, a view of society and the role of the individual in it that is distinctly antiliberal.

The influence of these characteristics appears to be negative rather than positive: neo-laissez-faire has been relatively weak when the political Right is fractionalized, or dominated by a Christian Democratic party. But where the political Right is unified and secular or Protestant, the strength of neo-laissez-faire has depended on further conditions relating to the tenure of the conservative party, discussed below, and the character of state/interest-group relations discussed in the next section.

The combination of variables that divide the party-political representation of the Right in Anglo-American societies from other Western societies is illustrated in figure 2.1, which represents the degree of fractionalization of the Right and the electoral strength of Christian democracy over the thirty-year period 1951 to 1980 as two independent dimensions of the political Right in the United States, Britain, and fifteen other advanced industrial societies. Alongside the Anglo-American societies, which have dominant Protestant-oriented con-

Figure 2.1   Christian Democratic Party Vote and Fractionalization of the
Right in Seventeen Countries, 1951–80

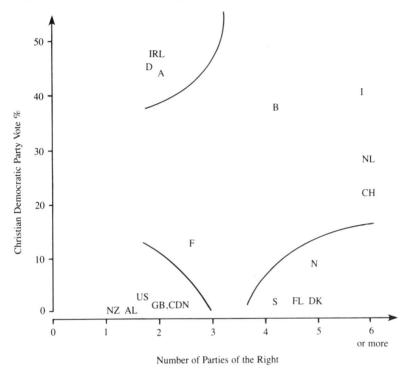

Key: (AL) Australia; (A) Austria; (B) Belgium; (CDN) Canada; (DK) Denmark; (FL) Finland;
(F) France; (D) West Germany; (IRL) Republic of Ireland; (I) Italy; (NL) Netherlands; (NZ) New
Zealand; (N) Norway; (S) Sweden; (CH) Switzerland; (GB) United Kingdom; (US) United States.

* Average number of parties of the Right required to form optimum rightist majority (optimum
here means the most right-wing majority coalition possible, except where the designated party
of the Right obtained a majority for itself). (Based on Sten G. Borg and Francis G. Castles,
"The Influence of the Political Right on Public Income Maintenance Expenditure and Equality,"
Political Studies 29, no. 4 [December 1981]: 610).

servative parties, two further distinct groupings emerge: the Northern European countries in which the political Right is fractionalized
into conservative, agrarian, and confessional parties; and West Germany, Austria, and Ireland, where Christian Democratic parties are
dominant. A fourth, more varied, grouping encompasses the Low
Countries and Switzerland, in which the Right is fractionalized along

both religious and ethnic lines, Italy, where a strong Christian Democratic party dominates a fractionalized Right, and France, in which the Right is split between the Union for French Democracy (UDF) and the Guallists.

Where the Right is deeply fractionalized, the liberal defense of laissez-faire capitalism has been weakened by party cleavages that cut across the left/right dimension of laissez-faire versus state intervention. Conservative or neoliberal parties representing the values of individualism, market competition, and a limited state have tended to adjust their strategy if they enter government coalitions with confessional, agrarian, or center parties oriented to crosscutting issues of party conflict. Moreover, even when they are out of office, the pressures of electoral competition within the Right may lead to a moderation of antistatism, as has been the case with the conservative parties of Scandinavia.[4] In societies where the Right is fractionalized, the strongest demands for neo-laissez-faire have been put forward by populist protest movements, such as the Progressive party in Denmark and the Anti-Tax party in Norway, that have combined antipathy for state regulation and welfare expenditures with a generalized antisystem sentiment.[5]

In several Western European societies, the political Right has historically been oriented around religious values. In Central and Southern Europe, Christian Democratic parties have formed the major parties of the Right, while in France, Christian democracy remains an important tendency within the Center-Right UDF. While ideological conflicts between Christian Democratic parties and parties of the Left remain sharp, Christian Democratic parties have not fostered the ethics of capitalist individualism or laissez-faire. Their heterogeneous bases of support and Catholic moorings have inhibited the development of class-based or ideologically coherent programs.[6]

This link seems to be confirmed in the case of West Germany, where the political salience of Catholicism has declined markedly since the Second World War and the Christian democratic alliance of the Christian Democratic Union (CDU) and the Christian Socialist Union (CSU) has become more sympathetic to the doctrines of liberal capitalism. After the Second World War, the CDU-CSU became a biconfessional party, uniting Protestants and Catholics, and like its counterpart in Austria, was able to provide the party-political basis for a relatively united Right. As R. E. M. Irving has observed in his study of the subject, "Those Christian Democratic parties which absorbed conservative parties—as has been the case in Germany and Austria—are now themselves essentially conservative parties. On the other hand, those Christian Democratic parties which still have to com-*pete* with conservative parties—as do the Italians with the MSI and PZI, the Belgians and Dutch with the Liberals, and the French with the *Guallistes* and *Giscardiens*—are essentially centrist in orientation."[7]

In the United States, the chief religious influence on parties of the Right has been Protestantism, which has emphasized the values of individualism, self-reliance, and moral self-responsibility for success or failure, values that are congruent with a market society. As Seymour Martin Lipset has noted in a discussion of the character of the American Right:

> As a new society and a new nation, formed as a society by settlers who rejected the hierarchically organized churches and fixed class system of Europe, and formed as a nation in a Revolution which rejected the alliance and dominance of throne and altar, the central ideology of the United States is anti-statist, individualistic, egalitarian and democratic. It glorifies the pioneer settler and the Protestant who is morally responsible directly to God.
>
> The anti-statist individualist emphasis which defined nineteenth-century Americanism has remained important. While the European conservatives have often supported increased state power in the form of a benevolent Tory welfare state, American conservatives have stressed individualism, local rights, and *laissez-faire*, even to the extent of describing their ideology as libertarian.[8]

Such values have been weaker in the British Conservative party, which has been closely associated with the established Church of England, and has generally been more sympathetic to the ethic of noblesse oblige. However, in both countries the relative weakness of institutionalized state/church relations, and the relatively loose ties of Protestant churches with their communities, has meant that religion itself has been a less important source of cleavage than in Catholic countries. By contrast with most continental European societies, the Anglo-American societies have been characterized by what Gabriel Almond has described as a "homogeneous, secular political culture."[9] With the partial exception of Canada, the main source of cleavage is socioeconomic, with the chief lines of party competition oriented around issues of state intervention in the economy, welfare, and equality.[10]

In Britain during the 1950s and early 1960s the intensity of party competition on these issues appeared to decline. After the Second World War, the Labour party led the way in promoting a new and broader vision of the role of the state in the economy, and elements of this vision—the notion of the welfare state and government ownership of certain monopolies and ailing industries—were adopted by the Conservative party from the late 1940s. This was made all the easier because these state interventions could be subsumed under traditional conservative doctrines that have been sympathetic to state paternalism and the pragmatic adaptation to change.

The period from the 1950s to the 1960s has generally been described in terms of a consensus on major aspects of government policy: both Conservative and Labour parties seemed to accept the desirability of the welfare state and full employment maintained through Keynesian policies of demand management. But this consensus never embraced the far wings of either of the major parties. The moderate, social democratic, Butlerite tendency within the Conservative party was always subject to criticism from the economic "purists," most notably Enoch Powell, Peter Thorneycroft, and Peter Birch, each of whom held, and resigned from, government office in these years. When conventional economic policies were seen to be failing in Britain in the late 1960s and 1970s, such criticisms, emphasizing the dangers of state control in society, gained legitimacy within the party.

The link between the dominance of socioeconomic lines of cleavage, right-wing unity, Protestantism, and conservative support for neolaissez-faire, is a complicated one. There are significant differences among the Anglo-American societies as well as between them and societies that fall into the groupings mapped out in figure 2.1. Conservative parties in all societies have an understandable concern to avoid being identified solely with socioeconomic issues which polarize the electorate along class lines, for the simple reason that if they do so they are likely to find themselves in a minority. Thus conservative parties have emphasized patriotism (and sometimes nationalism), administrative efficiency, questions of morality, and other issues that have potential appeal to lower class voters.

In Australia and New Zealand, and to a lesser extent in Britain, conservative parties have been able to connect their long tenure in government with the image that they are the "natural" party of government, best fitted to provide efficient government for the entire nation (as contrasted to labor parties depicted as representing solely the working class). In the postwar period this was conducive to an emphasis on social democracy, based on the conservatives' appeal as the party best able to administer an extensive government and welfare state in an atmosphere of class consensus.

It is perhaps no coincidence that the turn to neo-laissez-faire over the last twenty years has been strongest in conservative parties that have been turned out of government. In opposition, the appeal to the middle ground as the natural party of government is less convincing. The art of "conserving" is itself more problematic for a conservative party when a socialist government is in office. Under such circumstances, the distinction between conservatism and right-wing radicalism is harder to maintain, for once the continuity of conservative rule has been relinquished, the doctrine of conservatism may be more clearly defined by reference to a positive set of principles than to Burkean gradualism.

In Australia and New Zealand, conservative parties maintained a virtual monopoly of governmental power from the 1950s until the early 1970s. In both countries, conservative parties remained conspicuously unideological. Despite a diffuse sympathy with liberal ideals, neither the Australian Liberal Party nor the New Zealand National Party attempted to retrench the extensive role that the state had assumed. As Alan Robinson observed of the National party in 1967: "The National Party's course in the last twenty years has often been to try to reduce the effects of Labour's appeals by offering similar policies and by maintaining Labour policies, which it claims to administer more soundly."[11] In New Zealand and Australia, the strengthening of the commitment to active neo-laissez-faire within the National and Liberal parties first became evident in the early 1970s, when Labour parties formed governments in both countries.[12]

In the United States, the Republican party in the post–New Deal era has never succeeded in maintaining an image of itself as the natural party of government. Apart from Canada, in which the Conservative party is confronted by a strong centrist Liberal party, the United States is the only Anglo-American society in which the party of the Right has not won the dominant share of the vote in legislative elections for the thirty-year period 1951 to 1980.[13] The Republican party was the first right-wing party to turn to neo-laissez-faire in the post–Second World War period, and with only about 25 percent of the electorate identifying with it, has been both much smaller than the Democratic party and generally more ideological.[14]

In Britain, the periods of Conservative party opposition from 1964 to 1970 and from 1974 to 1979 have coincided with shifts in doctrine away from conservatism with a small "c" toward radical liberalism and neo-laissez-faire. One of the chief features of the British political system is that the penalty of opposition is powerlessness, and the penalty of powerlessness for the opposition leadership is susceptibility to ideological pressure, or even revolt, from the ranks. This has been particularly true for the Labour party in opposition, but it also has applied to the Conservative party in recent years. The revival of laissez-faire was clearly visible in the detailed blueprints for governmental economic policy drawn up under the leadership of Edward Heath in the late 1960s, when the party found itself in opposition after thirteen years of continuous rule. The turn to neo-laissez-faire was intensified in the period of opposition in the mid-1970s when Margaret Thatcher replaced Heath as leader of an opposition party.[15] Altogether, the Conservative party formed the government for less than half of the period from 1960 to 1980.

The revival of laissez-faire has amounted to a more radical change in right-wing doctrine in Britain than in the United States, and has been accompanied by profound changes in the role and self-image of the Conservative party. Over the last two decades, the Conservative party has rapidly shed the traditional image of the party of deference and of the establishment.[16] The decline of aristocratic participation at the upper levels of the party, the distancing of the party from traditional institutions of the establishment, particularly the Church of England, the universities, and the BBC, the introduction of explicit democratic arrangements for the election of the party leadership, and the election of two lower-middle-class leaders, Heath and Thatcher— all are part of a process in which, as Andrew Gamble has pointed out, "the Conservatives have been transformed from natural defenders of British institutions into frequent outsiders and critics."[17]

Political Constraints on Economic Policy

The revival of laissez-faire in the United States and Britain is related not only to the ideological predispositions of the political Right in these countries, but also to a diffuse rejection of conventional economic policy. As electoral studies have revealed, support for Mr. Reagan in 1980, and for Mrs. Thatcher and the Conservative party a year before, was less an expression of commitment to positive policy proposals than it was a reaction against the economic performance of existing governments. Governing parties, no matter what their ideological color, were hard pressed to win elections in the 1970s and early 1980s when the "misery index" of unemployment and inflation was high and generally rising. From this standpoint, the turn to neo-laissez-faire in the United States and Britain was part of a widespread rejection of conventional economic policies in societies where these policies failed to deliver "the goods."

The criticisms developed by the political Right centered on two aspects of conventional economic policy in particular: (1) the tendency to combat rising unemployment by stimulating the economy through government spending and monetary expansion, and (2) the extension of state intervention in the economy from the macro level to the micro level, through incomes policy and various forms of structural policy.

The rejection of expansionary fiscal policy lies at the heart of monetarism. In its minimal form, as a policy emphasizing the importance of price stability and control of monetary growth to achieve it, monetarism has gained acceptance within a broad political spectrum in a number of Western democracies. The view that no direct trade-off between inflation and unemployment exists in the short run, and that controlling inflation should be a priority of economic policy, filtered into conventional economic wisdom well before right-wing governments took office in Britain and the United States. Publicly set monetary targets were introduced in Germany in 1974, in the United States in 1975, in France in 1976, and in Britain in 1977, and are now the norm rather than the exception in the advanced democracies.[18]

The second criticism, based on a presumption against forms of state intervention in the economy beyond the most aggregate tools of economic management, is a particularly distinctive feature of neo-laissez-faire. It provides a key to understanding why the revival of laissez-faire has been stronger in the United States and Britain than in other countries whose economies have also performed poorly in the 1970s.

In the United States and Britain, the Keynesian approach to economic policy-making, combining aggregate demand management with a commitment to high levels of employment, was particularly vulnerable because of the constraints under which it was pursued. In neither country has it been possible for governments to supplement Keynesian macroeconomic policies with effective and discriminating microeconomic policies that influence economic interest group demands in line with national priorities of price stability, low unemployment, and economic growth. Although the reasons for this vary, in both the United States and Britain the decisions of major economic organizations, such as corporations and labor unions, have been far removed from effective state influence. The repeated failures of microeconomic policy, and particularly incomes policy, have strengthened the arguments of those in the Republican and Conservative parties who reject state economic intervention altogether.

From this standpoint, monetarism in its fullest form was recommended to the political Right in the United States and Britain by what it avoided, as well as by what it promised. Under monetarism, the principal instrument by which the state should influence economic outcomes is that of monetary policy—an aggregate tool that does not involve any institutionalized system of state/economy intermediation. W. W. Rostow, a critic of monetarism, makes this point incisively: "Here is a method which claims to reconcile high growth with control over inflation by the action of distant technocrats in a quasi-independent institution, the Federal Reserve. It does not interfere directly with existing institutions for setting prices and wages, and it takes responsibility and authority off the shoulders of politicians."[19]

Of course, monetarism and neo-laissez-faire are just one of a number of possible responses to the policy problems associated with Keynesianism in the 1960s and 1970s. In Britain, the Labour party has also rejected the postwar social democratic consensus on aggregate demand management and now favors a policy entailing increased government expenditure, the extension of state ownership of industry, and compulsory planning agreements, that, in its own way, is as radical as neo-laissez-faire. As David Coates has observed, "The persistence of the competitive weakness of British capitalism, and its accentuation during the world recession, had at least one important political consequence in the 1970s. It altered the weight of factional support within each major political party, strengthening within each party that faction which wished to make a sharp break with the form into which government economic policy had settled in the 1960s."[20]

As the limitations of aggregate macroeconomic policies became apparent in the 1960s and 1970s, governments in all Western democracies attempted to develop more discriminating instruments to regulate the economy. The institutional form of economic intervention varied, but common to all was the attempt on the part of the state to coordinate the decision-making of functional nongovernment organizations. By influencing wage settlements directly through incomes policy, governments hoped that wage inflation could be controlled directly, without recourse to recessionary policies that would affect the level of activity in the economy as a whole. In Britain, governments also introduced various planning mechanisms, which attempted to bring coherence and rationality to economic decision-making by coordinating investment decisions along intersectoral lines.

The challenge that governments must face in pursuing such a strategy involves gaining the support or acquiescence of interest groups to policies that impose selective or short-term costs to achieve general or long-run benefits. Or from the standpoint of the interest groups themselves: To what extent are nongovernmental economic organizations able and willing to block or defuse attempts on the part of the state to introduce microeconomic policies designed to coordinate sectoral claims in line with national priorities? This question is worth pursuing further, for it lies at the heart of economic strategies that have served as alternatives to neo-laissez-faire.

The question falls into two analytically distinct parts. First is the issue of the political leverage of economic interest groups: To what extent do interest groups in the sectors targeted by microeconomic policy have the political strength to resist government demands? This turns on the political resources commanded by interest groups, such as the legitimacy accorded to them in representing their constituency, and their level of organization, wealth, functional role, militancy, and internal unity. But the ability to resist state economic policy also depends on the political process itself, particularly the accessibility of decision-making arenas to interest group influence, and the dispersal of potential veto points, i.e., the degree to which resistance in one decision-making arena is convertible to veto power within the political process as a whole.

Second, there is the issue of interest group concertation, the extent to which the state is able to coordinate interest group demands in a particular sector or sectors through channels of consensual policy formulation and implementation. Here we are on ground well travelled by scholars of neocorporatism. Two conditions have been emphasized as especially important in creating and sustaining an exchange between interest groups and the state: a) interest group centralization, which conditions the ability of interest groups to implement bargains that are struck with the state at the national level; and b) a relationship of trust between the relevant interest groups and the government, which serves to assure that the state will actually compensate interest groups for their short-term sacrifices.[21] As Mancur Olson has convincingly argued, the centralization of authority in encompassing peak interest groups may also increase the likelihood that the interest group concerned will take into account the implications of its actions on society as a whole, and create an incentive "to make sacrifices up to a point for policies and activities that are sufficiently rewarding for the society as a whole."[22]

My conclusion is that the practice of microeconomic policy in the United States and Britain is caught between the stools of interest group leverage and concertability. Interest groups are able to resist attempts to coordinate their decisions (in Britain, mainly because they are strong; in the United States, mainly because the political system is so open to interest group influence), yet in neither country has it been possible to implement microeconomic policies consensually.

Before we go any further, a brief look at contrasting scenarios may make the argument clearer. Figure 2.2 dichotomizes interest group political leverage and concertability, yielding four possibilities for state/interest-group relations. As indicated above, the United States and Britain tend toward the pluralist cell. Two of the three remaining possibilities are closely approximated among contemporary democracies: the combination of high interest group leverage and high concertability is a distinguishing characteristic of societies in which state/economy linkages in key arenas of microeconomic policy are described as neocorporatist in the growing literature on the subject; and the combination of low interest group leverage and low concertability, which I have labeled dirigist, is most closely seen in France through the 1970s. For our purposes, we can set the fourth possibility aside, for the concertation of interest groups having little influence

Interest Group Political Leverage

		High	Low
Concertability	High	NEOCORPORATISM	QUASI-CORPORATISM
	Low	PLURALISM	DIRIGISM

Figure 2.2 Types of State/Economy Linkages

typifies the authoritarian variant of corporatism seen in some Western societies between the World Wars, but not reproduced among contemporary liberal democracies.[23]

Neocorporatist state/economy linkages are most closely approximated in the Northern Scandinavian countries, Austria, and to a lesser extent in Belgium and Finland. In these countries, labor unions and employers' organizations are strongly entrenched, and have the organizational density and financial muscle to make it very difficult for the state to force its will on them. However, these organizations are highly centralized, and they have been effective participants in bargaining at the national level. The close ties between governing socialist parties and trade union movements in these countries has provided a nexus between the state and the economy, a means through which the state may influence economic decision-making.[24]

Thus, in the context of concertation, a high level of interest group leverage may actually increase the ability of the state to coordinate the activities of economic organizations along intersectoral lines. Concertation allows the state to extend responsibility for public policy to organizations that have the power to veto or disrupt it. In Norway, Sweden, and Austria, governments have effectively integrated trade unions and employer associations into microeconomic policymaking as quasi-public agencies. This integration is based on the bargained cooperation of peak union and employer associations in formulating and administering broad incomes policies tying together wage decisions and key aspects of government economic policy, including manpower, fiscal, and tax policies. In these societies, state intervention in economic decision-making has generally taken place in the context of institutionalized class compromise between highly organized and entrenched workers and employers, mediated by social democratic participation in government.[25]

A contrasting form of state influence over economic decision-making is found in societies where economic interest groups are weak and fractionalized. In France, government influence has been exercised through tightly knit policy networks, involving state officials and representatives of capital, that have a large degree of autonomy from interest group demands. As John Zysman has pointed out in his study of economic policy-making in France: "Centralization of the state bureaucracy and at least partial insulation from outside interference . . . are critical features of the French system. . . . The centralization of the French state provides the possibility of unified and concerted government action, while its partial autonomy allows it to initiate policy and direct events rather than simply react to domestic pressure."[26]

The insulation of policy networks is partially a result of the weakness of interest groups, above all of labor unions, which are politically fractionalized, financially weak, and encompass less than a quarter of nonagricultural employees. The state bureaucracy, in contrast, is known for its coherence and self-confidence. The result is that "channels of influence are sufficiently narrowed so that many groups now feel themselves powerless to exert any political pressure within the state bureaucracy."[27]

From the 1960s, French government economic policy has been directed to promoting national economic power by increasing the international competitiveness of selected companies—the so-called policy of "national champions." As in Japan, the linkage between the state and economy reflects a mercantilist tradition of economic policy in which market activity is oriented to state objectives, summed up by Samuel Brittan as "a kind of right-wing dirigism—a common front between government and industrial organizations designed to bypass the market wherever possible."[28]

Neocorporatism and dirigism describe sharply contrasting types of state/economy linkages. Yet both facilitate microeconomic policies through which the state can influence the decision-making of nongovernmental economic organizations. If interest groups are strong and have the capacity to aggregate their members' demands to the national level, the state may bargain with them; if they are weak, the state may ignore them.

Developments of recent years in countries that have approximated these types show that the nexus between state and economy that each type facilitates can be undermined by the formation of new groupings, or the strengthening of old ones, that stand outside the established policy-making framework. In Sweden, the countermobilization of professional and managerial employees in their own unions, the SACO and the PTK, has introduced a new set of demands into industrial relations at odds with those represented by the established union federations, and has vastly complicated bargaining in the sphere of economic policy.[29] In France, the growth in the stature and power of the major union federations, the CGT and the CFDT, under socialist government, has made it much more difficult for the state to pursue microeconomic policy unilaterally.[30]

Both neocorporatist and dirigist state/economy linkages facilitate a highly structured relationship of the exercise of authority to the allocation of resources in the economy, which is to say that certain kinds of demands are channeled within the system, while others are excluded. The political tensions that this causes, as excluded groups raise new demands or clamor for entry into exclusive policy networks, are amply illustrated in the events of 1968 in France, and the less explosive, but equally eventful, rise of consumer groups and the antinuclear movement in Sweden in the 1970s. In these developments it may be possible to see a general trend in which the ability of governments to introduce their own priorities into organized economic decision-making has become more problematic. Neocorporatist and dirigist state/economy linkages appear inherently unstable in a period of competitive interest mobilization and countermobilization. The emergence of a range of previously unorganized or excluded groups over the last fifteen years has reduced some of the salient differences between these societies and others in which state/interest-group relations were always more pluralist.

In the United States and Britain, state/economy linkages can be described as highly pluralist, combining relatively high interest group influence with low concertability. Interest groups have the political capacity to block or defuse government economic policies that attempt to coordinate their activities, yet lack the coherence to become effective partners in creating and maintaining consensual policies.

Interest groups are not particularly strong in the United States when compared to those of Britain and the societies of Central and Northwestern Europe. In most sectors, including industry and agriculture, they are relatively weak in terms of internal unity and level of organization.[31] Labor union organization, for example, is moderately strong only among blue-collar workers in the manufacturing industries of the northern states. The overall level of union organization in the industrialized democracies is about 22 percent, with France perhaps having the lowest percentage. Moreover, the legitimacy accorded to interest group political activity in America is less than in most Western European countries, as is demonstrated in the conspicuous attacks on interest group influence made by President Carter in his Farewell Address, and on several occasions by President Reagan.[32] Major functional interest groups are more deeply and exclusively embedded in parties in Britain, and attacks made upon them by politicians tend to be highly partisan, directed to interests operating on "the other side."

But what interest groups in the United States lack in unity and organization, they can make up for by exploiting the uniquely fractionalized political process. As Harrison Salisbury has summarized, "The structural elements are familiar; federalism, separation of powers, legislators nominated and elected from single-member districts. The elements interact to perpetuate the pattern where groups have multiple access points and governmental officials find it extremely difficult to assemble enough authority to act on a comprehensive scale, whether it involves enacting policy or negotiating with a socio-economic sector."[33]

These factors, in combination with the weakness of parties, led to highly segmented policy-making, dominated by subgovernments of interest groups, bureaucratic agencies, and congressional and sub-congressional committees operating in iron triangles. Such a policy-making framework ensures sensitivity to the demands aggregated by the interests organized around a particular policy sector—in one observer's words, a "segmented responsiveness."[34] But, by the same token, the scope for intersectoral coordination is minimal. As Joel Aberbach, Robert Putnam, and Bert Rockman have pointed out: "The spirit of 'political government,' however, may be one of 'directionless conflict.' The transmission lines of political government carry voltage from society to government, but the absence of a central grid dissipates energy needed for sustained productive purpose. Polity surges in the United States often result from momentary energies, so that they typically remain unassimilated into a broader policy mosaic."[35]

In recent years, the autonomy of policy-making in iron triangles has declined. The growth of state economic intervention, both regulatory and redistributive, the increasing role of policy specialists, the intensification of interest group activity on the part of established groups, especially business groups, and the proliferation of new public interest groups, have together opened up, and immensely complicated, the practice of policy-making.[36] An overall judgment of the recent development of interest group politics would have to take into account certain advantages of the emerging system: more visible policy-making, the application of greater professionalism and expertise to policy-making, the effective representation of more, and more varied, interests on a broader range of issues. However, from the standpoint of formulating and implementing microeconomic policy, it is fairly clear that what was once difficult has become harder.

The failures of the Carter administration in pursuing an integrated energy policy are one illustration of the problems of defining and gaining consensus on a complex set of issues in a context of shifting policy networks involving a variety of interest groups—in this case, tax reformers, nuclear power specialists, and civil rights groups, alongside the oil corporations and consumer groups.[37] As Arnold Heidenheimer, Hugh Heclo, and Carolyn Teich Adams have pointed out: "Rather than straining for analogies, it is well to recognize that the U.S. national government has little capacity to pursue coherent courses of action below the most aggregate levels of economic management."[38]

The influence of the constraints of the American political system on economic policy debates is particularly clear on the issue of industrial policy. The establishment of agencies having responsibility for diagnosing specific problem areas and making differential grants, such as the Economic Development Organization and the Model Cities Program, led, in practice, to the multiplication of criteria for assistance and the wide dispersal of benefits.[39] As Charles Schultze has argued,

> The governmental choices that an industrial policy contemplates have little to do with fairness and much to do, at least ostensibly, with exacting economic criteria. . . . These are precisely the sorts of decisions that the American political system makes very poorly. . . .
> One does not have to be a cynic to forecast that the surest way to multiply unwarranted subsidies and protectionist measures is to legitimize them under the rubric of industrial policy.[40]

There are at least three strategies for dealing with this situation. First is the strategy of constitutional reform, which is based on altering the institutional constraints of economic policy-making. While specific proposals for reform may differ, the goal is to increase the autonomy of government from interest group influence. This, for example, lies behind Lester Thurow's advocacy of stronger political parties which could summon the will, and the congressional support, for policies that inevitably impose losses on some groups in society.[41] A second strategy is that of "mobilizing consensus," gaining a general normative agreement on fundamental issues underlying the role of the state in the economy. Such a strategy is put forward by Daniel Bell in his discussion of a "philosophy of the public household," of what would be necessary to create a more legitimate economic order.[42] The third strategy is neo-laissez-faire. This is based on the attempt to retrench the economic role of the state, to depoliticize the economy by returning decision-making as far as possible to the market. The response of a number of conservatives to the experience of economic policy-making in the 1960s and 1970s, as they have interpreted it, has been to adjust their policy agenda to the institutional constraints of the political system. Such a strategy is a central feature of what James Ceaser has described as the "conservative theory of governance" practiced by the Reagan administration, the chief features of which are simplifying the political agenda by concentrating on a few select policies; resisting an active policy-making orientation that views nonintervention to be as much a policy as intervention; and shifting responsibilities away from the federal government to states and localities, or to the private sector.[43]

In the United States, government is infiltrated by interest group demands because it lacks the fortification of centralized institutions or strong parties. In Britain, the fortifications of government are stronger, but so are the major functional interest groups that stand beyond. Interest group pressure in Britain is more narrowly focussed on the executive. Lobbying in the parliamentary arena has a more uncertain payoff, and, when pursued by a sectional interest group, is usually the sign of prior failure to sway civil servants or their ministers. However, the pattern of relations between interest groups and the executive is reminiscent, in some important respects, of that described in the literature on iron triangles, if we exclude the role of congressional committees. Group subgovernment, highly segmented policy-making, fragmentation of policy-making into issue communities, are terms that have been applied to the British system.[44]

The consequence of this for economic policy-making in Britain is aptly described as "arms length" government by Andrew Shonfield, a reliance on aggregate policy instruments that obviate the need to come to terms with entrenched economic interests. Where governments have introduced microeconomic planning agencies, these have been more concerned to gain the consensus of the relevant interest groups than to discriminate among firms in accordance with planning criteria. Planning in Britain has been guided by representational formulas of "fairness" rather than economic "rationality."[45] As Jack Hayward has observed:

> Firstly, there are no explicit, over-riding medium or long term objectives. Secondly, unplanned decision-making is incremental. Thirdly, humdrum or unplanned decisions are arrived at by a continuous process of mutual adjustment between a plurality of au-

tonomous policy-makers operating in the context of highly frag-
mented multiple flow of influence. Not only is plenty of scope
offered to interest group spokesmen to shape the outcome by
participation in the advisory process. The aim is to secure through
bargaining at least passive acceptance of the decision by the interest affected.[46]

While this remains an accurate description of policy-making in a
variety of spheres, it no longer applies with regard to industrial relations. Since the late 1960s, the corporate bias toward gradualism,
consensus, and the avoidance of crisis has been displaced by a series
of conflicts that have resulted from attempts on the part of the state
to concert unions and employers in incomes policies and to legally
restrict the powers of unions.[47] While the pluralist character of state/
economy linkages has not materially altered, the demands of governments for economic concertation have greatly increased. Moreover,
from the mid-1960s, these demands coincided with the rise of what
Samuel Beer has described as "romantic populism" in British political culture, which undermined the authority of union leaders and
fostered the autonomy of shop-floor organizations.[48]

These conflicts between unions and the state have had a decisive
influence on the turn to neo-laissez-faire in the Conservative party.
Neo-laissez-faire provided a means of pursuing economic objectives
without directly engaging trade unions in economic policy. Under
neo-laissez-faire, the chief instrument of economic policy is control
of the money supply which, unlike incomes policy, is completely beyond the organizational reach of entrenched economic interest groups.
Moreover, the consequence of Conservative monetary policy has been
significantly to increase the level of unemployment, which has reduced the economic leverage of unions.[49]

Labour governments have, on a number of occasions, been able to
gain the consent of the peak union organization, the Trades Union
Congress (TUC), to incomes policy, but that consent has meant little
because decision-making within British unions is so decentralized.
British unions lack the coherence to make class compromises on the
northern Scandinavian model, yet they are too powerful to be thrust
aside as in France in the 1960s and 1970s. They are represented in a
unitary peak organization, the TUC, but the TUC has little authority
over its union constituents. Beyond the seldom used power of expulsion, the TUC has to rely on its powers of persuasion to bring
recalcitrant unions into line with majority policy. Likewise, the Con-

federation of British Industry is extremely weak by contrast to peak employer associations in countries where neocorporatist state/economy linkages are found. Moreover, employer interests are not informally coordinated within a centralized and encompassing banking system, as they are in West Germany, where the *Deutsche Bundesbank* serves to influence the decision-making of economic organizations in line with the priorities of public policy.[50]

In the sphere of incomes policy, the difficulties associated with gaining and sustaining union consent to voluntary incomes policies have led governments to impose incomes policies unilaterally and enforce them statutorily. But where governments have used legislative authority to coerce labor market outcomes in the face of union hostility, the result has been to broaden labor market conflicts into overt political conflicts concerning the legitimacy of government authority.

The dilemma of pursuing an incomes policy in Britain was faced most acutely by the Conservative government between 1972 and 1974. The dramatic failure of the policy in the great coalminers' strike of 1973–74, and the subsequent loss of the General Election in February 1974, had a profound effect on the willingness of the Conservative party to contemplate a return to microeconomic intervention in the labor market.

While all Western democracies experienced worsening economic performance from the late 1960s, governments in the United States and Britain had to respond under the particularly severe constraints of high interest group political leverage with little possibility of bridging interest group demands through consensual bargaining. Support for neo-laissez-faire developed as part of a learning process, forged in the policy experiences of the 1960s and 1970s. However, the "lessons" of this period are by no means objective facets of an independent social reality. The strength of neo-laissez-faire in the United States and Britain should be understood not only by looking at the experiences of the period, but, as discussed earlier in this chapter, by looking at the character of the conservative parties that were interpreting those experiences.

Conclusion

The growth of government intervention in the economy in the twentieth century has been part of a process in which social and economic outcomes have been viewed as legitimate objects of purposive control. In Anthony King's formulation: "Once upon a time man looked to God to order the world. Then he looked to the market. Now he looks to government."[51] In this chapter, I have argued that the effectiveness of that control is dependent on the institutional configuration of state and interest groups, which serve to constrain economic policy quite independently of the quality of the knowledge that is available about the relationship of economic means to ends. In the United States and Britain, concertation of private economic decision-making would be problematic, even if we knew what the ideally best policy was, because of the fragmentation of the institutions responsible for aggregating interest in these societies.

This is not to say that concertation is impossible under all circumstances. In both the United States and Britain, as in other societies that have undergone total war, national solidarity and the widely perceived need to rapidly mobilize human and material resources allowed governments to concert economic decision-making largely on the basis of consent.[52] But the purposive incentives generated in total war are not matched by those roused by talk of an economic "war" against inflation or unemployment. Even when unions and employers have been favorably disposed to voluntary incomes policies, their support has soon collapsed because these groups have no means to make binding collective decisions. Where the links between the state and labor market organizations are pluralist, governments have been most prone to fall back on the force of law when they have attempted to influence labor market outcomes.[53]

The realism of neo-laissez-faire is that it does not involve the task of coordinating economic decision-making in society. The market, not the political process, is viewed as the arbiter of competing economic demands. This, as I have tried to show, was an important inducement in the turn to neo-laissez-faire on the part of conservatives in the United States and Britain. In this sense, neo-laissez-faire is an adjustment to circumstances, to the constraints that the political system and interest groups place on government action in society. However, from another standpoint, neo-laissez-faire is a radical doctrine, for it is founded on the attempt to establish the autonomy of the market from politics in an age where, as Ernest Gellner has pointed out, we can recognize the market as a social artifact, as a set of relations that is manipulated in a variety of ways to serve a variety of interests.[54]

Although there are parallels in the turn to laissez-faire in the United States and Britain, there are important differences also. In both countries, neo-laissez-faire was recommended to the political Right in the context of what I have described as pluralist state/economy linkages. However, in the United States, the problem of state influence over organized economic decision-making issues from basic elements of the American constitution—federalism, the separation of powers, the weakness of political parties. In Britain, the turn to neo-laissez-faire was influenced by the existence of strong interest groups, particularly trade unions, that were unwilling or unable to be concerted in line with government economic priorities. Thus in Britain, neo-laissez-faire is a policy that has been pursued in a more confrontational way, in explicit opposition to entrenched unions. It is partially the outcome of a series of industrial battles between the Conservative party and trade unions, and has been accompanied by a refusal on the part of the Thatcher government to continue the informal channels of union consultation that were established in the early 1940s. In the British context, neo-laissez-faire forms part of what S. E. Finer has described as adversary politics.[55] The Labour party promises to reverse much of the Conservative policy should it come to power, and groups of workers that stand to lose most from the introduction of market norms, namely those in the least competitive, traditional industries, especially the coalmining industry, have fought battles almost as intense as those fought by similarly condemned groups in the nineteenth century—the handloom weavers come to mind.

In the United States the turn to neo-laissez-faire has been hotly disputed by a variety of groups, but is congruent with certain deeply rooted aspects of American political culture, particularly suspicion of government and the traditionally strong emphasis on individualism. By and large, there has not been sustained opposition to neo-laissez-faire among the groups and constituencies of the Republican party itself. In Britain, the revival of laissez-faire has taken place at a time of great change in the Conservative party and its role in society. Even within the Conservative party the doctrine, as pursued by the Thatcher government, has been a highly contentious one, and has contributed to a profound division within the party, as well as in the society at large.

In writing and revising this chapter I have had the benefit of comments from too many friends and colleagues to mention here by name. However, I would like to thank my fellow participants in the British/American Festival, especially James Ceaser and Richard Hodder-Williams, for constructive criticism. The writing of this chapter was generously aided by a University of Virginia Summer Grant.

3

Changes in Party Systems and Public Philosophies

DENNIS KAVANAGH

———

In this chapter, Dennis Kavanagh develops some of the concerns of the first two chapters, for his analysis of political parties relates directly to executive-legislative relations and to policy choices. He notes at the outset several similarities in the recent experience of parties in the United States and Great Britain: dealignment, difficult experiences with reform, the erosion of an elite consensus on basic policy issues, and the rise of issues as cues to party preferences. The explanation for these similar developments lies essentially in the perceived failures of government in the 1970s. The weakening of the parties, more advanced in the United States where party control of presidential candidates is almost entirely absent, reflects a widespread erosion in both countries of the enduring links which bound social groups to particular parties. One consequence is that parties now perform far less satisfactorily one of the classic functions assigned to them by political analysts of the last generation, namely to act as institutional channels for translating popular policy preferences into governmental action. Kavanagh makes three important warnings: first, it is dangerous to confuse rhetoric with reality and both in the United States and in the United Kingdom the extent to which a new agenda and priorities actually determine policy output can be exaggerated; second, it is important not to get seduced by seeming similarities and therefore ignore the major differences in the nature of "the Right" in the two countries; third, it is essential, as Rasmussen also asserted, to realize that institutions are clearly tied to the culture and society in which they exist and therefore that the likelihood of successful institutional transfer is not great.

Introduction

The United States and Britain are among the handful of two-party systems in the world today.[1] But a common nomenclature only disguises important differences. Although Anglo-American political and party systems are often distinguished from their West European counterparts, the American and British party systems are also often studied as a contrast. For example, it is often noted that the British parties have certain attributes which the American parties lack. The former, for example, are programmatic, disciplined, centralized, and responsible, in contrast to the latter. Appreciation of the different character of the respective party systems is important in understanding the different ways constitutional democracy operates in the two countries. In one they are part of a power-concentrating political system, one in which Parliament is sovereign, unconstrained by formal checks and balances, federalism, written constitution, courts, or a powerful second chamber. In the other, they are part and parcel of a power-dispersing system; the cultural suspicion of government, constitutional separation of powers, absence of centralized authority, and diversity of society all combine to hinder strong government. In Britain, as L. J. Sharpe has observed, the emphasis is on functional effectiveness, on the idea that government should have sufficient power to carry out its policies. In the United States, by contrast, democracy attaches a higher importance to placing limits and controls on public power.[2]

Similarity and contrast have stimulated many comparative studies of the political systems of the two countries. Such studies of the political parties have often had a practical or reformist bent, usually focussing on what the United States could learn from Britain.[3] In his exploration of the intellectual history of "The British Party Model" in the *American Political Science Review*, Leon Epstein has noted how the majoritarian features of the responsible party model in Britain have appealed to many Americans.[4] The fusion of the executive and legislature, facilitated by the British party system, has provided the opportunity for clear and responsible political leadership. By contrast, the Madisonian model has produced frequent bouts of deadlock between Congress and President; the parties failed to join together what the Constitution had separated. Reformers advocated the importation of many features of the British party system, and this was perhaps most fully explicated in the famous 1950 APSA Report *Towards a More Responsible Two-Party System*. On the whole, however, defenders of the status quo in the United States have had the better of the argument. Acutely aware of the different sociopolitical environments of the two countries they have claimed that American parties derive from a particular social, cultural, and constitutional context, and to a large extent cannot be other than they are.[5]

A political party is not a single unitary actor or institution. We may variously refer to a party in government (a Republican administration, or Labour government), the party in the legislature, the party organization and its bureaucracy, the party membership, or, perhaps even the party in the electorate. Each of these usages refers to different party actors and roles. In the United States the differences between the presidential and congressional wings of the parties have traditionally been so marked that U.S. politics has actually been described as a four-party system.[6] Federalism in the United States has also hindered the integration of state party structures. Political parties are complex, not simple; this is particularly so in the United States.

This chapter compares British and American parties in different contexts. First, it examines how the parties perform the function of expressing popular preferences in the two societies. Second, it examines how the parties have responded to pressures to become more "open" and democratic institutions. Third, it examines the impact of parties on government; parties, after all, are unique in claiming an electoral mandate to control government. Finally, it considers the relations between the parties and the climate of opinion in the two countries. It therefore examines the parties' electoral followings, memberships, and leaderships. There are a number of similar trends in the two systems, but even these are expressed in rather different ways.

The Parties and Popular Preferences

A key task of political parties in a democracy is to present policy alternatives and organize choices for the electorate. There are, however, many signs that the major parties in Britain and America are weakening in their ability to structure the vote. If we take account of the declining support and the fall in turnout compared to the early 1950s, the decline of the Conservative and Labour parties is quite marked. In 1951 80 percent of the total electorate voted Conservative or Labour, compared to only 50.5 percent in 1983. But the disproportional effects of the electoral system has meant that the decline has not been reflected in a fall in seats in the House of Commons.

In the United States the more important factor has not been the rise of a third party (although George Wallace in 1968 and, to a lesser extent, John Anderson in 1980 attracted considerable support) but abstention. The proportion of eligible voters turning out in presidential elections has fallen steadily from 62 percent in 1952 to 52 percent in 1980 (table 3.1). A number of surveys have shown that

Table 3.1   Proportion of Electorate Voting for the Two Major Parties in General Elections (Britain) and Presidential Elections (United States), 1950–84

Great Britain percentage of the electorate voting either Conservative or Labour		United States percentage of the resident voting-age population voting for either the Democratic or Republican presidential candidate	
1950	75.5		
1951	80.3		
		1952	61.0
1955	74.3		
		1956	58.7
1959	73.8		
		1960	62.8
1964	67.7	1964	61.9
1966	68.7		
		1968	52.4
1970	64.8		
		1972	54.9
February 1974	60.7		
October 1974	56.1		
		1976	53.2
1979	62.9		
		1980	47.8
1983	50.5		

electoral participation in the United States is perhaps the lowest of Western countries.[7] The low turnout figure is less a consequence of political alienation than the complex registration requirements of the United States, the mobility of the electorate, and the extension of voting rights to blacks and young voters (who tend to register less enthusiastically than most other groups).

If we turn to party membership there has also clearly been a decline in the case of Britain. The Conservative party does not keep a register of individual members, but most informed assessments claim that the membership has fallen from approximately 3 million in the mid-1950s to 1.2 million in 1983. The individual membership of the Labour party has fallen from nearly a million in 1953 to approximately 250,000 in 1983. Before the 1983 election the Labour party had the lowest ratio of individual members to voters in any West European socialist party.[8] The United States has never had European-style mass membership parties, so it is not possible to monitor trends. The decline in membership has occurred at the same time as the parties, to differing degrees, are giving a greater say to members in leadership selection and policy formation. (It raises the question of whether a smaller membership becomes less representative of a party's voters in general.)

It is also apparent that party identification or partisanship has declined in the two countries (see tables 3.2 and 3.3). In the United States 75 percent of voters claimed to be Republican or Democrat in 1952 but the figure fell to 61 percent in 1980. The so-called Independents swelled in the same period from 23 percent to 38 percent. In Britain the proportion identifying with Conservative and Labour has fallen between 1964 and 1983 from 81 percent to 70 percent. More impressively, the number of "very strong" identifiers with the two main parties has fallen from 36 percent to 23 percent in the United States between 1952 and 1980, and from 38 percent to 23 percent between 1964 and 1983 in Britain. In both countries this weakening of partisanship is more marked among the younger voters, so it may well turn out that, because partisanship is to some extent inherited, there will be fewer partisans in the electorates of the future.

It is not easy to explain these trends. In Britain the fall in party membership has not been matched by a declining activity in voluntary organizations. In the United States the decline in electoral participation and partisanship and growth of cynicism must, in a similar way, be related to contrary survey evidence of an increase in interest in politics and other forms of political and electoral activities, higher

Table 3.2   Trends in the Incidence and Strength of Major Party
Identification in Great Britain (in percentages)

	1964	1966	1970	February & October 1974 (average)	1979	1983
Percentage of electorate with:						
A party identification	93	91	90	90	90	86
A Conservative or Labour identification	81	81	82	75	76	70
A "very strong" Conservative/Labour identification	38	40	40	25	19	23
A "fairly strong" Conservative/Labour identification	34	32	33	35	39	29
A "not very strong" Conservative/Labour identification	9	9	9	15	18	18

Sources: Reanalysis of data from David Butler and Donald Stokes, *Political Change in Britain* (New York: St. Martin's Press, 1976) for 1964, 1966, and 1970 cross-sectional surveys; the February 1974, October 1974, and 1979 British Election Study cross-sectional surveys; and the 1983 BBC/Gallup election survey.

Table 3.3   Trends in the Incidence and Strength of Major Party
Identification in the United States (in percentages)

	1952	1956	1960	1964	1968	1972	1976	1980
Percentage of electorate who are:								
Independents*	23	23	23	23	30	35	37	38
Republicans or Democrats	75	73	75	77	70	64	63	61
"Strong" Democrats or Republicans	36	36	36	38	30	25	24	(n.a.)

Sources: 1952–76: Arthur H. Miller and Edward J. Schneider, *American National Election Studies Data Sourcebook* (Cambridge, Mass.: Harvard University Press, 1980), p. 81; 1980: National Opinion Research Centre General Social Survey.
* Includes those "leaning" to the Republicans or Democrats.

levels of education and ideology among voters, and the numerous dramatic political events in the 1960s and 1970s.[9] Richard Brody writes of the "puzzle of political participation in America" and notes: "One has the impression, although good data do not exist, that organisational membership, in general, and politically relevant interests groups have been trending upwards."[10]

Political participation may differ in the two countries in one important respect: it is generally less oriented to political parties and elections in the United States (although recent developments in Britain suggest that more political activity takes place outside the party structures than was once the case). Lipset has drawn attention to a paradox of American politics, namely that the oldest major political parties in the world have coexisted with an immense variety of social movements.[11] Political participation in the United States is multidimensional in that different modes or patterns of political activity give rise to different types of participants: voting specialists, party specialists, communal activists, and group specialists.[12] In Britain the great majority (some two-thirds) of participants are voting specialists; that is, they confine their political activity to voting, the "easiest" activity. Americans have many more opportunities to vote: primary elections, local referendums, elections for different federal, state, county, and town jurisdictions, choices on a long ballot, and separate voting for the executive and legislature. A smaller proportion of Americans vote in elections but they are more active politically, being involved across a wide range of other modes of political action.

The social bases of support for the parties are also changing. The traditional two-party systems were both rooted in class divisions and socioeconomic issues though region and religion were also important in the United States. The Democratic and Labour parties had strong support among the manual working class and Republicans and Conservatives among the middle class or white-collar section. Of course, one has to qualify this statement, not least for the third or so of the working class who regularly voted Conservative. In the United States features like religion and ethnicity also qualified the class basis of the party system. Yet there was a clear socioeconomic basis to the old party systems, even if the level of class consciousness was different.

This has changed somewhat in recent elections. In the case of the Labour party, the usual three-fifths of the working class vote which it gained between 1945 and 1970 fell to 50 percent between 1974 and 1979, and fell further to 38 percent in 1983. And among the growing section of the working class (those living in the South, working in the private sector, and increasingly owner-occupiers or mortgagees), the Conservatives had a commanding lead in 1983. In the United States the Democratic party has become less Catholic, less working class, less trade unionist, less Southern, and less white. This is another way of describing the erosion of the old New Deal coalition at the presidential level. George Wallace made inroads among the working class vote in the South and the North in 1968 on such social issues as law and order and race. This trend was further accentuated in 1972 after the nomination of Senator McGovern. By 1980 there were only small differences between the proportions of Catholics and Protestants voting for each of the parties and class differences were the narrowest of any postwar presidential election.[13] The new liberalism which has found a home in the Democratic party attracts increasing support from the middle class and well-educated professionals, while the new conservatism has gained more blue-collar workers for the Republicans.

Another change has been in the regional distribution of party strength. In the United States the existence of the solid South made sectionalism a salient feature of American politics and society. But the growing penetration of the South by the Republican party—dating back to 1964 at the presidential level and subsequently, though more modestly, at the congressional level—and the growth of Democratic support in New England has made the party system more competitive nationally.

In Britain there has long been a division between the north, which is largely Labour, and the south, which is overwhelmingly Conservative. The division has increased in recent years with northern, urban, and inner city seats moving more sharply to Labour at times of a national swing to Labour and less so to the Conservative party at a time of national pro-Conservative swing. Seats in the south, suburbs, and rural areas have steadily become more Conservative. After the 1983 election Labour seats outnumbered the Conservatives two to one in northern England, while Conservative seats outnumbered Labour four to one in southern England. Third-party interventions in constituencies have frequently drawn support away from the weaker of the two main political parties. A consequence has been a decline of two-party competitiveness across the country and a reduction in the number of marginal seats. The division between a Labour North Britain and a Conservative South Britain of course correlates with areas of heavy manufacturing versus new industries and high versus low unemployment, respectively. The different sociogeographic bases of the two parties calls into question their ability to aggregate interests across the nation.

In both countries the decline of traditional stabilizing forces—party identification, social class, and other social factors—has allowed more scope for issues, personality, and events before and during the campaign to make the electorate more volatile. In the United States, Vietnam, race, the "social agenda," and the economy in 1980 have all been important. In Britain, the political agenda has been less dramatic, but inflation and industrial relations (accompanied by major industrial unrest in February 1974 and early 1979) were also decisive. In 1979 and 1983 the Labour party policies were spectacularly out of line with the views of many Labour voters, just as McGovern's policies were out of line with many Democrats in 1972. In the United States the trends have given rise to a paradox. There has been a closer alignment between party identification and issue preferences and an increase in ideology and attitude consistency among voters.[14] Yet this has occurred while parties have been getting weaker. The paradox has been well expressed by Jeane Kirkpatrick as one in which party politics "becomes more ideological and less institutionalized."[15]

Yet the role of political personality remains an important difference between the two countries. In the United States the expansion of party primaries at the presidential level, indeed the presidential election itself, accentuates the importance of personality. In congressional elections, party factors have declined in significance and incumbency has become more important. In Britain, however, issues remain more important than personality. In 1979 Mr. Callaghan outscored Mrs. Thatcher on popularity yet Labour decisively lost the election. In 1983, although Margaret Thatcher was preferred as the party leader by 55 to 15 points over Michael Foot (and less than half of Labour's voters thought he would make the best Prime Minister), the margin between the Conservative and Labour parties was much smaller.

Some years ago talk of an "Americanization" of political parties in Western Europe referred to a trend in which the personalities of party leaders, public relations, and mass media became more important in elections and party loyalty weakened among the electorate. Kirchheimer perhaps had this in mind when referring to the spread of "catchall" parties in Western Europe.[16] In the United States the expansion of the primary system has rendered the parties less able to control the nomination process; as Austin Ranney notes, "parties are prizes, not judges."[17] To an increasing extent candidates for office recruit their own campaign teams, are more reliant on the mass media to promote their visibility and "name-recognition," and often canvass the support of particular cause groups. These trends have been exacerbated by financial reforms at the federal level which mean that money goes directly to the candidate not to the party. Moreover, American parties can to some extent be reshaped every four years with the emergence of a new nominee for the presidency. The important role played by opinion pollsters and campaign consultants in suggesting and refining policy positions is an effect of the weakness of party. The British parties have private pollsters but there are no counterparts to Caddell or Wirthlin, who are presidential pollsters and campaign advisers. The professional campaign consultant is unknown in Britain.

Britain has not become "Americanized." In the first place British political parties as organizations have a more continuous existence between general elections and a more established bureaucracy, regardless of changes of leader. Expenditure on advertising and opinion polling is modest compared to the United States. Political advertising on television is precluded anyway, and there are strict legal limits on the expenses which constituency candidates may incur. In real terms candidates are spending less than they were in 1950. There is also no equivalent to the lengthy primary campaign trail. Although television has increased the visibility and dominance of the party leaders in election campaigns, talk of the "marketing" of Mrs. Thatcher is exaggerated. She was indeed receptive to the advice of her managers when it came to scheduling her campaign speeches and activities in 1979 and 1983, a characteristic which differentiated her from other recent party leaders like Mr. Heath, Mr. Callaghan, or Mr. Foot.

Some of the trends Kirchheimer noted about Western political parties twenty years ago have been confirmed. Kirchheimer regretted the passing of the traditional parties and their declining role in integrating individuals into the political system and framing coherent policy choices for society. He feared that, because voters' loyalties were too loose, the political party would become "too blunt to serve as a link with the functional power holders of society."[18] No doubt he would regard the United States today as having confirmed his fears.

Parties and Electoral Realignment

In both countries there has been much academic and journalistic comment about the prospects for a realignment of the party system. The term realignment refers to a durable change in the balance of strength between established political parties or the emergence of a new party and party system. In the case of the United States Burnham has suggested that realignment is "the American surrogate for revolution," a means by which the parties adjust to and cope with major changes in the social and economic environment.[19] Party realignments occurred in the past in 1860, 1896, and 1932, the latter coming about when Roosevelt forged the New Deal Democratic majority. On this historical trend a realignment should have emerged in the late 1960s. It did not.

No such cyclical pattern is discernable in the case of Britain. In the 1920s the Conservative/Labour duopoly replaced the pre-1914 multi-party system of the Liberals, Irish Nationalists, Conservatives, and Labour. In both countries the factors which have precipitated a realignment were dramatic events like war, or economic depression, or issues (such as Irish Home Rule) which often split a major party, or a change in the composition of the electorate (like the growth of the working class electorate in Britain after 1918).

Yet there are many forces making for the continuity of the party system. Competitive political parties are adaptive; they choose candidates and issues which advance their prospects of winning elections. In addition, partisanship, or the established party loyalty of many voters, disposes them to continue to support their party, regardless of disagreements or reservations about various features. Finally, there is the role of the first-past-the-post electoral system. Its effect in protecting the British two-party system can be seen in the general election of 1983; the Labour and Conservative parties collected 95 percent of the seats for only 70 percent of the votes while the SDP–Liberal Alliance with 25.4 percent of the votes gained 3.5 percent of the seats. Indeed, it is the continued dominance since the 1920s of the two main parties in Britain and the United States that makes both countries distinctive compared to many other West European states. In France, Italy, and Germany, for example, internal collapse as a result of defeat in war, and the introduction of new constitutions and electoral systems, have been a means of fashioning new political party systems.

In the United States the thesis of realignment has generated a veritable academic industry. The signs of political realignment in recent years include: the emergence of issues which cut across the political parties; the growth of split ticket voting; the greater influence on voting behavior of candidate and issue factors compared with party identification; the increased volatility of the electorate. But to date the realignment has obstinately refused to occur. Speculation has centered on one of three possibilities. The first is the replacement of the Democrats by the Republicans as the natural or normal majority party. Since 1944 the Democrats have obtained more than 50 percent of the presidential vote only twice. Indeed, in presidential elections since 1948 the Republicans have amassed more votes than Democrats (292 million to 268 million). The Democratic party has also lost its hold on the once solid South. A key element in the thesis of the emergence of a new Republican majority is the idea that there is a sun-belt majority, based upon the migration of population and new industries to the South and Southwest and the decline of old industrial areas.[20] On this analysis the minority Democratic party will be confined largely to the Northeast and Pacific Northwest.

Yet in terms of congressional voting, most levels of officeholding, and party identification the Democrats continue to do much better than they do in presidential elections and much better than Republicans. On party identification they were in the 1970s still nearly two-to-one ahead. The Republicans have managed to overcome their partisan deficit by outscoring the Democrats on candidate and issue factors. Moreover, much evidence suggests that Reagan's victory in 1980 was more a repudiation of Carter than an endorsement of his own policies. If the Conservatives are the majority party in Britain, the GOP is not, unless the 1984 exit poll figures translate into enduring identifications, which did not occur after 1980.

A second possibility is that there will be a clearer emergence of the New Deal pattern.[21] Many liberal voters who were Republican have been shifting to the Democrats and conservative Democrats in the South have been shifting to the Republicans. In the 1950s many people cast their votes on the basis of party loyalty or evaluations of the candidate. But from 1964 onwards the issue preferences of voters became a more important influence on voting behavior and were increasingly related to partisan allegiances.[22] In 1980 Ronald Reagan took clear right-wing positions on many issues and voters did see important differences between the political parties.[23]

The final possibility is that there will not be realignment at all. Dean Burnham, among others, has suggested that the American party system is actually undergoing a process of dealignment, one in which both parties lose support without a new pattern emerging. The two parties appear to be too weak, too detached from the loyalties of the voters to force a realignment, and electoral change actually works *against* and not *through* the established political parties.

In Britain the symptoms of change are fewer, but one may point to: the greater electoral volatility; the decline in the aggregate electoral support for the two main parties—from 90 percent in 1970 down to 70 percent in 1983—and growing support for other parties; the record low electoral levels of support for each of the main parties in recent years—27 percent for Labour in 1983 and 36 percent for Conservatives in October 1974.

Liberals and Scottish Nationalists both made inroads on the two parties' support in the 1970s. A more significant breakthrough occurred in 1981–82 with the emergence of the new Social Democratic party. In alliance with the Liberals its support soared in opinion polls and by-elections and posed the greatest postwar threat to the established two-party system. The Alliance gained 25.4 percent of the vote in 1983. With a proportional electoral system it would have gained 160 seats and smashed the system. Instead it got a handful of seats.

Notwithstanding the formidable hurdle of the electoral system, the evidence is still negative that the Alliance has made a breakthrough in the electorate. Neither party in the Alliance has managed to attract support from a distinctive social group, or people concerned about particular issues, or established a large group of partisans. Its electoral support is remarkably evenly drawn across social groups and constituencies, a sure sign of protest voting.[24] Much of the popular support for the SDP, as with the Liberals, is based on perceptions of its political style and political leaders. Crewe fairly concludes that it is a "soft" vote and as likely to fade away as it is to rise.

The Labour party certainly appears to be in secular decline. In all general elections since 1951, bar one, it has lost a slice of the electorate. In each of the three elections between 1974 and 1979 it gained less than 40 percent of the vote and fell even further in 1983. There were a number of special factors which harmed Labour in 1983; the impact of the Falklands War, Michael Foot's unappealing leadership, the bitterly divisive campaign for the deputy leadership of the party in 1981, the split over the constitutional changes, and the inept election campaign were a remarkable and possibly unique combination of adversities. But none of these can gainsay Labour's long-term problems.

What support then is there for the thesis of a Conservative hegemony? In 1983, Mrs. Thatcher's government was the first since 1959 to win reelection after a full term of office and its victory was achieved by the largest margin in seats and votes in any postwar general election. The party's 42 percent share of the vote, however, was not only slightly less than it had gained in 1979 but just about equaled its average share of the vote in postwar elections, and the proportion of Conservative identifiers, at 38 percent, was the same as in 1979. The Conservatives gained a landslide by default in 1983, and owed more to Labour's incompetence than to the electorate's appreciation of the government.[25] But one also has to note a number of Conservative strengths. First of all, the Conservative dominance of the vote for the leading two parties—61 percent to 39 percent—is the most marked of any postwar election. Second, the government withstood usual claims of "time for a change" and the electoral liability of having three million people unemployed. All this happened at a time when adverse economic circumstances and incumbency had weakened governments in elections in most other Western states. Third, there has been an undeniable shift to the right in mood and attitudes among the British electorate and a shift away from the many Labour policies over the past decade (see below). Finally, the rise of the Alliance, though it may have harmed Labour more than the Conservatives, still drew votes away from the latter party.

In both countries, therefore, the evidence for a realignment is not clear-cut. Reliable support for the main parties has weakened and there are many signs of electoral dissatisfaction with the choices on offer. But a new line up of parties has not emerged, although in Britain there is a large following for the new Alliance party. If anything, the evidence in both countries is more supportive for the thesis of there being a partisan dealignment, or a withdrawal of support from the two main political parties.

Parties and Reform

Party reform usually covers two broad categories of phenomena. It includes, first, changes in the rules affecting the internal workings of a political party, and second, attempts to change the relationship between a party and the wider sociopolitical environment in which it operates. In the course of the twentieth century, party reform in Britain and the United States has generally tried to further one or more of the following objectives:

(1) *Particular policies.* In Britain, for example, advocates of proportional representation (and, by implication, more than two significant parties in Parliament) argue that it will limit the opportunity for any one party in government, backed by less than 50 percent of the voters, to introduce "extreme" policies. In the United States many supporters of "responsible party government" have hoped not only to reshape the choice offered to American voters but also to promote policies associated with the liberal wing of the Democratic party.

(2) *Intra-party democracy.* Significant and sustained efforts to give members, usually the activists, a greater say in the decisions of the party have been largely confined to the Democratic and Labour parties. In the former, efforts have centered on the nomination process, in the latter primarily on the determination of policy, though also on nominations.

(3) *Anti-party proposals.* These attempt to depoliticize issues by limiting the remit of political parties. In the United States this outlook dates back to the Founding Fathers' fear of factions and suspicion of power which might be abused. It was later espoused by proponents of "good" (i.e., nonpartisan) government. Before 1914, the spread of the primary system and other devices of direct democracy, together with municipal reform and nonpartisan elections, were designed to correct abuses in parties as well as to weaken them. Although Britain has long been regarded as the home of party government, it is worth noting the existence also of a tradition of the national interest or a government of national unity which would decide issues free from partisanship. The mood has been seen in wartime and in the economic crisis of 1931, in the formation of government coalitions, as well as in the traditional bipartisanship over foreign and defense policies. More recent calls for coalition governments, referendums, a written constitution, policy-making via royal commissions, bargaining between government and major economic interests, or a greater role for the judiciary or the civil service, often reflect explicitly or implicitly a suspicion of party government.

In the past two decades there have been important changes in the power structures of the major parties in the two countries. In the United States the extension of the primary system for the selection of a candidate for the presidency has increased the power of party voters and members at the expense of the party "notables." In the Conservative party the introduction in 1965 of a ballot among MPS for the election and in 1975 for re-selection of the party leader has increased the power of MPS. In the Labour party, various constitutional changes have reduced the influence of MPS and increased that of extraparliamentary groups and activists.

In Britain important issues have been raised by the Labour party's reform. The party's constitution, because it gives formal authority over party policy to the annual Conference, has been judged by some commentators to be incompatible with the sovereignty of Parliament. Robert McKenzie, however, had demonstrated in his classic *Modern British Political Parties* that, when in office, the Labour party had regularly flouted the principle of intra-party democracy and Labour Prime Ministers and cabinets had exercised the perquisites of office in a manner similar to that of Conservative leaders and governments.[26] Yet there were other factors, underplayed by McKenzie, which supported that balance of power. One was the broad agreement among party and union leaders on party policy. Another was the control exercised by leaders of the major trade unions over their delegations to support the parliamentary leadership. Between 1945 and 1969 the platform had hardly lost a vote at the annual party Conference. When it did, the parliamentary leaders defied it with impunity, and the authority of the Conference ebbed.

Yet from the late 1960s onward the trade unions were more divided and there was less agreement on policy. Between 1970 and 1979 the platform lost thirty-two votes, many of them against the wishes of the parliamentary leadership.[27] Whereas the Conference and the National Executive Committee (NEC) had traditionally been used to squash the left-wing dissent in the parliamentary party and in the constituencies, in the 1970s they reinforced left-wing dissent. On many issues the Conference and the Labour government spoke with two different voices, leading to a disastrous confrontation over incomes policy with many public sector trade unions in the winter of discontent in 1979. This climaxed the mood of disappointment of many Conference activists at the record of Labour governments between 1964 and 1979.[28]

The lesson which the activists learned from the experience was that there was little point in winning policy battles in opposition if Labour governments did not implement the policies. They concluded that what was needed was a means of ensuring that the balance of power in the party remained constant, whether the party was in opposition or in office. Too often, the activists claimed, ministers wriggled out of manifesto commitments on the grounds of political acceptability, timing, administrative practicability, lack of resources, and so on. They decided therefore to try and change the structure of the party to make the parliamentary party more subordinate to the Conference and to ensure that party policies were carried out.

Demand for constitutional reform centered on three features: NEC control of the election manifesto, mandatory re-selection of MPS within the lifetime of Parliament, and election of a leader by party members. Between 1979 and 1981 the second two were achieved. This was the most serious attempt by the Left to smash the old "rules of the game" and translate the opposition style into the power structure of the party. The call for greater party democracy was mounted by the left wing to make the Parliamentary Labour party (PLP) more accountable to the Conference and MPS more accountable to local party activists. Shifting the balance of power in the party became the Left's preferred way of closing the gap between the Conference and the PLP and preventing any alleged "betrayal" by the latter. It was also a way of closing the gap between myth and reality that McKenzie had made so much of.

The reforms had a number of consequences. Several right-wing Labour MPS found these proposals objectionable. Plans for a breakaway party were already advanced but the constitutional change was an important factor in encouraging the formation of the Social Democratic Party. By 1981 the idea of a new party had attracted the support of nearly thirty Labour MPS. The machinery for electing the leader of the Labour Party was tested throughout 1981 in a long and bitter struggle for the deputy leadership, in which Denis Healey narrowly defeated Tony Benn, a classic Right versus Left political contest. In 1983 the procedures were tested again when the membership voted overwhelmingly to elect Neil Kinnock, of the Left, in preference to Roy Hattersley, of the Right, as leader, and the latter as deputy leader. As the main contenders sought votes among constituency parties and trade union conferences, the system resembled the American primary. The new balance of power was also reflected in the way the manifesto was drawn up for the 1983 election. Under Clause 5 of the party constitution the NEC and the PLP jointly draw up the manifesto. In recent elections this meeting had been used by the parliamentary leadership to veto proposals which they found objectionable. For example, in 1979 Mr. Callaghan, as Prime Minister, had refused to include various policies which were popular with the

Left and supported by the annual Conference. In 1983, however, Mr. Michael Foot took the lead in suggesting to his shadow cabinet that the draft campaign document drawn up by the NEC should be accepted as the manifesto. Surveys indicate that the program was disliked by many Labour voters. Leaving aside the merits of the reforms themselves, there is no doubt that the spectacular divisions they occasioned, the encouragement they gave to the formation of the SDP, and the policies they encouraged have been electorally disastrous for the party.

There are various reasons why the Labour party has shifted to the Left and the power of activists has increased in recent years. The performance of Labour governments, the behavior of party leaders, changes in the role and structure of trade unions, and changes in electoral behavior have all contributed. Particularly important has been the myth of "betrayal" by the parliamentary leadership. The most articulate spokesman for the view that successive Labour governments have betrayed the policies and ideals of the movement has been Tony Benn. The charge aroused a sympathetic hearing among many party activists. Impressionistic evidence and survey data suggest that Labour activists in the late 1970s were increasingly middle class, articulate, ideological, assertive, and disproportionately left-wing.[29] There were also important changes within the trade unions. Mr. Callaghan, like earlier Labour leaders, originally relied upon the major unions to control the annual Conference. But in the 1970s the unions became more politicized, their executives moved to the left, and union leaders were no longer able to control their delegations as they had twenty or thirty years earlier. Another factor is that, though the PLP remained to the political right of other party organizations, it was itself gradually shifting to the left, mainly as a result of retirements and replacements of sitting MPs. The view that revisionism and so-called consensus politics had been tried by the party's right wing and failed also gained ground—as it did in the Conservative party. There were remarkably few defenders of the economic policies of the Labour governments of 1964–70 and 1974–79.

In the United States the great expansion of activist power was reflected in the post-1968 changes in the presidential nomination process of the Democratic party. Hubert Humphrey was nominated in 1968. He had not run in any of the primaries, however, and critics claimed that the way in which he gained the nomination epitomized many of the shortcomings of the traditional system. At the Chicago convention in 1968 the party agreed to set up a commission, later known as the McGovern-Fraser Commission, to examine the selection of delegates. Its new guidelines were accepted in 1971 by the Democratic National Committee and came into effect in 1972.[30] The new guidelines introduced, inter alia, written rules for the selection of delegates, abolition of instructions to state delegates and of the automatic selection of party notables, an end to the winner-take-all primaries, and, finally and most controversially, a requirement that state primaries should take affirmative action so that "minority groups, women and young people would be selected in reasonable relationship to their presence in the population of the state."

The reforms had a number of effects. They have certainly resulted in more socially representative party conventions since 1972. There were in 1972 more blacks, young people, and women, as well as fewer party notables; changes which produced what Jeane Kirkpatrick has called "a new presidential elite." She also notes that the new rules reflected a demographic view of representation over alternative versions, such as authorization and accountability. The extension of the primary system increased the number of participants in the nomination process; by 1980 more than three-quarters of the delegates were selected through the primaries. The new rules also weakened the influence of the state party over the nomination. Finally, they encouraged outsiders to contest the nomination. The Democratic party had formidable insurgent candidates in 1972, 1976, 1980, and 1984 as did the Republicans in 1976. On the other hand, there was more central party control over delegate selection, as national party rules took precedence over those of the state.

Some of the effects were unintended or unanticipated by the reformers. For example, many McGovern-Fraser Commission members did not wish to increase the number of states using presidential primaries or to advance the prospects of a national presidential primary. In the event, more states adopted presidential primaries and in turn this encouraged demands for a national primary. The decision to allocate delegates on a proportional basis to candidates who gained 15 percent or more of the vote also encouraged candidates to contest primaries and possibly fragment the party.

The growth of activist power in the Democratic and Labour parties has raised a number of questions about the representative function of political parties. Do they, in particular, speak for the voters or the party members? The strength of Goldwater in 1964, McGovern in 1972 (and Benn in the British context) shows the importance of activist support for a candidate who may have little strength among the established party voters. For several years now, survey evidence has suggested that activists are distinct from rank and file voters on many policy matters. Recent studies have shown that while Democratic voters are fairly evenly divided between self-avowed conservatives and liberals, party activists are almost exclusively liberals. Republican voters are more united in their outlooks, being conservative by a two-to-one margin, and Republican activists skewed even more to a conservative outlook, by a margin of four-to-one. Giving more say to the Democratic activists—a starting point of the 1970s reforms—ran the risk of taking the party's nominee and politics further away from the values of ordinary voters. The high point of this divergence was seen in McGovern's candidacy in 1972. In the presidential election that year, the Republican Richard Nixon was actually closer to the views of Democratic voters on ten of eleven issues surveyed by the CBS election study.[31] Moreover, the reforms disproportionately attracted "purist" rather than "professional" activists to the 1972 Democratic convention. "Purists" were concerned primarily about issues and candidates rather than the political party. Compared to the "professionals" they attached less importance to party unity or winning the election. The "professionals" wanted to select candidates and platforms that would unite the party and win elections. Subsequent studies suggest, however, that that convention may have been atypical.[32]

In Britain there has been a similar problem and once again it has been more acute among the party of the Left. For some years now surveys have shown that many Labour voters actually agree more with Conservative policies than those of Labour.[33] There has been a long-term decline among Labour loyalists for bedrock planks of Labour party policy, including the powers of trade unions, greater public ownership, and increased spending on social services. A good illustration of the disjunction between the views of Labour voters and those of activists was the referendum in 1975 on Britain's continued membership of the EEC. By large majorities the spokesmen for Labour members (the annual party Conference, the party's NEC, and the Trade Union Congress), voted for withdrawal from the market. The PLP was pretty evenly divided while the cabinet favored continued membership by a margin of two-to-one. In the referendum Labour voters approved the terms by 53 percent to 47 percent.

In both countries there have been similar issues raised by recent party reforms. In neither case could it be claimed that the reforms advanced such party goals as deliberation, consensus-building, or winning votes. Interestingly, subsequent changes in the Democratic party have reduced the number of primaries and primary-elected delegates and allowed for ex-officio delegates, such as party notables, to attend the convention. Changes in the Conservative and Republican rules about nomination have not been nearly so divisive.

Disagreement about the rules of the game in political parties and factionalism have encouraged a retreat from the political process itself in resolving intra-party disputes. In the United States, disappointed activists have increasingly turned to litigation. The courts there have ruled on such delicate internal party topics as the apportionment of convention delegates, conflicts between state and national party statutes on the selection of delegates, and the definition of a party member. In Britain the courts were involved in the protracted dispute over the re-selection of an incumbent Labour MP in the Newham North constituency in 1977–78. Members of the editorial board of the *Militant* newspaper resorted to the courts to contest their expulsion from the Labour party in 1982. In 1983 a Conservative MP successfully turned to the courts when he failed to be re-selected by his constituency party. In the same year the Labour party, for the first time, went to the courts to dispute the Boundary Commission's recommendations for the redrawing of constituencies. In this case the courts made clear their wish not to be involved in such clearly political issues—a contrast to the willingness of the Supreme Court to set the pace on apportionment.

Parties and Policies

What difference, if any, does it make that one party rather than another controls the executive? After all, voters choose between competing parties at elections and the assumption—if elections count—is that there is a genuine choice between parties and that party makes a difference to what government does. How successful are parties in producing intended consequences on society and economy?

It is usual to talk of cabinet or parliamentary government in Britain. Yet both the cabinet and House of Commons take their character from political party, and in effect one may talk of party government in Britain. (This is a consequence of one party usually having a majority in Parliament and forming the government of the day.) In the United States—given the separation between Congress and President and weak party discipline—this is not the case, as advocates of responsible party government have appreciated. The problem facing the President or party leaders is to build a coalition to pass a measure. Whereas a number of observers have complained that parties may have too much of an impact in Britain, the more frequent complaint in the United States is that they may have too little.

In the United States, the Republican party largely came to terms with the New Deal and certainly accepted America's postwar assumption of the leadership of the Western alliance. Except for 1964 and 1980, the Republicans did not nominate candidates who challenged these assumptions, and so sharp programmatic differences between presidential candidates in the postwar period were limited. For most of the time Republicans have nominated "me-too" candidates. And only in 1972 did the Democrats nominate a candidate appreciably distant from the consensus. In Britain also, the dominant groups in the two main parties accepted the package of so-called "consensus" policies supporting the welfare state and mixed economy. David Robertson has shown how party programs at elections did converge and there was a steady increase until 1964 in the proportion of voters regarding the political parties as "much of a muchness" and agreeing that it did not make a great deal of difference which party won the election.[34] All this appeared to confirm Anthony Downs's analysis, advanced in *An Economic Theory of Democracy*, that in a largely consensual electorate, two evenly matched parties would converge in their policies to win the decisive votes of the floating voters.

But in recent general elections the manifestos of the Conservative and Labour parties have differed on many policies. In the 1980 presidential election Reagan's position was also more "conservative" than most of his Republican predecessors. In both countries there has been a sharpening of the electoral choice provided by the major parties.

One test of the government's effectiveness is to look at its success in getting its legislation passed. American Presidents, as Rasmussen shows in his book, do not always get a high percentage of their requests to Congress accepted. To some extent the lower success rate in the 1970s was a product of Republican Presidents Nixon and Ford facing large Democratic majorities in the House and the Senate. In Britain, as Patterson notes, such a situation "would precipitate a governmental crisis and general election."[35] But it is normal in the United States.

In Britain the government effectively controls the House of Commons. The number of front-bench members of the government plus parliamentary secretaries (MPs who are unpaid, but bound to support the government) amounts to over one-third of the votes required for a parliamentary majority. The dominance of government is seen in an average rate of approval for its legislation since 1945 of 96.6 percent, one of the highest success rates in any Western system. The crucial factor in the British case is partly loyalty. MPs in the governing party know that defeat on a key parliamentary vote may unseat it, or advertise party divisions and court election defeat, or make their own re-selection as a candidate difficult. These constraints are only weakly, if at all, present in the United States. Another difference is that many back-bench MPs hope to gain a place in the government. By contrast, Congress is a counter-government in itself. Senior congressmen such as party leaders and committee chairmen have their own established positions and in many ways are the equivalent of the British cabinet minister. Moreover, they do not owe their position to the President in the way that a British cabinet minister is appointed by and beholden to the Prime Minister.

There are signs, however, that British MPs have become more independent in recent years. They are certainly more prone to defy the three-line whip and even to vote with other parties. Norton has charted in painstaking detail the growth of Conservative dissent in the early 1970s.[36] He explains this in terms of the Heath government's reversals of policy, Heath's authoritarian style of leadership which provoked resentment, and also the new breed of MPs who are less willing to act as lobby fodder. Rebellions have continued under Mrs. Thatcher. Dissent also reached high levels under the 1974–79 Labour government. It is possible that a further fragmentation of the party system and the emergence of minority or coalition government might further increase the influence of the House of Commons vis-à-vis the executive. There was a short-lived minority government in 1974 and the Labour government lacked an assured party majority between 1976 and 1979. For the present, however, the government controls the legislative process.

In Britain, two rival views about the effects of parties on public policy have been advanced by academics and politicians. The first claims that the "adversary" form of a two-party system, combined with the all or nothing nature of the electoral system, one-party government, and the growing polarization of parties, produces abrupt reversals of policy as one set of partisans replaces another in government.[37] This view claims that parties do influence government although, regrettably, for short-term and ideological motives. It is a thesis about the interaction of the two parties in which the adoption of radical policies in one party stimulates a radical response from the other. Critics of these abrupt changes have recommended the adoption of proportional representation. The probably resultant coalitions will, it is claimed, be a means of slowing down the abrupt changes and the translation of excessive partisanship into public policy.

A different view is that the same recurring problems and similar constraints force parties, regardless of their ideological leanings, into following a broadly similar set of policies. Richard Rose has demonstrated that if one relates party incumbency to various economic outputs—rates of inflation, unemployment, economic growth, prosperity, changes in the distribution of income and wealth, and the size of government deficits—it is striking how slight are the differences which are associated with party control of government. If parties do not have much impact, this is not, Rose adds, because of agreement, but, because "necessity more than ideological consensus is the explanation for similarities in behaviour."[38] Stop-go economic policies, attempts at reforms of trade unions and industrial relations, incomes policies, public spending cuts, and cash limits have not been the prerogative of any one party in office. We may also observe that nearly as many discontinuities in economic policies have taken place within the lifetime of a government as between changes of government. The more relevant point, however, is that these continuities occurred in spite of the parties' attempts to try different policies. My own view, developed elsewhere, is that the adversarial critique has some relevance to explaining the early stages of a government but that Rose's "moving consensus" is more pertinent to understanding the long-term trends.

We can advance various reasons for the moving consensus: the conservatizing impact of the civil service and the political wisdom it conveys; the role of the established lobbies and interests represented in the terms "pluralist democracy" and "group politics"; the pressures of international factors; the poor preparation of parties in opposition; the limited turnover of elites in the commanding heights of the economy and society when a new government assumes office; the long-term commitment of resources in advance and the inertia effects of so many statutory expenditures and policy routines. This is all summed up in the late Sir William Armstrong's reference to "ongoing reality" as a great limitation on what any government can do. However powerful modern government is thought to be, a great deal of continuity flows from the political limits and checks and balances on government in any pluralistic society. We may also explain the limited differences in terms of political ins and outs, in which the balance of ideas and personalities within a party changes as it moves between government and opposition; it is a cycle of radicalism in opposition giving way to caution in government.

It is difficult to argue, however, in the light of experience since 1979, that a determined government still makes little difference in Britain. Many observers have been impressed at how radical the present government has remained in practice. Mrs. Thatcher has certainly challenged many of the assumptions of those who participate, either as actors or observers, in the British political process. The reduction in the legal immunities and rights of trade unions, according priority to the abatement of inflation, even with unemployment at over three million, introduction of privatization and the changed framework in which traditionally public services are carried out, far-reaching controls over local government, use of patronage to appoint political sympathizers to public bodies, open hostility to the civil service and large parts of the public sector and service, and attack on some professions' monopoly of services, amount to a major change. It is more difficult to demonstrate a durable change in popular mood, operating assumptions of decisionmakers, and terms of public debate. But I would be surprised if these also have not moved.

In the case of the United States there have been important continuities of economic policy which defy both the rhetoric of the parties and public expectations, as well as little relationship between spending, taxing, and regulation and the party of the President.[39] For example, there have been larger budget deficits as a percentage of GNP under Republican Presidents Ford, Nixon, and of course Reagan, than under Democrats. There have not been the expected differences when it comes to increases in public expenditure. National defense expenditure increased faster under postwar Democratic administrations and spending on education, health, and income security faster under Republicans. Republican presidents, as expected, were better at keeping tax increases down, and did slightly better on inflation and slightly worse on unemployment. Since Congress has a significant part to play in policy-making and has not been controlled by the Republicans for thirty years, relating outcomes to party is in any case hazardous.

Given the weakness of party government in the United States such findings should not occasion too much surprise. They confirm the broad drift of several studies over a number of years which show that, in American studies, socioeconomic factors (per capita income, urbanization, and industrialization) are more important in explaining the outputs of state governments than are many party political factors.

Party and Ideological Realignment

There are many signs of the erosion of the traditional "consensus" politics in both Britain and the United States. In Britain it is widely accepted that Mrs. Thatcher is determined to break with the postwar consensus on the mixed economy and welfare state. In the United States, Beer has written of the decline of the New Deal public philosophy and the search for a replacement.[40] By public philosophy he refers to a widely accepted outlook on public affairs which defines both the salient problems and broad lines of policy for resolving them. Clearly, political parties, because of their role in aggregating preferences, proposing platforms, and, uniquely, seeking responsibility for implementing them after, are important in this context.

The package of policies in the British consensus is familiar enough: full employment budgets; the greater acceptance, even conciliation, of the trade unions, whose bargaining position was enhanced through a larger membership and the achievement of full employment; public ownership of basic or monopoly services and industries; state provision of social welfare, requiring in turn high public expenditure and taxation; and economic planning of a sort via a large public sector and a reduced role for the market. Government was seen to have a positive and purposive role: as employer, taxer, and distributor of benefits. This is the vocabulary, as it were, of modern British capitalism and of social democracy. The ideas of Keynes, Beveridge, and the proponents of the mixed economy became the new social democratic consensus.

Many of these ideas have been in retreat for some time now. I do not propose to examine each one of them but some orienting features of the new mood are worth comment.[41] One is the call to roll back the government. It is difficult to quantify this and if one looks at Mrs. Thatcher's record on public spending and taxation then the thesis does not stand up at all. Some part of the attack on "big government," "bureaucracy," and taxation is just rhetoric. But the retreat is in part a reaction to the recession and slowdown of economic growth and the resultant problems of funding government programs, particularly in the welfare state. In a slow growth economy like Britain's, pressures for increases in public spending have collided with pressures to protect take-home pay. Governments have sought to cope with the inflationary pressure by various forms of incomes policies and there is some evidence that the policies were resented by the work force and led to industrial disruption.

There has also been evidence in Western Europe that political protest movements have been strongest and industrial disruption most marked where direct or visible taxes have increased the most: the tax backlash phenomenon. In Britain Conservative promises of tax cuts in the 1979 election were important in attracting former Labour voters. The litany of the new political economy is now well known: tax cuts, reductions in public spending, cash limits, encouragement of market forces, and privatization of state services and industries. The present government has been concerned to stand aside from industrial disputes and wage negotiations, and has abandoned the commitment to full employment. The argument for governments conducting such a retreat is that it is a way of protecting themselves from political trouble.

But the abandonment of the consensus must also be connected with the internal dynamics of the two main political parties. In both, the traditional policy minorities made advances, partly in response to the alleged failures of earlier governments. By the mid-1970s there was a growing body of opinion in both political parties that wanted to break with the postwar consensus. In the Labour party, revisionists had dominated Labour governments. They had defied the party Conference and pursued policies on the grounds that these were (a) economically necessary and (b) the way to win elections. Revisionism was as much a theory about electoral sociology as about economic management. The Labour leaders, however, did not deliver economic growth, lost elections in 1970 and 1979, and spectacularly divided the movement in 1969 and 1978–79. Constitutional reformers, invoking the language of accountability, the authority of the annual party Conference, and the values of intra-party democracy, overturned the party's constitution in 1980 and 1981 and moved the party sharply to the left. There were remarkably few defenders of the governments' records. The only significant response to this was not "voice" but "exit," in the form of the creation of the SDP.

Mrs. Thatcher similarly challenged many of the operating ideas and practices of her Conservative predecessors.[42] They had been accommodating and defensive, believing it politically necessary to maintain the welfare state, full employment, and high levels of public expenditure, while conciliating the trade unions. She has a different set of ideas—individualism, thrift, self-reliance, and the superiority of the market over socialism and neocorporate deals with the major interests. Government, she believes, has a limited capacity to do good, but a great capacity to do harm, not least by distorting or interfering with the "natural" working of society and the market economy. In contrast to Baldwin and the immediate postwar generation of Conservative leaders she has no sense of "guilt" for the mass unemployment of the 1930s. When she became leader in 1975 the Conservatives, for long the natural party of government, had lost four of the previous five general elections and appeared to have no politically acceptable answer to the problems of inflation and trade union power. Monetarism seemed to provide a policy for curbing inflation without negotiating with the trade unions. She was inevitably a divisive leader for her party, given that so many of her senior colleagues had been closely involved in the policies of earlier Conservative governments. In terms of programs the parties in 1979 and 1983 were further apart than for many elections. The emergence of a "new left" was matched by a "new right" and a "new center" party in the form of the Liberal-SDP Alliance.

But what evidence is there for the emergence among the public of a new set of values, Thatcherite or otherwise? We know that for some elections now many people have voted Labour in spite of its policies. What has contributed to the sharp decline in Labour's electoral fortunes is that declining identification with the party and diminishing working class loyalty has left it exposed on policies, many of which fail to find a response among voters. In 1979 and 1983 clear majorities of voters agreed with many of the Conservative policies, and majorities of Labour voters were often in agreement with a number of Conservative policies.

But this is not to say that there was a ringing endorsement of the ideas of the new right. There has long been clear support for Conservative positions on populist-authoritarian issues like law and order and immigration. In 1983 there was also majority support for a number of Thatcherite values. But the major programs of the welfare state still evoke strong support. For some years surveys have found that a majority of voters are willing to pay higher taxes to fund more welfare programs. Blanket attacks on the market and on the state, by the Labour and Conservative parties respectively, find echoes from few voters. It is not a case of the public being divided between defense of a state economy and state welfare on the one hand, versus defenders of the free market and private provision of welfare on the other. The great majority of people want the market to provide wealth but the state to guarantee the welfare and are willing to pay more taxes to expand the welfare state. The public supports the market for generating wealth while wanting the government to use a share of the wealth for social purposes. It is a case of two and a half cheers for the market and for the welfare state.[43]

But, overall, the evidence is that the electorate has become more conservative over the past decade. David Robertson has recently monitored changes of opinion on many questions that were asked in identical form in October 1974 and May 1979.[44] Of seventeen questions that can be directly compared, the electorate moved to a more right-wing average position on fifteen, and to the left only on the question of increasing cash to the National Health Service. He claims "the brute evidence is that the rightwards shift of the Conservative policy in the 1970s was at least matched by a similar shift in mass opinion."

In the United States it is some of the New Deal assumptions which appear to be in retreat. Those assumptions and policies encompassed active government, particularly in economic planning, use of government controls and regulations, encouragement of trade unions, and promotion of welfare and redistribution. They encouraged the expectation among many voters that the federal government would take national action to tackle economic problems. We have noted that the electoral coalition which supported these policies combined many of the blue-collar workers in the big cities with the South, and provided rich political dividends for the Democratic party. The key test of the acceptability of new policies is whether their opponents come to accept them—either on grounds of conviction or electoral expediency. The Republicans quickly came to terms with the New Deal consensus and, except for Goldwater in 1964, nominated "me-too" candidates.

Preserving the New Deal electoral coalition for the Democrats depended in part on suppressing the race issue. From the mid-1960s this was no longer possible, and Southern whites bolted from the party. But Vietnam, the "social issue," and the so-called "New Politics" also contributed to the disruption of the party's electoral coalition and public philosophy. The "Old Liberalism" was concerned with *material* benefits, that is, economic redistribution from the "haves" to the many "have-nots," and appealed to blue-collar workers. The "New Liberalism" has been more interested in *post material* issues of minority rights, civil liberties, environmental protection, and greater opportunities for participation and self-expression, and has appealed particularly to the college-educated high-income groups. The divorce between the two groups was seen in 1972 with the support of the latter for McGovern and the desertion of many of the former for Nixon.

In 1980 the election of Ronald Reagan as President and talk of Reaganism both as political style and a set of ideas, and the disarray of the Democrats all seem to provide some parallels to what has been happening in Britain. In the United States there were similar themes; namely, tax cuts and spending cuts, alongside support for increasing expenditure on defense, law and order, deregulation (a parallel to privatization in Britain), decentralization, and a reaction against social engineering and "Great Society" social programs.

In both the Republican and Democratic parties traditional policy minorities came to the fore. This was most clearly the case with the emergence of Reagan in 1980 (and with his near success in gaining the party's nomination in 1976). The Republican party's platforms in 1976 and 1980 moved to the right, just as the Conservative party's have in Britain in 1979 and 1983. In the United States this was also associated with a revival of neo-Conservative ideas.[45] There was much discussion of government being overloaded with demands, of the deficiencies of government as a problem solver, and of the limits of reform. In Britain the experience of wages policies, economic planning, regional policy, high-rise council estates, and policies for economic growth did not inspire confidence in social engineering. In the United States there was similar disillusionment with the results of the various Great Society programs to promote educational standards and quality and combat poverty. The massive Coleman Report in the 1960s had demonstrated that differences in the input of resources and facilities had little or no or, sometimes, even inverse relationships to students' academic achievements. One can readily see how this research has fueled fiscal conservatism in many countries and doubts that complex social problems can be solved through the investment of yet more resources. It is a case of the monitoring role of social science being used to confute the problem-solving claims of techfix and professionalism. A remarkable number of disenchanted American liberals have contributed to the journal *Public Interest*.

Yet in the United States, there is also a populist new right, which is particularly concerned about social permissiveness, abortion and pornography, resisting communism, and articulating fundamentalist religious values. This has no counterpart in Britain. Anticommunism and social issues, particularly those of race, busing, abortion, equal rights, birth control, and pornography, have not been salient issues in Britain. Indeed the politics of the so-called new right in the two countries have been rather different.

It is less clear that there has been a swing to the political right in the case of the United States compared to Britain. Survey evidence suggests that on a number of issues opinion has not moved to the right at all and indeed may have become more liberal. This applies particularly to attitudes on active government, abortion, women's liberation, civil rights, and many government social programs. Everett Ladd notes that the public still wants the government to carry out many of its traditional tasks while not being very confident about its ability to do so. The election of 1980 was a "Brittle Mandate" for the Right.[46] The victory was more of a repudiation of Carter personally and a reflection of dissatisfaction with his handling of the economy than an endorsement of the ideas of the new right. Beer is correct in referring to "the search" for, rather than development of, a new public philosophy.

Conclusion

What lessons, if any, may one system learn from the other? Comparative study may be justified on grounds of intellectual interest, finding out if and how things work differently or better elsewhere. Alternatively, it may be directed to a search for "lessons." One has to tread carefully in this area. Britain and America provide two different models of liberal democracy. Political institutions are not easily transplanted from one context to another. We are aware of how the importation of a "fragment" of values or population from a settler society to a new one may look very different in the latter. Yet for all its political inventiveness America has proved remarkably inimitable. Few other countries have admired or looked to it for its political institutions—least of all its political parties. The great age of the export of British political institutions was during the postwar transition of colonies to independence. Many of the new states were gifted with Westminster-type institutions. Yet today all but a few of them are under one-party or military rule.

Political parties are not independent actors. Because political parties mediate between government and society they are affected by both. My starting point has been that the differences in governmental structure and society between the two countries are so radically different that there is not much that one can usefully import from the other. Many generalizations about British parties (for example, that they are disciplined, programmatic, or responsible) can be qualified. But they are in these respects outstanding when we compare them with parties in the United States. We should not overstress the centralization of power of British political parties. Local political parties largely go their own way, without much reference to the national party in Parliament, and neither party leadership is able to control the process of nomination which rests, except in very special instances, securely with local constituency parties. Yet they are obviously centralized when compared with their American counterparts. In the latter, political bargaining, compromise, and coalition building are necessary to take account of the divided political structure, federalism, and social pluralism.

This chapter has noted some similar trends in the party systems of the two countries. In both there is evidence of a declining public attachment to the parties. The Democratic and Labour parties have "democratized" their operations, giving more say to active members, and with results that have been politically divisive, electorally unpopular, and imperfectly representative in choices of leaders and policies. In both countries the advent of Mrs. Thatcher and Ronald Reagan have produced sustained attacks on a number of aspects of the postwar political consensus.

The difficulties of parties do appear to be more serious in the United States. A party not in control of the presidential nomination process lacks a major attribute of a party. Recent reforms of the nomination process, particularly in the Democratic party, have compounded the problems. In elections the rise of political action committees, mass media, cause groups, and candidate-oriented groups have helped to fill the vacuum and provided further incentives for candidates, particularly at the presidential level, to distance themselves from parties. Compared to the British, American parties can be significantly reshaped every four years, when the party's standard-bearer for the presidency can impress his values, concerns, and policies on the image of the party. All this strikes and concerns a British observer, as it does some Americans.

The American parties have been remarkably successful in integrating diverse groups of people into the political system. The likely costs, in terms of party splits and multi-party politics, greater sectionalism, and further difficulties in governing through Congress, which would follow from more centralized, disciplined, and programmatic parties, may outweigh the gains. I repeat: it is difficult to isolate an institution from its context, particularly an American one. The United States has managed with weak political parties (indeed, political parties which would hardly be recognized as such by most Europeans) for a long time.

4

Whitehall and Washington Revisited: An Essay in Constitutional Lore

HUGH HECLO

———

In this chapter, Hugh Heclo moves inside the governmental structure itself to compare the bureaucracies of the two countries. He
concentrates his focus on what he calls "constitutional lore," the unwritten and implicit rules which guide the behavior of civil servants
and their political masters. This traditional understanding participants have about the way their world of government works is well
developed in Whitehall and is, indeed, so central a feature of the
nation's political culture that it can endure major changes in governmental ideology and external conditions. Such "lore" barely exists in
Washington. The reasons are related to the historical development of
the particular institutional forms in each country, but they derive
ultimately from different philosophies long since established about
the administrator's proper role and the dissimilar notions of accountability in Great Britain and the United States. Heclo concludes by
looking at the attempts made by both Mrs. Thatcher and Mr. Reagan
to cut back on government. Generally, he feels that, although neither
has succeeded in large measure, the British system has gained more
from Mrs. Thatcher's intervention than the American system has
gained from Mr. Reagan's.

This essay has profited immensely from the comments of the participants at our
round table discussion and from the insights of colleagues who read this essay in
draft form. So much is this the case that I am afraid one blanket acknowledg-
ment will have to suffice for a host of intellectual obligations.

Introduction

Britain and America might be said to be two nations divided by a common political tradition. In this chapter I would like to explore this political tradition as it finds expression in the civil services of Washington and Whitehall.

The civil service is a useful point of comparison for it sheds light both on relations inside government and on ties between government and the larger society. If our countries were too much alike, comparisons would hold little interest for us; if they were too different, the incommensurabilities would make no sense. My impression is that Washingtonians who have spent any time in observing Whitehall feel about the same way as do London officials trying to make their way among our Potomac puzzle palaces: each feels that the other is strange but knowable.

The political tradition that we share seems obvious enough, at least when seen against the background of all the non-English-speaking nations of the world. Britain and America share a political culture that is liberal and democratic. This tradition implies two related ideas: that government actions are ultimately based on the consent of the people, and that the people are understood as individuals possessing rights beyond the reach of government. To be sure, these are not simple or unambiguous principles. But they do set the tone for everything else that follows politically in the two countries. What follows for the permanent officialdoms of Washington and Whitehall is a fundamental subordination of official power to elected political authority.

I realize that in making such an observation I risk being branded as naive by those who, with good evidence, can point to the large and growing power of bureaucracies in modern society. Still, I would argue that the basic point holds, especially when Britain and the United States are compared with continental nations, or nondemocratic regimes. In Washington and Whitehall bureaucratic power is real, but it is more furtive than assertive. It is hedged about with myths and practices that, while they may disagree in form between the two countries, serve to express a common agreement about the desirability of subordinating unelected to elected officials. This subordination is widely regarded as proper even if it is not always observed in practice. Imagine trying to institute a political revolution. My guess is that to seize power successfully in London and Washington, it would be much wiser to take over the almost 1,200 positions held by elected representatives in the two capitals than an equivalent number of unelected positions in the bureaucracies. In most other countries one would probably do better to occupy the unelected bureaucratic top spots and brush aside the assortment of assemblymen, elected deputies, and ceremonial presidents.

The Washington/Whitehall comparison is a well-trodden path with illustrious guides. One thinks of Bryce and Lowell or, in another literary tradition, of the works by Henry James and Henry Adams. It is a route traveled by the Americans Dorman Eaton (in his influential 1880 report on the British civil service) and Louis Brownlow (who in 1937 imported the famous "passion for anonymity" phrase from Tom Jones in the British Cabinet Office to apply to FDR's new administrative assistants). More recently in the same circuit one finds insightful observations from British ambassadors to Washington (usually made upon departure), from Henry Farlie, Geoffrey Hodgson, and from visiting parliamentarians who have come to learn from our congressional committee system or the Congressional Budget Office. And in one of the small gems of this genre, Richard E. Neustadt offers some of the most useful advice before starting on such a journey: namely, always to base comparisons on functional equivalents and never simply on similarities of nomenclature.[1] For we are of course also divided by common language as well as by common political tradition.

In that most exact of sciences called hindsight, it is now common to disparage some of the earlier efforts at British-American political comparisons. American reformers are said to have been too eager to apply the British concept of elite, generalist administrators to an inhospitable Washington context; British observers can be charged with not really appreciating the requirements of political administration in a democratic society. Rather than trying to settle these arguments, I will offer a personal puzzle that serves as my point of departure. It is an observation that will possibly offend some American colleagues. In traveling between Washington and Whitehall, I have always been impressed by the quality of the information gained from interviews with British officials when I ask about the workings of their government. And I have usually been disappointed with the information to be gained from even double the number of interviews in Washington. One possible explanation is that the British are simply more intelligent and reflective than American officials, an interpretation favored in London circles. But I doubt there is much difference in native abilities. The best of the American officials I meet are governmentally street smart in the sense of knowing how to get things done and how to stay out of trouble. My point is that so often this is all they know about the workings of their government.

What I find to be present in Whitehall and missing—or at most existing in quite attenuated form—in Washington is something that might be called "constitutional lore." Constitutional lore is the traditional understandings that participants share about the way their world of government works and should work. It resembles what Durkheim meant in another context when he said that the most important part of a written contract is what does not appear in the contract. Constitutional lore is more general than situational knowledge and personal strategies for getting along (plenty of that in the subgovernments of Washington!). It is less grand than formal principles and written constitutional documents. The lore in question has to do with shared conceptions of how authority is constituted and shared standards of appropriate conduct in exercising such authority—a fancy way of saying that constitutional lore lets people in government know their place and what's expected of them. Such lore serves as connecting tissue between ideas and institutions, between political thought and political structures. It is a government community's self-understandings.

These self-understandings about the way government life is constituted may not be exactly true. That is to say, they may not correspond to actual practice at all places or times. Indeed, constitutional lore may be most useful because it is partially made up of untruths serving, like manners in personal affairs, as the little lies of daily life that make social intercourse possible. The following sections of this paper explore the differing contents of constitutional lore nestled in our common political tradition.

Exclusive versus Extensive Government

A phrase that is sometimes used to describe the political revolution set in motion in Britain almost four hundred years ago is "government by discussion." It is a fruitful phrase because it invites us to think about political institutions as devices for organizing a conversation about the work of government. British and American political practices grow out of this common ancestral idea that governing must not be based merely upon assertions of political will or authority but ultimately on the deliberations of citizens and their representatives.

And yet it is also clear that Britain and America have set about organizing the essential conversation in rather different ways. Life in Whitehall is experienced as a community of government. Life in Washington is experienced as an association of convenience. This is the first and most fundamental point.

If we could cast our minds back to the early days in Washington and look in simultaneously on London, the contrast would be observable in its purest form. Nineteenth-century Washington is a town of boardinghouses for the political transients who wash in and out of the city, some rootless, some ambassadors from a home locality, but each on the make in his own way. Governmentally speaking, London at the same time is a town of clubs where decisions are taken in small circles of acquaintances, pecking orders are well known and accepted, and careers advanced by playing by the rules. No wonder the refined Adams progeny (John Quincy, Charles, and Henry) felt more at home in London than Washington!

Of course I exaggerate somewhat, but consider the way civil service reform was advanced when each nation began overturning the patronage system in the last half of the nineteenth century. In Britain one finds a small circle of persons working inside the governing community, sometimes in administrative positions, sometimes in Parliament, but always in the small, close-knit world of London political society.[2] There is Macaulay, a celebrated historian, MP, part-time administrative official, law member of the Supreme Council of India; there is his brother-in-law Charles Edward Trevelyan, former official in the East India Company and zealous administrative investigator in Whitehall; William Gladstone, MP for Oxford University and as Chancellor of the Exchequer Trevelyan's political superior; Stafford Northcote, Gladstone's private secretary; Rev. Jowett, head of Balliol College at Oxford; and a few others. These "official men" as they sometimes called themselves were largely persons from middle class backgrounds whose accomplishments led them to be inducted into London's elite. Their reform efforts, first with the Indian civil service in the 1850s and then the home civil service in the 1870s, served to transform rather than disband a governing elite by bringing to it an exclusivity based on talent rather than aristocratic privilege and favoritism. Writing in the 1870s, Trevelyan's son George caught the flavor of what happened:

It was one thing for [our leading politicians] to deprive the East India Directors of their patronage, and quite another to surrender their own. . . . Aware of the growling and blustering through all the clubs and boardrooms between Piccadilly and Parliament Streets, [Macaulay] was extremely uneasy on his brother-in-law's account. . . . Macaulay was never so depressed as when he had been spending part of his afternoon at Brooks's.[3]

Charles Trevelyan himself wrote to the American reformers:

these early supporters of [civil service reform] might be counted upon the fingers, and if the matter had been put to the vote in London society, or the clubs, or even in Parliament itself by secret voting, the new system would have been rejected by an overwhelming majority. Nevertheless, whenever adverse motions were made in the House of Commons we always had a majority in favor of the plan. This at first caused us some surprise; but on investigation the case turned out to be thus: Large as the number of persons who profited by the former system of patronage were, those who were left out in the cold were still larger, and these included some of the best classes of our population—busy professional persons of every kind, lawyers, ministers of religion of every persuasion, schoolmasters, farmers, shopkeepers etc.[4]

American reformers used many of the same terms—open competition, merit, examination of qualifications—but the words meant something different and the route to civil service reform expressed that difference. The pressures for change originated outside Washington rather than in small governing circles of the nation's capital. Our version of middle class reformers was a loose association of influential persons scattered among the northern and western states who turned their attention from the recently successful campaign against slavery and founded a no less moralistic "single issue" group to mobilize public support for personnel reform. Their deepest aims had little to do with the needs of government; indeed very few of the reform leaders had any working knowledge of the national administration. The fundamental aim was to purge the American political process of practices that were corrupting popular government. In his 1871 speech before the Senate, reform leader Carl Schurz contended:

The question whether the Departments at Washington are managed well or badly, is, in proportion to the whole problem, an insignificant question after all. Neither does the question whether our civil service is as efficient as it ought to be, cover the whole ground. The most important point to my mind is, how can we remove that element of demoralization which the now prevailing mode of distributing office had introduced into the body politic.

Fellow reform leader George William Curtis described the nature of this demoralization in the vivid language of the times;

> The "spoils" system . . . destroys confidence in the method of popular government by party. It creates a mercenary political class, an oligarchy of stipendiaries, a bureaucracy of the worst kind. . . . It is a system which, by requiring complete servility to the will of the oligarchy, both as the tenure of minor place and as the condition of political promotion, destroys the individual political independence which is the last defence of liberty. An election thus becomes merely the registry of the decree of a cabal. Government by the people, four-fifths of whom simply vote for the ticket or the measures prepared by the oligarchy, sinks practically into the empire of a corrupt ring. In a country where every citizen ought to take an active part in practical politics, this system disgusts with politics, and repels from them good citizens who cannot compete with the professional political class which gives all its time to the pursuit by which it profits.[5]

Contrast this with the opening thoughts of the 1854 Northcote-Trevelyan report, an assertion meant to carry weight in London circles, not to mobilize a mass reform movement:

> It cannot be necessary to enter into any lengthened argument for the purpose of showing the high importance of the Permanent Civil Service of the country in the present day. The great and increasing accumulation of public business, and the consequent pressure upon the Government, need only to be alluded to; and the inconveniences which are inseparable from the frequent changes which take place in the responsible administration are matter of sufficient notoriety. It may safely be asserted that, as matters now stand, the Government of the country could not be carried on without the aid of an efficient body of permanent officers, occupying a position duly subordinate to that of the Ministers who are directly responsible to the Crown and to Parliament, yet possessing sufficient independence, character, ability, and experience to be able to advise, assist, and, to some extent, influence, those who are from time to time set over them.[6]

Lacking the space to go into further detail, let me encapsulate the main points. The British viewed civil service mainly in terms of the needs of government; Americans saw it mainly in terms of the needs of popular democracy. "Merit" in Britain meant a superior quality of person, a person fit to share in the powers of governing. Merit in America referred to getting one's deserts through the results of a minimum competence test. Openness in Britain meant providing new entree for talent to a well-defined community of government. In the United States it meant free access by individuals to a collection of government jobs. The competitive examination established by the British was, especially above the level of mechanical clerical work, to test one's proficiency in branches of knowledge appropriate to an English gentleman—studies bearing no immediate connection with the business of any profession and whose effect had been "to open, to invigorate, and to enrich the mind." The examination topics for the first group of applicants in the reformed civil service of the East India Company looked as follows (the numbers referring to the weighting given each topic):[7]

English Language and Literature:
Composition	500
English Literature and History, including that of the Laws and Constitution	1,000
Subtotal:	1,500
Language, Literature, and History of: Greece	750
Rome	750
France	375
Germany	375
Italy	375
Mathematics, pure and mixed	1,000
Natural Science, that is, Chemistry, Electricity and Magnetism, Natural History, Geology, and Mineralogy	500
Moral Sciences, that is, Logic, Mental, Moral, and Political Philosophy	500
Sanscrit Language and Literature	375
Arabic Language and Literature	375
Total	6,875

In America by contrast the competitive examination for the civil service has from its earliest days been conceived as a test of minimal skills to do the government job at hand. Prodded by congressmen, here is what the Civil Service Commission said about *its* examinations in the first Commission Report:

> except in the very few examinations needed for places requiring technical or scientific knowledge, no questions more difficult have been used. The examples in arithmetic do not go beyond the needs of the public business. Every question in geography, history or government is confined to that of the United States. Not a word of a foreign language, nor a technical term of art or science, nor any example in algebra, geometry or trigonometry has been employed in any of the general or limited examinations. . . .[8]

I am saying nothing novel in concluding that the British conceptions affirmed inequality, the American equality. More to the point, civil service reform in Whitehall represented a modernizing bureaucracy molding itself around a class system. Updated to meet the needs of an industrial society for more organized, sophisticated government, the new civil service lay in a direct line of descent from the older tradition of gentry rule—rule by those with the general abilities of one's betters, those with a talent for governing. In essence a governing class was responding to the new instabilities created by a more democratic political process and doing so by reforming itself and its channels to power. In Washington civil service reform was the expression of a preexistent political and social democracy imprinting itself on the diffuse apparatus of a more thoroughly popular government. The claim was not one of finding one's betters to govern but of cleansing democratic processes of impurities they had acquired. As the social and economic problems of industrialization gathered force in America, this appeal to democratic morality was supplemented with appeals for scientific, nonpolitical expertise in government—a kind of government with professionals but not professional governers.

Today it is possible to find many of the same tendencies in Washington and Whitehall. Academics have an unfortunate taste for excessive abstraction. Much of what I am talking about is manifested in the very concrete ways people manage their lives and careers. In fact, a good case could be made that understanding government is mostly about understanding how real, living human beings are led to make various calculations about their own personal prospects.

The personal prospects in question here have to do with the shaping of careers at and near the top of executive organizations in the two countries. The total number of persons involved are not all that different in Washington and Whitehall, ranging from 600 to 2,000 persons in each place (depending on how broadly or narrowly one wishes to define the ranks of political administration).[9] There is likewise a similarity in length of service. Britain's top executive officials spend two to three years in any given job; for presidential appointees in the United States it is not much different. But these statistics tell us little. The real difference between the nations lies in the nature of the careers, the life commitments, and resulting understandings of government that prevail.

In Britain, there is a career government both at the civil service level of officials and at the political level of ministers. Elected politicians succeed or fail by rising through the ranks of their party in Parliament, orienting their lives around the career ladder of ministerial positions if their party is in power or the structures of loyal opposition if their party is not in power. Career civil servants at the top of their own profession—a profession of policy advice and general management oversight—have survived an extensive filtering process run mainly by civil servants themselves. The 750 or so highest civil servants in London have careers that are more or less centrally managed on a government-wide basis (i.e., above the departmental level) by career officials much like themselves.

In Washington elective political careers are made by individual political entrepreneurs. Their personal prospects have nothing to do with becoming members of an aspiring executive team and everything to do with carving out a niche among large numbers of legislators with their own handmade careers. And where shall we look for the counterparts to London's higher civil servants? Certainly not to the career members of the formal U.S. civil service, who are generally kept well down in the bowels of executive organizations, or at least outside the normal range of political administration. As Richard Neustadt pointed out in the 1960s, the counterpart to British officialdom is to be found by looking at the current 600 to 2,000 "in-and-outers" (depending on how widely one wishes to cast the net) who man the executive machinery in presidentially appointed or sub-presidentially appointed positions.

What does all this mean? It means that in Britain there is a kind of inner life to government. Those who are "in" are in by virtue of an almost monastic quality of shared commitments and collective separateness. Relations with other people may of course exist, but these are outsiders with their own collective identities and certainly not to be regarded as coequal with the charmed circle of government. This attitude has deep roots in British political culture. Career experiences outside one's profession tend to be regarded as threats, not opportunities. The idea of composing a career out of stints, say, in academia, business, think tanks, and so on is alien, and nowhere more so than among the best and brightest of Whitehall's highly meritocratic civil service. In Washington, it is quite different. The in-and-outers who make up the de facto higher civil service in America capture the spirit of a government with a meager "inner life" but a powerful tendency to radiate outwards into external political communities—communities of interest and communities of interpretation that make up the conversation called public policy. New presidential appointees come to Washington trailing clouds of externally recruited staffers. Their work in government and their many roosting places outside government are expressions of a lateral openness in American political society, just as Britain's civil service has historically represented a kind of vertical openness to talent channeled along predetermined lines. Of course, all this is only a very broad characterization. There have been and still are places of so-called inner life in American national government—deep in the bureaus, in particular scientific and technical agencies, in the Supreme Court, in more or less enduring networks of policy professionals dealing with given issue areas. But unlike Britain, there are no elective and career communities for the government as a whole. Rather than there being a monopoly of governmental folklore within government, such lore as exists is spread all over and within easy commuting distance of Washington.

Perhaps now the initial puzzle with which I began is a little clearer. Why *should* one expect people in Washington to reflect on doctrines of behavior within government? Government is not a career calling; it is an empty vessel into which other affiliations and professions are poured. How could you expect mere participants to think like communicants?

Policy, Politics, and Administration

In his 1940s doctoral dissertation Reinhard Bendix scored telling sociological points about the nature of bureaucratic power: he argued that there were mutually contradictory and simultaneous tendencies for modern administrators to be subservient *and* discretionary by virtue of possessing indispensable skills.[10] Beyond their skills, which might not be strictly irreplaceable, lay the real source of bureaucrats' power: namely, a common social philosophy. But for all Bendix's research and interviews with higher civil servants in Washington in 1940, the common philosophy never quite materialized. Thirty years later, Aberbach, Putnam, and Rockman returned to Washington with a major international study to test the attitudes of bureaucrats and politicians.[11] They soon gave up trying to identify the up and coming "high-fliers" in the civil service, simply because no one could tell the social scientists who these might be. And when it came to the Washingtonians' self-confessed "role focus," the researchers had to resort to the label "aberrant" in comparison with European bureaucrats and politicians. Everything seemed all mixed up, to wit:

> American bureaucrats are clearly more political in their role focus than their European counterparts, and American congressional politicians are apt to be more technically oriented than are European parliamentary politicians. The fragile and uncertain nature of political authority in America makes for bureaucratic orientations that emphasize the building of political support. But the policy-shaping responsibilities given to the legislative body in the American system of government help to make legislators more sensitive to the technical details of policy. In this system of fragmented responsibilities each institutional actor plays a major role and each, to a degree unknown in Europe, has come to speak the other's language.

It should be noted that the same mixed role focus among executives was found by Aberbach et al. to apply to both senior career officials and politically appointed bureaucrats in Washington during 1970–71.

Comes now the 1980s. The new Reagan administration in 1981 appointed a Maryland political scientist and political supporter, Donald Devine, to head the government's central Office of Personnel Management, and the new director admonished an audience of public administrators with this statement:

> I believe we have strayed too far from the foundations of public administration. As is the case in the larger political society, I believe it is time for change, for a looking back to tradition, to a restoration of working with basic liberal-democratic principles. . . . I believe it is time to turn to Max Weber. . . . Of course, the line between policy and administration will always be blurred in the real world. On "tap" and on "top" is too simplistic—but it makes an important point. But the distinction is absolutely

critical in the theoretical world. This distinction between policy and administration rests upon the broader distinction between the policy-making elected public official and the responsive civil servant, upon which democracy rests.[12]

There is something slightly schizophrenic going on here. If ever there were a place where policy, politics, and administration are intertwined, it is in Washington. And yet in trying to cope intellectually and politically with this fact Americans seem unable to do anything other than retreat to the unconstructive distinction between administration on one hand and policy and politics on the other. Doing so is simply a denial rather than a working conception of the relationship between political and civil service leadership.

On the surface there is a certain similarity. British administrators, like their American counterparts, can frequently be heard drawing the distinction between administrative work which they do and political work which they shun. But the term "political" is being used in a much more narrow way in Whitehall than it is in Washington. Where British civil servants draw the line is at *party* political work. Activities having to do with the everyday workings of party organizations (local party meetings, electoral campaigning, drawing up of party platforms, etc.) are the point at which higher civil servants normally refuse to become involved in helping their political superiors. But this leaves open a vast sphere of political policy work to British careerists. The fact that civil servants will be heavily involved in advising ministers on all aspects of policy—including the strategies and argumentation to sustain the government's policy against the opposition in Parliament—has traditionally been accepted on all sides in London.

While ministers may be seen to make the major policy decisions in some final sense, the fact is that the vast bulk of the policy conversation in Whitehall is devoted to civil servants creating, presenting, and bargaining about what is known as the departmental view. And beyond departmental jurisdictions, in the central machinery of government where the elite of the higher civil service dwell, there has traditionally been an even more elevated conception of the civil servant's political role. Given British history, it is possible for senior civil servants to see themselves as officers of the Crown. This can be taken to mean that they owe a loyalty to something over and above the party governments that come and go. Senior career officials can and have asserted that there is a continuity in the public interest of which they are the ultimate guardians. Of course carried to extremes, such an identification of a self-contained career profession with the public interest is a recipe for arrogance. Within bounds, however, it can produce a self-consciousness and pride in public service that is valuable and largely unknown in Washington.

While civil servants in Washington have power, it rarely arises from any widely accepted role as policy advisers to top political executives and certainly not from any professed calling to administer the public interest. Instead, civil servants have traditionally made their way in the U.S. constitutional system by advancing two claims, one overtly and one unspoken. The first is a claim to carry out specific, more or less technical, functions requiring professional expertise. As far as Congress is concerned, this notion of bureaucrats having no role in political policy-making beyond the supply of technical information has been the sine qua non of support for the civil service. This was true at the beginnings of civil service reform one hundred years ago, and it remains true today when congressmen very occasionally interest themselves in the Reagan inroads into "nonpolitical" civil service functions. A second source of civil servants' power—never explicitly advanced when they claim protection from partisan influences—accrues from the influence gained by being strategically placed at the intersections of America's separated political institutions. The enduring divisions between executive and legislative branches, national and subnational political arenas, have produced many opportunities in the modern era of activist government for bureaucrats to become involved in a large number of lateral alliances. These may link congressional committees, interest groups, and government bureau chiefs in the classic image of "iron triangles" or the alliances may simply put in touch with each other the people who are most conversant on the technical intricacies of particular programs wherever these people may be located.

This situation casts career bureaucrats in roles with both narrowly technical content and a good deal of political policy work at the lower realms, well below the levels of presidential and departmental decision-making. In this environment it is easy and advantageous to cling to myths of separate responsibility for politics, policy, and administration. Elected politicians in Congress and the White House can claim to be in charge; careerists can claim that their nonpartisan expertise entitles them to job security.

And what of those at the higher executive levels, the swarm of temporary presidential and other political appointees who are the real counterparts of Britain's higher civil service? To be sure, in this assorted cast of characters there are individual role conceptions and interpretations of the unwritten constitution making up life in Washington. The crucial point is that these conceptions and interpretations are not shared. They are more or less idiosyncratic, both to the political executives themselves and to those with whom they must interact. What is the "proper" self-conception of an American undersecretary or assistant secretary? No one knows. For there to be any lore even approximately comparable to what exists in Britain's higher civil service, presidential appointees would have to have some shared conception of themselves as a group, some sense of appropriate behavior, duties, and reciprocal obligations. Most appointees have no such textured approach to governmental affairs, and their lack of interest in such things is reciprocated by the congressional staffers, trade association officials, Washington lawyers, think tank academics, and journalists with whom they deal. One makes one's way as best as one can, not in a vacuum but in a primeval soup of unstructured political expectations. For presidential appointees the easiest mental demarcation is the hoary image of their role as majordomos of national public policy and all career subordinates as so many hired hands for administration. But there is a kind of nonexistential quality in all this; government-as-experienced never corroborates any neat distinctions among politics, policy, and high-level administration. British writers of fiction can compose wholly plausible stories based on the contrasting world views of politicians (i.e., ministers) and civil servants.[13] No American can even attempt the theme because without collectively understood "roles" in Washington there can be no "play."

Without some historical understanding, it is a wholly unsolvable puzzle: Why should Americans, who really invented the notions of pragmatism and comingled powers, have proven so resistant to the idea that civil servants are something more than routine employees or professional technocrats with no real role in the political debate or public policy? In constructing an explanation one could have reference to grand theories of *Das State* and Lockean philosophy but let me be more mundane. At the level of proximate explanations, the Anglo-American divergence in dealing with policy, politics, and administration has to do mainly with the evolving difference between cabinet government and congressional government—a subject of not only historical curiosity but also real contemporary relevance.

In the nineteenth century, British civil servants emerged at the higher levels of political management as advisers to ministers in what was really a parliamentary debating club. It was in this century that, along with the growth of cabinet government, a division began to occur between two types of aides to the ministers of the day: a parliamentary undersecretary (an MP helping the minister deal with the business of the House) and what became known as a permanent undersecretary advising the minister on departmental business. This latter form of advice was always offered in the context of having to advance and defend executive policy before the Houses of Commons and Lords, with all the attendant risks of political embarrassment for the party-based team of ministers in question. In this situation, it could make no sense at all to have imagined that the departmental adviser, the prototype of today's Whitehall mandarin, was not involved in policy and its political ramifications. In fact it made more sense to argue that the parliamentary secretary was not involved in administration and to this day these junior ministers (as they became known) have never succeeded in gaining significant control over departmental business.

Contrast this with the American system of government, where congressmen often have been the most important policymakers. In such a system the politics/administration dichotomy does have a usefulness, but a usefulness for relations between the branches, not within the executive. For the distinction has allowed officials to get on with administering (and building political coalitions with parts of the Congress) while always pledging their liege to the idea that it is democratically elected politicians who set the policy course. Unlike Britain, the United States is a country where mass democracy preceded the development of a significant bureaucracy. The result was to deny legitimacy to any nonelectorally derived claims to govern. Civil service reform in America has never really been about governing as such—that is to say, trying to find an appropriate rearrangement of political authority. Instead the U.S. civil service has been seen mainly as a question of how to get mass services delivered more competently in a popular democracy.

Thus as noted at the outset, Britain and America share a political tradition that insists on the myth of separation between policy and administration, namely, that unelected should be subordinated to elected officials. However, this myth is translated into different civil service norms by concrete differences in the constitutional structure of power in the two nations. The result is two distinctive conceptions of neutral competence in government. It is worth pausing to appreciate this difference.

Cabinet government in Britain provides a clear demarcation between a government of unified powers possessing full authority in executive and legislative affairs, on one hand, and an opposition left essentially to criticize and await its own turn at governing, on the other. In such a regime of government and opposition, a system of career officials reaching to the very apex of departmental organization can be generally accepted as being "neutral" between the political parties precisely because it is thoroughly unneutral as between the party in opposition and the government of the day. Serving the party in power to the fullest of one's professional competence, and then doing the same for any successor government becomes an affirmation, not a denial, of political neutrality.

In America the separation of legislative and executive institutions ensures that, except in rare instances when tightly disciplined party government bridges the two branches, there is no central point for decision-making. Responsibility is diffused. If senior officials are to be politically neutral, who in Washington is the government and who the opposition? Reformers who in the past have wanted to copy the British civil service have usually ended up assuming that the President stands atop an executive hierarchy. As a practical matter, however, it has been impossible to deny that Congress—in its many parts—is often able to exert greater influence over departmental work than is any President.

With the powers of national government constituted in such a way, senior executive officials are in an inherently ambiguous position. They cannot simply serve one government of the day but must instead accommodate a number of different power centers. They cannot live in an insulated departmental setting such as Whitehall but must be in constant liaison with the legislature. They cannot hide under a doctrine of neutrality between succeeding governments because mini-governments—the ruling coalitions organized around one issue and then another—are constantly in action and often changing. It is implausible to think that permanent, Whitehall-type careers can be built on this political tightrope strung between two jealous branches of government. It is far easier for civil servants to retreat into a different kind of neutrality—a neutrality claiming to offer technical, professional, and scientific services with little overt role in advising one's political masters on policy and political matters.

The task facing civil service reformers has been correspondingly different in the two nations. British reformers have had great difficulty imparting more specialized expertise and policy knowledge into an administrative class preoccupied with the internal workings of government. There is immense value for Britain in having available the skills of Whitehall: the sense of detached loyalty and independence of mind, the sense of historical lessons and concern for future precedents. However, it is also true that London officialdom is bursting with people who have practiced government and little else. The substance of policy problems going on "out there" in the wider world is not necessarily the same thing as government's internal conversation with itself.

American reformers have had no easier sledding. They have had to find a formulation for something—namely, a permanent bureaucracy required by modern social conditions—that could easily be seen as running counter to their nation's dominant democratic philosophy. The answer lay in the concept of scientific/technical neutrality rather than political neutrality in the British sense. I do not think it is any accident that Woodrow Wilson embraced the politics/administration distinction as he reflected on the nature of congressional government in the late nineteenth century. In fact, let me suggest a perhaps eccentric notion. Probably the only way Americans could have created a civil service without embracing the mythical policy/administration distinction would have been if civil servants had evolved out of the advisory staff of congressmen. Only then would the political and policy roles of career advisers have developed as something integral to their self-conception and been defensible against democratic political pressures to the contrary. But instead, for most of our history, the national government was doing far too little for congressmen ever to need much staff.

It comes down to this paradox. The British have been able to blend political and administrative functions so intimately because they made it a point to separate two top-to-bottom career lines in administration and politics so clearly. Cabinet government—with its nested doctrines of responsibility—has been the "enforcer" of this system, directly by disciplining the political career lines in Parliament and indirectly by organizing the implicit contract of mutual dependence with civil servants. The Americans shared powers among divided institutions, with Congress sharing more equally than others, and this had the effect of leaving career lines more or less open and disorganized rather than exclusive and monolithic. And so we return to my original puzzle from another angle. In Washington, the policy-administration myth that helps mollify relations between branches also serves to confuse serious reflection on roles within the executive.

On the one hand, civil service officials, who are generally not privy to high level political and policy deliberations, do not know enough to be particularly informative about the large sweep of government affairs. On the other hand, temporary political appointees often have not been around long enough and are too bound up in myths about policy-making to have much perspective on what they are saying.

Micro- and Macroaccountability

The Anglo-American political tradition puts great store in the concept of accountability. Indeed the government apparatus of each country could be regarded as little more than huge machines for generating accountability. However, the notion of accountability has rather different meanings in the two nations.

Just previously I spoke of cabinet government in Britain as being made up of nested doctrines of responsibility. These are really a series of hoary but quite useful constitutional myths that come easily to the tongue in Whitehall. In the limited space available I will simply headline them.

—Under the doctrine of collective responsibility, cabinet ministers are said to be jointly accountable for the actions of the government. This in turn helps create the expectation that bureaucrats should help the government as a whole defend itself against the opposition's constant drumbeat of attacks in Parliament and then turn with equal aplomb to do the same when that opposition party comes to power.

—Ministerial responsibility is taken to mean that the political department head is fully responsible for all decisions taken in his department. Since there is no way ministers can know about all the actions for which they are going to have to take the heat in public, they have a strong incentive to listen to officials' advice that may keep them out of trouble. By the same token, career officials have strong reason to try to keep their departmental champion from being embarrassed in Parliament and are expected to pay for this political protection by serving ministers loyally or at least without recourse to "irregular" channels (namely, other politicians in the executive or Parliament, journalists, and interest groups; informal contact with civil servants in other departments is more accepted practice for coping with one's minister).

—The highest civil servant of the department, the permanent secretary, has traditionally been regarded as the principal accounting of-

ficer in the sense of being responsible to the Parliament's Public
Accounts Committee for the proper and lawful expenditure of public funds. This doctrine in turn has been used to justify keeping elite
civil servants in exclusive control of internal departmental management and to deny political ministers any real role in administrative
management.

Of course, all this is much too neat to provide anything like a full,
descriptive account of British government. But there is great usefulness (and an operational reality of sorts) in having this lore to repair
to in the daily crush of government activity. Accountability in Britain is a cumulative concept. In its purest form, broad areas of discretion are granted and the trustee called to account for the ultimate
results of his stewardship. This kind of accountability—macroaccountability I will call it—works through the making of a very few
but very large decisions. Although pure forms may not necessarily occur in practice, I would still argue that this concept sets the guideline
for much of British political practice. Election results produce, and
voting rules are framed to help ensure they do produce, a big decision
that gives unified control of the legislature and executive to a single
party. That government party, in theory at least, is accountable to the
House through trying to avoid another single big decision, a vote of
no confidence. And like collective responsibility, ministerial responsibility for all decisions and permanent undersecretaries' accounting responsibility also partake of such macroaccountability. "Merit" in civil
service reform in Britain had the meaning it had precisely because
persons entrusted with the broad discretionary power of governing
under unwritten rules had to be fit to govern. In the case of career
civil servants, there are huge numbers of unwritten, minute rules of
conduct, and because they are uncodified, such common law understandings add to the exclusivity of being in the charmed circle of government. Such informality has a disciplining quality, for it takes time
to learn these things, to test the ground for hidden norms, to become
"one of us." One is expected and trusted to learn to know these rules
or else—the big club in the closet—one is simply out and not considered a proper chap. In Whitehall when you're in you're in and when
you're not you're not.

I do not know if Americans are more suspicious of government
power than Britons (after all, it was they who taught us about government as the rule of law). But it does seem clear that Americans
have chosen different means to give expression to their suspicions.

Hear the voice of an authentic believer in microaccountability, W. Dudley Foulke, as he reflected on his life as a civil service reformer:

> Our experience in constitutional restrictions shows that the evils of government are always least where its powers are limited by certain fixed laws; that it is wiser to trust our rights to general preestablished rules than to leave them to be determined by the irresponsible will of another. Accordingly, in general matters of law we leave as little discretion as possible to our judges, our governors, and political officials. We consider that fixed rules, however imperfect, are better than arbitrary power. . . . What the civil service reformer asks is that still other limitations should be prescribed. . . . If you ask then why I want appointments controlled by rules and examinations; why I am not willing to trust the discretion of the executive or even of the Legislature, I answer: "for the same reasons that you insist that the judge that passes upon your life, liberty and property shall be governed by fixed rules of law. . . ."[14]

The striking thing about the American formulation is its either/or choice, either fixed rules or the inevitable misuse of power. The British make do with a civil service that has virtually no statutory basis from the legislature and whose regulation and control is almost entirely a matter of informal conventions within the executive (again the existence of a Royal bureaucracy prior to the creation of popularly representative institutions is important). The Americans have a civil service in Washington that is rich in statutes, personnel rules, and specified regulations in a hopeless attempt to cover every contingency of political life and administration.

Microaccountability does not mean the absence of delegation. It means delegation with lots and lots of formal strings rather than one big club in the closet. Microaccountability pursued through written rules has increasingly been the norm in Washington as even minimal levels of trust between the branches and between appointees and bureaucrats have waned. The Civil Service Reform Act of 1978 goes to great lengths to identify the purposes of the Senior Executive Service, to separate career-reserved from general executive positions, to limit the number of noncareer appointments in the ses, and to establish mechanisms for judging and rewarding bureaucrats' performance. For political executives the resources for pursuing microaccountability

have been greatly strengthened, just as Congress has sought to mul-
tiply its strings through legislative vetoes, annual authorizations, the
War Powers Resolution, budget reform, oversight committees, the
1978 Ethics in Government Act, and other devices. Whether multi-
plying the pieces of accountability has increased or in fact diminished the sum total of accountability in the system as a whole is a
good question.

What does seem clear is that within the executive branch all the
new management tools for performance appraisals and financial incentives have been accompanied by more distant rather than closer
working relations between political appointees and career executives,
particularly in the first term of the Reagan administration. At the
end of 1983, two-thirds of the alumni of the Federal Executive Institute reported the "political/career interface" as having a negative effect on management effectiveness (in April 1981 the percentage had
been 40 percent).[15] In another survey of public executive attitudes, a
majority of respondents felt that their agencies' performance ap-
praisal system had little effect on performance, had not improved
communication between superiors and subordinates, and was not
worth the cost of administration. After five years' operation, 40 percent of those who originally joined the new Senior Executive Service
in 1979 had left government. And early in 1984 the public interest
lobby Common Cause reported from a series of in-depth interviews
that while overt politicization was rare, there was a clear tendency
(particularly in nontechnical agencies) for political executives to cir-
cumvent rather than consult with and use career executives. To manage in this way is in fact the substance of the advice offered by the
conservative Heritage Foundation to the Reagan administration to
guide its second four years in office.

Where there is the tradition of a governing community, it is possible to assume some degree of mutual confidence and delegations of
authority that show a genuine readiness to permit discretion.[16] Whitehall has generally been such a place; Washington has not been. Microaccountability begins from the premise of distrust. It then rein-
forces that premise by withholding all incentives to develop mutual
understanding. Reliance on detailed supervision seems to make it unnecessary to nurture ongoing relationships—the middle ground that
can exist between what Foulke termed fixed rules and arbitrary
power. Discretion, which is not the same thing as license, chal-
lenges people to think about responsibilities. With mere supervision
there is little need to think about or try to understand such subtle-

ties. No wonder it is more interesting to conduct interviews in Whitehall.

Nipping at Behemoth

The bulk of this essay has been devoted to what I would regard as more or less enduring characteristics in Washington and Whitehall. Both systems of political administration have immense inertial power, not in some abstract academic sense but in the very real ways careers and understandings of government are shaped in people's lives. While occasional news accounts may speak of a Thatcher "shakeup" or Reagan "revolution" in government, the personal efforts of individual politicians are likely to change inherited structures and practices only at the margins. Still, these margins are important since they can nudge bureaucratic cultures in different directions. Given the strong ideological, antigovernment predispositions of the Reagan and Thatcher administrations, it is worthwhile paying some attention to recent developments.

By the end of the 1970s, the strengths and weaknesses in British and American national government were, roughly speaking, the mirror images of each other. In Washington there was a great deal of openness to outside policy expertise and popular political pressures; the problem was how to provide a means in this system for experienced career people with institutional memory to play their part in the ongoing and often erratic policy conversation. For public consumption the 1978 Civil Service Reform Act was presented as a means of increasing bureaucratic responsiveness in an era of anti-Washington feelings. Privately, the Washington administrators who largely put together the Act were hoping to revive the status of career civil servants. In Whitehall the situation was the reverse: how to get more porousness in a system where civil servants seemed to monopolize so much of government life. More than that, a widespread impression had grown that a certain arrogance of power prevailed in Whitehall. Politicians could be heard to complain publicly that the mandarins were unresponsive, if not a little contemptuous of political ministers. In the wider public, civil servants aroused ire by behaving like any other vested interest group interested mainly in the terms and conditions of employment. Given bureaucrats' job tenure, wages, and inflation-proofed benefits, the latter charge cut deep with Britain's economically battered population. The contempt for politicians may have had some justification in light of British leaders' tendency to gum rather than bite bullets in economic policy over the past twenty years; but it was hardly discreet to have expressed such feelings.

It was into this situation that the Reagan and Thatcher governments launched their efforts to change the direction of government. Both leaders claimed to carry the banner of conservatism, but both Thatcher and Reagan are more appropriately classified as radicals when it comes to government institutions. Conservatives are thought to believe in the value of precedent, of observing historically tested routine, of prudence in experimenting with new forms; in short, conservatives are meant to believe in the value of established institutions. The free market ideology of the Reagan and Thatcher regimes has little time for such considerations. Of primary concern in their leadership are the policies that flow from their political program for reducing the role of government. Institutional functions tend to be regarded as mere means to these ends. From this radical-"conservative" perspective, the defense of continuity is seen as simply a defense of the values shaped by the opposing party and other friends of big government.

Since Washington and Whitehall are rather different places, one should expect that the arrival of two ideologically similar governments in 1979–80 should be producing somewhat different effects. Because there is little real constitutional lore on the shores of the Potomac, Reaganism has had fewer institutional understandings to disturb in pushing its policy program. For Whitehall the effect of Thatcherism has been more jarring but also probably more healthy.

In 1981 the Reagan administration arrived in Washington with a self-declared mandate to cut back on the domestic role of the federal government. That policy objective has been pursued with what amounts to great singleness of purpose in the American context of traditionally nonprogrammatic parties. In doing so, the administration has probably had less fundamental effect on domestic policy than most partisan rhetoric would imply but more institutional consequences than many people realize. Consider only a few examples.[17] The national budget process has been used first one way and then another by the administration in order to gain short-term strategic advantages in dealing with Congress and influencing public opinion. This has put tremendous strains on the congressional budget process as an ongoing institutional mechanism. By the same token the President's Office of Management and Budget, the one central agency where civil service norms had acquired a tenuous foothold since the

1930s, has tended to find itself cast in the role of a politically dominated body of research assistants (analogous to a congressman's office) rather than a professional staff arm of the presidency. Career
officials throughout the domestic departments and agencies have apparently been even more excluded than they always were from major
policy deliberations. Hiring freezes and other budget-cutting exercises
have hit at the most politically vulnerable aspects of support for career institutions, such as recruitment, training, travel, and career
development.

As I see it, the problem is that all of the Reagan administration's
institutional effects and insensitivity pushes government life in Washington in precisely the direction it has already been tending in of its
own accord. It is a direction that denegrates the career public service
as a calling fit to attract the most talented in America. It teaches participants and would-be participants that the only game in town is the
game of making one's policy preferences prevail, a lesson already
well-established in Washington. It is a direction that shows bright
people who are interested in having an impact on public policy that
they are foolish to consider civil service careers. Allowing the career
civil service to go to seed sets up the preconditions for a self-fulfilling
prophecy of governmental incompetence.

In other words, the American problem is that there is no problem.
It is not widely acknowledged to be a sign of trouble that something
like a higher civil service function is performed only sporadically in
Washington, if at all. And yet if everybody is a policy partisan and
activist, how shall we hear from those who worry mainly about keeping the government machinery running in good working order, about
administrative feasibilities, or about the lessons from the past and
legacies for a future beyond the life of the current administration?
Surely these concerns should be a prominent, though obviously not
necessarily dominant, part of the policy conversation. Until American
political society has grasped that as a problem, it makes little sense to
talk of solutions. The Reagan administration's institutional impact
has been perverse precisely because—in the single-minded pursuit of
a policy agenda—it has reinforced the Washington and American
tendency to turn a blind eye to institutional values in the national
government.[18]

The effect of Mrs. Thatcher in Whitehall offers a curious and informative contrast. Mrs. Thatcher is said to work very effectively
through individual civil servants who have acquired her trust, which
is to say a mandarin whose policy preferences run along lines such as

to make him "one of us" from the perspective of Number 10 Downing Street. But the civil service as such is apparently anathema, since it represents a vested interest in maintaining all the erroneous presumptions (and presumptuousness) of big government. Before in London it had always been the socialist Left that complained about a bureaucratic conspiracy to frustrate a political program. Mrs. Thatcher has made antibureaucratic paranoia a bipartisan issue.

Since 1979 the Thatcher brand of "conservative" radicalism has sent the kind of shock wave through government that can occur only where there is an inner life to the governing political community.[19] In deciding upon senior civil service promotions, the Prime Minister has reached down into the bureaucratic pecking order to elevate those who tend to agree with her style and management views and to encourage into early retirement those who do not. While formally within the Prime Minister's power, such actions have few modern precedents. All of this has cheered Mrs. Thatcher's friends and alarmed civil service traditionalists, whom the Prime Minister tends to regard as fuddy-duddies.

The Whitehall grapevine is especially sensitive to developments that affect "chaps" and their careers, but there have been important changes of a less personal nature as well. Anti–civil service rhetoric has been officially sanctioned from Downing Street and credit proudly taken for reducing the total number of civil servants to a peacetime low. The Civil Service Department has been unceremoniously abolished and its functions split two ways. Manpower resources have merged into the Treasury, which can be expected to be mainly interested in controlling personnel costs. Questions of personnel management (recruitment, training, organization, and efficiency) have gone to the Cabinet Office led by the Cabinet Secretary as Official Head of the Civil Service and thus placed more directly accountable to the Prime Minister.

Outside businessmen have received a more prominent role in trying to bring better management practices into government departments. After the abolition of the Central Policy Review Staff (a central unit intended to help the cabinet engage in longer-term policy planning and evaluation), the Prime Minister's personal staff under the leadership of an outside businessman was nearly doubled in size.

These developments are part of a larger context of changing practices that nudge the British system in the direction of more openness to lateral influences outside the traditional executive community of government. In part because they feel less assured of topside political backing, civil servants have become more prone to leak information to the press and no longer so unquestioningly accept the strictures of the Official Secrets Act. But politicians, too, in an apparent weakening of the rules of the game more generally, have become more "leaky" regarding supposedly·secret cabinet deliberations. Parliamentary committees have become more prominent in monitoring and debating particular policy areas and in a small way have begun challenging the executive monopoly in policy analysis. Members of the House of Commons (though still virtually unstaffed by American legislative standards) are acquiring more personal staff support from ex–civil servants and other sources, including young American college students on internship programs. Reacting to the latter unpaid research assistants with six-month terms, a group of Tory MPs (true conservative traditionalists in this case) complained of "un-English over-enthusiasm and pushiness" and of "bombarding the postal service with free franked mail and feeding MPs with unnecessary questions to ask Whitehall departments." And there may indeed be some evidence that individual MPs have become more prone to rely on constituency services as well as the normal party hierarchies to assure their election prospects.

All of these are merely straws in the wind. Such is the strength of Whitehall traditions and constitutional lore that it would be a mistake to assume that these developments have pushed British government very far in the American direction. In my view the effects of Thatcherism and its accompanying changes have, on balance, been wholesome for British government. Unlike the Reagan years in Washington, Thatcher's tenure has tended, often unintentionally, to push the British system in a more or less desirable direction—toward more openness—that it would not have moved toward of its own account. The Prime Minister's sustained backing of efforts to trim the public payroll and increase efficiency has undercut some of the prevailing snobbishness in Whitehall about senior civil servants concerning themselves with matters of "mere management."[20] Contrary to the Thatcher government's desires, parliamentary committees have developed a certain independence in seriously examining important policy issues (such as Thatcher's beloved monetarist doctrines) and occasionally challenged the executive to produce less shallow justifications for its actions. Undoubtedly the most dramatic development has been the growing "leakiness," the passing of unauthorized information from inside Whitehall to outsiders. This has occurred at the hands not only of political ministers (an unruly lot even in the best of times) but also of normally circumspect senior civil servants. Several of these officials (never a minister) have been prosecuted under Section 2 of the Official Secrets Act for revealing to Parliament information showing that the government had been untruthful, or at least extremely devious, in presenting facts to the legislature.[21] The resulting furor has touched off an important debate about the nature of civil service loyalty and the largely implicit contract among officials, ministers and MPS.

I would argue that this outbreak of debate, in its effects if not its causes, is a healthy thing for British politics. The effect is to open up and give public airing to the inbred processes of central government in London. Former civil servants, political advisers to ministers, academics, and others have felt compelled to join in the debate. Doctrines of civil service loyalty even in support of ministerial deviousness, once the province of internal Whitehall memoranda and unwritten lore, have had to emerge in public light to be given consideration for what they are—part of the public's business.[22] So much the better.

Nevertheless, it is important to recognize the dangers of pushing too far, and some of these dangers would already seem to be discernible. Without appropriate procedures (e.g., through a modernized Official Secrets Act that was, after all, designed in the Victorian and Edwardian ages to meet the foreign policy requirements of an Imperial Britain), the openness achieved through leaks can simply become a byword for renegade information-passing that destroys responsibility.

Similarly, breaking the civil service monopoly on advice and analysis should not be regarded as the same thing as breaking the civil service ethos in Whitehall. It is a great asset for any nation to have a group of its most talented people engaged in the kind of public service that meets the needs of temporary ministers for matured advice and the public's need for institutional continuity beyond the life of any one government. Despite the recent, popularized accounts of mandarin power, the fact is that such a high level civil service function is a very fragile presence in modern democracies, even in Britain. Looking after a generalized sense of the public interest is a role that has to be exercised without being openly proclaimed. The higher civil service is vulnerable essentially because such a claim fits poorly with contemporary standards of democratic legitimacy.

While judgments in this highly interpretive area will understandably differ, my reading of the situation leads me to think that there is cause for worry. In recent years, for the first time in living memory, civil service recruiters have found it very difficult to attract sufficient numbers of first rate university graduates to fill its rolls. (Of course to an American observer the extraordinary thing is that civil service leaders should expect to acquire only the very top quality university graduates and not have to accept those who are "merely" adequate.) This suggests something not only about the attractiveness of private sector business and professional careers but also about the damage that has been done to the image of the higher civil service. And there are other reasons to worry. Civil servants at the strategic career point (usually the early forties) when major promotion decisions begin to be made have watched the picking and choosing among senior mandarins by Downing Street. Looking at their career prospects for a second five-year Thatcher term and perhaps beyond, some or perhaps many may have decided to trim their views so as not to appear disloyal. The British term for this is "toadying," and it fits poorly with the concept of a higher civil service. A good many other civil servants in their late thirties and early forties have left the service because of blocked promotion prospects, an aversion to view-trimming, and so on.

Friends of the civil service ethos in Whitehall may also have cause to worry because of the longer-term change that seems to be occurring in British parties. On both the political right represented by Thatcher and the political left represented by Labour, a much more ideological, programmatic spirit has taken over. Like Thatcher, future government leaders may well feel that there is little need to listen to civil servants and that those who advise them to act contrary to their own inclinations on policy matters are in some sense disloyal. If civil servants are expected to offer simply responsiveness, efficient management, and technical detail and not to work on policy issues, then it undoubtedly will prove impossible to attract the best talent to the service. At that point the American Disease will have set in for sure.

What Difference Does It Make?

I began by suggesting that constitutional lore was a way of thinking about the connections between ideas and institutions. To make that point I have tried to unravel some of the lore that helps explain how our common Anglo-American liberal tradition can produce such divergent practices. Basically, what is at stake has to do with attitudes regarding authority. Compared with other nations, Britain and America certainly do resemble each other in terms of their skepticism about political authority, particularly as such authority might extend into spheres of personal liberty, civil rights, family life, and so on. But these family resemblances notwithstanding, we are not the same people. The civil service issues touched upon in this essay are but one facet of the different ways in which our two nations approach the concept of authority and faith in authority. The British put great store in properly constituted authority, the Americans in properly constrained authority.

To deal further with these issues would take us back centuries to differing traditions of religious dissent, the Scottish Enlightenment, patterns of faith in the scientific perspective, and so on. These are very deep waters which have been admirably explored recently by Don K. Price and into which I will not dare to venture.[23] The point worth noting here is simply this. The same willingness and need to reflect on doctrines of practice—the thing that I personally find so interesting in Whitehall interviews—can also be found in the history of religion and science in Britain. And because American traditions of dissent worry much more about the checking of authority, they do not evolve the doctrinal lore that goes along with faith nurtured in the proper constitution of authority (which is another term for establishments).

What difference does it all make? There are obviously strengths and weaknesses in both systems. The American system appears vigorous and open, but also erratic and rootless; the British system appears civilized and predictable but also stodgy and detached from the larger society. Washington tends to produce generalists without a real stake in the larger government enterprise, while Whitehall tends to breed specialists who know their world of government all right, but not much else. The unanswered question is whether each system can move somewhat more in the direction of the other without losing its distinctive virtues.

Without plunging into that conundrum, what I have really wanted to draw attention to is the importance of the existence of some broadly shared constitutional lore, rather than its exact contents. For without this, government itself risks becoming anomic, which is to say, lacking in normative standards of conduct and belief. To make such a statement is, of course, to run across the grain of much of the American political tradition. That tradition has tended to hold that the only legitimate standards are derived from the will of the people rather than the needs and self-understandings of the governors themselves.

And yet I would contend that there is public profit to be gained from allowing public officials to have some breathing room from externally imposed preferences, that is, to have what I have called an inner life to government. At least this seems to be true if we are willing to believe that affairs of state have to do not only with a struggle for power but also a struggle to achieve cooperation. In the more rigorous social sciences there is frequent recourse to the Prisoners' Dilemma Model. In this image two prisoners are offered reduced sentences for implicating the other; both can gain by cooperating and not squealing on each other, but each can also gain more by way of a lighter sentence if he double-crosses the other. Political life seems to present itself more often as this kind of mixed motive game—where the results depend on what the players choose to do—rather than any kind of predetermined zero or positive sum game.

Social scientists have suggested that in these kinds of situations cooperation will be likely to evolve, not by allowing the prisoners to talk with each other, or even by allowing them a certain number of repeat plays of the game. Rather, what matters is that the participants must have a reasonable expectation that they are going to have to go on dealing with each other for an indefinite period.[24] Members of organized crime by and large do not squeal on each other; businesses that can expect repeat customers are less likely to try and gouge them; armies with fixed front lines are more likely to engage in informal truces than are roving guerrilla bands. I do not think it is too farfetched to think that something like these larger understandings is what evolves as constitutional lore where that is allowed to happen within government.

As with the dilemma-bound prisoners, the evolution of constructive forms of political interaction within government is a very tenuous process. It needs to be constantly nurtured because of the kind of perverse asymmetry that exists in political affairs. Constructive cooperation and bargaining in good faith require a great deal of effort. It is almost always easier to be politically "smart" and institutionally foolish. Finding ways to resist that tendency, ways of making it easier for individual interests to serve collective needs, is one of the supreme acts of governance.

5

The Conduct of British Economic Policy 1974–79

BERNARD DONOUGHUE

In this chapter, the only noncomparative contribution to this volume, Bernard Donoughue uses his unique experience as head of the Policy Unit in 10 Downing Street from 1974 to 1979 to examine two major policy decisions taken by the Labour government, under two different Prime Ministers, during this period. Its special interest lies not only in the detail surrounding the processes from which these significant decisions emerged but also in the light it throws on prime ministerial power (discussed by Rasmussen in chapter 1), the beginnings of "monetarism" (one focus of Marks's chapter), the role of party in Britain (alluded to by Kavanagh in chapter 3), and civil service attitudes (a central concern of Heclo's chapter 4). The case study thus integrates several of the themes in this book, illustrating well how the interests of scholars concerned with one analytically separable part of the total political system can have a real relevance for those examining specific instances of important national policymaking. Conversely, the case study provides the necessary data for testing general theories as well as often providing cautionary data against too facile generalizations about the operation of government. While Donoughue attaches considerable importance to formal structures, the bureaucratic culture, and the role of political parties, he stresses particularly the significance of external events and the personal qualities of the central actors involved.

This chapter is concerned with economic policy-making in Britain during the 1970s and is based upon my experience as senior policy adviser to the Prime Minister and head of the Policy Unit in Downing Street from March 1974 until May 1979.

My policy view from Downing Street was, and is, both oblique and central. It was inevitably oblique because economic policy in Britain has for long been the primary concern of Her Majesty's Treasury situated on the corner block of Whitehall and Great George Street. The greatest part of any British government's thinking on economic policy is generated along the high curving corridors of that appropriately somber building. Internally, the Treasury is separated under deputy secretaries into divisions which conduct the various substrata of economic policy: domestic, overseas, financial, monetary, public sector, industrial, etc. These minikingdoms may rise and fall in importance or may extend or contract their subject boundaries, according to present fashion or the priorities of the elected government of the day (and the list of divisions I give is simply illustrative and not comprehensive for any point in time).

During war the Treasury's normal priorities have been temporarily subordinated to the overriding priorities of national military survival. But during the twentieth century, with the increase of central government intervention in the nation's affairs, the Treasury's overall power and functions have steadily and significantly expanded, as have its members, though it remains small relative to the rest of Whitehall (around 1,800 in central Treasury functions, excluding catering and computer communications). The Treasury has been and remains today the preeminent domestic department. At the political/ministerial level the Chancellor is in principle, and normally in practice, the most senior departmental minister within the government because he controls the resources available to other ministers—though the circumstances of personality, or of party or national influence could conceivably leave a home secretary or foreign secretary with more effective political power.

At the official level, Treasury civil servants are normally chosen from the highest caliber of applicants to the central bureaucracy. They can be criticized, with justice, for creating a departmental culture of monastic unworldliness. They may appear to spend their lives mixing only with other Treasury men. Certainly they are foolishly proud of being untainted or uncorrupted by contact with or practical knowledge of the soiled outside world into whose fiscal and monetary affairs they intervene with often devastating impact. However, their overall ability is very high and they rightly dominate central government. This intellectual dominance is assisted by a shrewd policy of territorial colonization across Whitehall. Able Treasury men are often placed into senior positions in other Whitehall departments (and are also dispatched onto the staff of the Prime Minister in Downing Street and of the governor of the Bank of England in the City). Even after thus transferring, the Treasury culture continues to condition their approach to government problems and policies: once a Treasury man always a Treasury man. Nor is that necessarily a bad thing. As special adviser, coming from the outside academic world into a suspicious Whitehall environment, I personally found the Treasury men ultimately the most satisfactory and most open to deal with. Admittedly it is also true that my most brutal initial bureaucratic battles were with them. But once they are convinced that an adviser intends to be a serious player in the Whitehall game (and successfully carries some policy clout), I found that they opened up and played. They did so with little of the irritatingly snooty hostility to outside expertise which too often characterizes those in the lower layers and lesser ministries of Whitehall who apparently feel most threatened by outside intruders. As often in life, it is ultimately easiest to deal with the best.

I have mentioned the Treasury first because it is the department of economic policy. However economic policy is not conducted in isolation by the Treasury. The Prime Minister in Downing Street is at the heart of the central capability of British government and therefore the view from Downing Street is a central one. Indeed the Prime Minister is formally the First Lord of the Treasury. It will be a central theme of this analysis to describe how that often nominal and "dignified" role of First Lord of the Treasury became increasingly an effective role during the 1970s as the Prime Minister became more actively engaged in policy-making.

Prime ministerial interventions to exercise influence on policy vary according to many factors of which these four are particularly important: the temperament and career background of the Prime Minister of the day; his (or her) power and standing relative to fellow cabinet ministers; the advisory services available personally to the Prime Minister; and the nature and pressure of events arising within a policy field.

Turning first to the question of prime ministerial temperament and career-conditioning as a factor in the policy-making process, the political analyst is of course in danger of entering naively into a psychological minefield. I will try to tread lightly. Except in the exigencies of war when leaders (as Lloyd George and Churchill) emerge because of their particular temperamental suitability, British Prime Ministers have been selected through the party and parliamentary process for political rather than personality reasons. A wide range of personalities have therefore presided over the cabinet in 10 Downing Street. The two Prime Ministers whom I served (Harold Wilson 1974–76 and James Callaghan 1976–79) were each by then extremely experienced in politics and government. It is a feature of British government (and I believe a strength compared with, for example, the American system) that long apprenticeship is usually necessary in order to acquire high office. Wilson and Callaghan had each been in Parliament since 1945. Each held office in the postwar Labour government, Wilson in the cabinet, Callaghan as a junior minister. Wilson had been Prime Minister for six years in the 1960s and Callaghan was almost unique in having held all three senior offices of state (the Treasury, the Home Office, and the Foreign Office) before he became Prime Minister. If there was an important difference of career background it was that Wilson, although long on prime ministerial experience, had run only one Whitehall department and that the relatively junior one of Trade. This perhaps led to his being extremely reluctant to intervene in the affairs of the senior departments, especially the Treasury which he held in some awe. Callaghan on the other hand had "seen it all before" as a minister and especially did not share Wilson's deference toward the Treasury. On the contrary, he was acutely aware of the defects in Treasury advice to him when Chancellor in 1964–67 and so was personally skeptical of the "Treasury mystique."

This difference in departmental background and departmental conditioning was reinforced by their difference of personality. Wilson was clever and subtle, but he was temperamentally soft and disliked confrontation. By the time I joined him in 1974 he was also suffering from a sense of déjà vu, finding the treadmill of recurring problems and stale policy solutions relating to Britain's decline boringly familiar. Both he and Callaghan were totally political animals, though the latter was more deeply rooted in the labor movement with stronger trade union affiliations than his predecessor. There was undoubtedly significance in the fact that, whereas Wilson began life as a university don at Oxford and a Cabinet Office official, Callaghan did not go to university but began work as a trade union organizer in the Inland Revenue. This led to differences of style and of interest. Certainly

Wilson absorbed figures and arguments with greater, incredible speed. But it would be a mistake to underestimate Callaghan's formidable, if unrefined, intellectual capacity (a mistake of which he was himself always guilty, but nobody who worked for him for long could be). Where Callaghan was most strikingly different was, first, in his very deep interest in the policy issues which came before him as Prime Minister and, second, in the temperament, tough, dogged, and often authoritarian, which led him to face problems head-on and to get personally involved in the policy solutions. He had not always appeared so tough. Earlier in his career he projected a rather rumbustious image and was accused of having more wind than marbles. And of course at the conclusion of his office in 1979, paralyzed by trade union militancy in the winter of discontent, he seemed tired and ineffective. But for most of the time I served him he was impressively, dauntingly tough and decisive. Civil servants were actually afraid of him. As one Labour politician who had known Callaghan all his parliamentary career remarked to me in 1978: "Jim has over the years toughened from the outside in."

Therefore, in terms of personality, Callaghan was much more than Wilson temperamentally inclined, and by ministerial experience qualified, to interfere with departmental policies and impose his will upon them. But for any Prime Minister to be able to do this he must have power and standing over his fellow ministers, and in particular over the Chancellor in the field of economic policy. Some of this authority comes automatically with the office. Holding the prestigious position of Prime Minister, having the power to appoint and sack ministers, and chairing the cabinet and its senior cabinet committees, all add weight to the Prime Minister should he wish to exercise a policy role. But they do not guarantee a decisive influence. For instance, a Prime Minister who lacks an independent political power base and who clearly holds office only on the tolerance of his cabinet colleagues would not be in a strong position to exercise this policy role and probably would not undertake it. In fact both Wilson and Callaghan had the authority and prestige to influence their colleagues decisively. Each was a widely accepted and respected leader and had a strong party base (allowing for the impossibilities of any Labour leader ever attaining total acceptance across the whole breadth of ideologies which constitute Labour's coalition). Wilson probably faced more senior and imposing cabinet colleagues than his successor—Jenkins, Castle, Crosland, Callaghan himself, and even Ross were all of greater stature than the younger men who succeeded them at their ministries in 1976 when Wilson retired and Callaghan reshuffled the cabinet. But if Wilson was less actively interventionist, it was not because he was constrained by weighty colleagues but because he chose to be so. He allocated to himself the title "primus inter pares" or, in his frequent football terminology, the role of "defensive sweeper up" rather than as an attacking forward in the cabinet team. This was not necessary. In fact, had he chosen to be more active, he had one great advantage relative to Callaghan: he had led his party to success in four general elections, whereas his successor lost his only campaign in 1979. There is no doubt that the electorate's mandate does, for a year or so into a new Parliament, convey an authority and legitimacy to a Prime Minister. Wilson had that electoral authority from 1974–76, even if his victories then were narrow; but he did not exploit it. Callaghan lacked it but still dominated his colleagues much more than his predecessor did (although Wilson was by repute much more aggressive in 1964–70).

As for the Chancellor with whom each of my Prime Ministers dealt in the economic field, Denis Healey was a formidable member of the cabinet. He had been a strong and successful minister of defence in the 1960s. At first as Chancellor he appeared uncharacteristically reticent and uncertain. But he was a powerful personality, with remarkable intellectual and physical stamina. For any Prime Minister to exercise significant influence over him and the heavyweight Treasury forces backing him required considerable will and convincing arguments.

The provision of arguments to a British Prime Minister has been the subject of much academic debate, because in Whitehall there is no separate and permanent Prime Minister's Department. Number 10 Downing Street is simply a large house (technically two town houses backing on one another, joined together). It contains a large apartment for the Prime Minister's family (though residence is optional and Wilson did not live there in 1974–76) and various offices, reception rooms, and bedrooms scattered over its five floors. There is room for only some one hundred staff, including messengers, typists, and policemen. Therefore the number of staff in senior advisory roles is inevitably small. These latter broke down into four main functional groups:

1. the Private Office secretaries, who are temporarily loaned to No. 10 by other Whitehall departments and who conduct the Prime Minister's official relations with Whitehall, Parliament, and the public in his capacity as Head of Government;

2. the Press Office, which handles the Prime Minister's relations with the media;
3. the Political Office, which conducts the Prime Minister's affairs in his capacity as a Member of Parliament and as leader of a political party;
4. the Policy Unit, which advises the Prime Minister on all areas of government policy.

One of Harold Wilson's many contributions to the machinery of government in Britain was to strengthen these supportive mechanisms working for the Prime Minister in Downing Street. In particular, in 1974 he created the Policy Unit staffed with outside specialists ranking as temporary civil servants. Previous Prime Ministers had employed individual advisers. But until then the Prime Minister did not have systematic policy analysis separate from the regular civil service machine and working solely for himself. This has proved a most important reform in the central machinery of British government and it is significant that not only did Wilson's successor, Callaghan, retain the Policy Unit, but his Tory successor, Margaret Thatcher, continued and strengthened it. The particular point of importance for our argument here, however, is that by introducing a Policy Unit Wilson increased the Prime Minister's capacity for effective personal intervention in other ministers' policies. Previous Prime Ministers certainly had views, and even occasional influence on economic issues, but it is simply not possible to maintain sustained influence over economic policy without conducting a long and successful debate with the Treasury. Prime Ministers do of course have ultimate power to override the Chancellor and insist on particular policies; but under democratic cabinet government that arbitrary approach is not one that a prudent Prime Minister would for long pursue, or a self-respecting Chancellor for long allow. In Britain, as in America and most accountable democracies, government is a long process of argument, at times lapsing into departmental trench warfare, and the Treasury normally carries the heaviest numerical ammunition and weapons of debate. A Prime Minister in debate with his Chancellor needs more than his willpower and status. He needs the provision of good arguments and alternative facts and figures. That is the potential arsenal which Harold Wilson added to the British Prime Minister's firepower when he established the Downing Street Policy Unit. The irony is that Wilson himself did not make sufficient use of it. Probably for the reasons of temperament and career-conditioning I have already mentioned, for long periods he preferred to stay out of Whitehall economic policy-making, leaving the Treasury to propose and his cabinet to dispose. When he did finally and decisively intervene over pay policy, as described below, he did make great use of his Policy Unit, as James Callaghan did consistently from 1976 to 1979.

The fourth and final major factor which I initially suggest may determine the extent to which prime ministerial interventions exercise influence on economic policy-making is the nature and pressure of events arising which pertain to economics. To a considerable extent this is unquantifiable. Economic events are threatening or manageable to some extent according to how the government itself sees or assesses them. But there is an objective difference between, on the one hand, the routine management of existing policies and, on the other, a crisis threatening the whole economic strategy of a government. The former will normally be conducted by the Treasury with the Chancellor only periodically reporting to the cabinet and to Parliament. The latter however requires the active involvement of the cabinet. Ministers may find their departmental programs in jeopardy. New crisis solutions will require continuing cabinet support against inevitable political unpopularity. The Treasury now has only two ministers out of nearly two dozen in the cabinet and, until Joel Barnett was included in 1977, had only one. It cannot operate new policies without cabinet approval and therefore needs to gain the approval of at least a dozen non-Treasury ministers, many of whom may suffer from the impact of the proposed new policies and some of whom may even have their eyes on the Chancellor's job. It is especially in this crisis situation that a Prime Minister has the supreme opportunity to intervene and influence. The Chancellor needs the Prime Minister to deliver ministerial support. It is then that a Prime Minister, providing he has the inclination, and the will, and the authority over his colleagues (and the ideas and the economic arguments) can decisively influence economic policy. It may be helpful to illustrate that analysis by references to economic policy-making in Britain during the period 1974–79.

Constructing an Income Policy 1975–76

The most striking feature of the first months of Harold Wilson's third and fourth administrations in 1974–75 was the almost total absence of collective discussion of economic policy. Between the formation of the minority government in March 1974 and the second general election in October the government was primarily concerned with getting itself into a political position to win that election. Peace was made with the striking miners. A flood of "green" discussion papers were produced indicating lines of attractive policy which re-elected Labour government would pursue. Particular emphasis was placed on industrial policy, with proposals for extending public ownership, central planning, and government financial aid, all with the purpose of regenerating British industry. Actually, to a great extent, this interventionist industrial policy was Labour's most visible economic policy. But in the sense of fiscal or monetary management, or direct measures to deal with the problem of burgeoning wage inflation and public expenditure, there was virtually no cabinet debate. A senior Treasury official told me in the summer of 1974 that the Treasury was holding its hand and waiting till after the second general election clarified the political situation and that then it would bring forward a crisis package of economic measures. But even after the October 1974 election (when Labour secured a small though only temporary majority) the renewed Wilson government did not grapple with the darkening economic situation. Its attention was immediately turned to foreign affairs, where the negotiations with our European partners and the preparations for the impending referendum on whether Britain should remain in the EEC dominated the cabinet's time into the spring of 1975. The issue of the devolution of constitutional powers to Scotland and Wales also absorbed ministerial time. Prime Minister Wilson seemed to be content to be diverted in this way and was possibly reluctant to face up to the growing economic crisis. The Treasury was still willing to wait for that crisis to erupt, cynically convinced that ministers would deal with it realistically and ruthlessly only when the pressure of events left no alternative.

There was anyway a major political problem concerning economic policy which faced the Chancellor, the Treasury, the cabinet, and the Prime Minister alike. The 1974 elections had been fought by Labour on party manifestos which committed the government to pursue full employment, higher economic growth, greater public expenditure, and industrial consensus through a "Social Contract" with the trade unions. Incomes policy was specifically rejected, at least in the conventional and assumed sense of a statutory policy. The kind of rigorous policies required to deal with a situation where inflation was rocketing toward 30 percent and the budget and trading deficits were forecast to rise beyond the nation's capacity to finance them was bound to require breaches of all of those election promises. It is therefore not surprising that Labour cabinet ministers hesitated before confronting the economic crisis. In fact, to my recollection, there was no meaningful collective discussion of economic policy by ministers until late March 1975 when the Chancellor proposed to the cabinet cuts in public expenditure of £1 billion as part of his coming budget. In mid-April his budget included these cuts and some tax increases, representing a deflation of £1.75 billion, but there was still only desultory ministerial discussion—and Prime Minister Wilson appeared to hold very few, if any, private talks with his Chancellor on substantive economic policy.

The economic crisis under Labour in the mid-1970s had two clear aspects: wage inflation and public expenditure inflation (there were of course other very important problems concerning competitiveness and productivity but the government is less directly involved in these). The wage crisis erupted in the spring and summer of 1975 and this precipitated the first major intervention by Prime Minister Wilson in central economic policy and involved defeat for the Treasury in terms of policy preferences.

In June 1975 the cabinet approved a disastrous 30 percent pay increase for railwaymen, having earlier rejected a Treasury proposal for £3 billion cuts in public expenditure. By June sterling was under considerable pressure and the Prime Minister told me privately that he now felt that "something must be done about wages" and asked for suggestions. The Policy Unit in No. 10, which then contained half-a-dozen distinguished policy analysts, quickly devised and put to the Prime Minister a major policy paper (to which the Prime Minister's very able press secretary, Joe Haines, made a major contribution). It suggested an economic package containing a Voluntary Pay Policy based on a simple £5 norm increase for everybody and backed by a "battery of sanctions." These tax penalties, discrimination in government contracts, a price code, etc., would ensure that the policy, although nominally voluntary, was obeyed. The Prime Minister was immediately attracted by this approach, which enabled him (and trade union leaders) to appear not to breach his election commitments against a *statutory* pay policy while still introducing an effective incomes policy. He broadly took this position during cabinet discussions at Chequers and in Downing Street during late June. The Treasury, however, wanted a fully statutory policy backed by criminal sanctions and the Prime Minister began to swing toward this position. On 30 June, in the context of sterling collapsing and a crisis visit to No. 10 by the governor of the Bank of England, the Treasury circulated papers to the cabinet proposing that on the very next day the Chancellor should introduce a statutory incomes policy into Parliament. However, after some midnight wavering, and strong pressure from his press officer and his senior policy advisers, the Prime Minister decided against the Treasury, informed the Chancellor of this early next morning, and then led the cabinet to reject the Treasury papers and to pursue a voluntary incomes policy approach as originally suggested by the Policy Unit. Prime Minister Wilson had finally decided to intervene in the economic crisis, had been provided with the arguments for his own policy approach, and had defeated the Treasury and imposed his own broad policy on the government.

During this crisis period not only Treasury thinking, but in fact the whole Whitehall machinery for discussing and deciding economic policy, was proved inadequate. This was partly because the Treasury had always actively discouraged the development of cross-departmental mechanisms for discussing major items of economic policy. As with the handling of the annual budget, it preferred to keep economic discussions tight within its corridors and then launch its conclusions onto (and through) unprepared and unbriefed ministers—a hallowed Whitehall tactic known affectionately to all insiders as "the Treasury bounce." Such tactics are most likely to succeed in a climate of crisis, such as a sterling collapse (real or inspired), when ministers are usually too paralyzed with fear to ask searching questions.

But even such economic policy-making machinery as existed was not used properly. The main economic committee of the cabinet (at the time called MES for "Ministerial Economic Strategy") met infrequently until the late spring and even then rarely discussed seriously the central problem of inflation. A separate cabinet committee considered external economic policy; and though its agenda, covering items such as oil pricing, was often strongly related to the inflationary crisis, its discussions were not treated as such. Together with the official committee on Prices and Incomes (PIO), these cabinet committees (on which I sat) merely watched passively the slide toward hyperinflation during the spring and early summer of 1975. Once the Prime Minister accepted the need for an incomes policy a further small ad hoc committee of ministers (Misc 91) was established to consider pay inflation. There was little coherence or coordination between these various economic committees. On one day in June 1976 two separate committees met, one discussing increases in school teachers' pay and the other discussing increases in university teachers' pay, with no contact or coordination between the two. Economic policy items were spread over this tangle of committees in a very ad hoc way. Individual wage settlements were considered in various places, but never the whole inflation picture. Particular public expenditure cuts were pursued but their unemployment consequences were never properly presented. Indeed unemployment as such was never, I believe, discussed by the cabinet until October 1975 (and then only after I had prompted a sympathetic minister to raise the issue). What was needed, and later emerged, was to have one senior ministerial committee actively considering economic strategy and to have, beneath that committee, ministerial and official subcommittees systematically covering all categories of micropolicy.

Such was the inadequacy of the existing economic policy-making machinery that during the spring of 1975 the Cabinet Office began to move into this policy vacuum. The able and aggressive cabinet secretary, Sir John Hunt, secured that overall consideration of public expenditure cuts should henceforward be brought from the Treasury under Cabinet Office dominion. It was also arranged that the Central Policy Review Staff, the policy think tank established in the Cabinet Office in 1971 by the Conservative Prime Minister Heath, should actively formulate and circulate economic policy papers. The Policy Unit in Downing Street also began frequently to brief the Prime Minister on economic policy issues; it also began discreetly to canvass and brief other cabinet ministers.

It is not surprising, given this tangle of committees and sources of advice, that the process of economic policy-making during the inflation crisis of 1975 was a little confused. At the end of June and beginning of July the Treasury was circulating papers to ministers in the cabinet economic strategy committee (MES) and in the special pay committee (Misc 91) on the firm assumption that, despite the Prime Minister's initial reaction, the government was in fact moving toward a full statutory incomes policy. The Policy Unit, however, was advising the Prime Minister on having a voluntary policy backed by sanctions while the official committee on Prices and Incomes (PIO) was scrutinizing the particular policy implications of that voluntary policy on the assumption that it was the government's policy. Meanwhile, certain senior cabinet ministers (especially Michael Foot at Employment) were separately pursuing advanced negotiations with the trade union movement for a completely voluntary incomes policy conducted by the TUC (Trades Union Congress) itself. This anarchy seemed concluded when the Prime Minister issued a firm prime ministerial directive supporting our voluntary policy backed by sanctions. But even then, when the Treasury produced the draft White Paper for this policy, its lack of enthusiasm was so transparent that the draft was rejected by the Prime Minister and the Policy Unit had to write a new draft White Paper within twenty-four hours.

These policy battles inevitably had consequences for those involved. The Chancellor, Denis Healey, was bruised, if only temporarily (his recuperative powers were astonishing). Prime Minister Wilson reemerged into the forefront of economic policy-making and personally unveiled the new policy to wide approval on 11 July 1975. Actually he remained active and more prominent in this field until his long-planned retirement in April 1976, working skillfully to unite ministers and trade union leaders behind the new pay policy as it was hammered out and modified over the months ahead (eventually the pay norm was raised to £6 and most of the "battery of sanctions" were kept as reserve powers). The Cabinet Office and the No. 10 Policy Unit had each made a big impact in the economic policy field and were henceforward to remain active and influential through their different channels and in their different styles. The cabinet secretary's appetite for policy influence was certainly further encouraged by his victorious battles with the Treasury at this time. The Treasury by contrast had lost its monopoly grip on economic policy-making. It was for a time clearly diminished in the Whitehall power-game and showed its resentments. When I met the head of the Treasury at the Reform Club in late July to make peace, he was still very touchy and quite adamant that my Policy Unit would not be incorporated into the formal economic policy-making process (although the Bank of England, the Central Policy Review Staff [CPRS], and even the marginal Central Office of Information were included on the Treasury's key Short-Term Economic Policy Committee). No. 10 was apparently still to be shut out. But in practice from this time onward the active relations between myself and other Policy Unit members and the Treasury grew closer at all working levels. Now that the Prime Minister had shown himself active in economic policy, and the Policy Unit had demonstrated that it had a significant influence on the Prime Minister, the realities of the Whitehall policy process had their logical consequence. The Prime Minister and the Policy Unit (and the Cabinet Office) were now clearly in the economic policy game and so most Treasury men henceforward treated No. 10 staff as serious players.

The IMF Crisis of 1976

The second strand of Britain's economic crisis in the mid-1970s concerned the dramatically increasing public sector and external financing deficits. This problem came to a head under Prime Minister Callaghan and gave him a major opportunity to impose his authority over the Treasury and to conduct economic policy from Downing Street. But the critical situation was in fact already manifest under Harold Wilson. In October 1975 he had called together the same secret inner group of ministers who had earlier considered pay policy to discuss what to do about the latest Treasury forecasts showing that the Public Sector Borrowing Requirement (PSBR) in 1975–76 would increase to £12 billion instead of the target £9 billion, and that the external deficit of £1 billion was rising. The Chancellor presented to them three policy options: import controls, or a 7 percent devaluation, or an approach to the IMF for a large loan. They decided to approach the IMF. Significantly, James Callaghan, then foreign secretary, pressed the committee to "do the tough things now." During the following weeks the cabinet did indeed repeatedly discuss tough things: the Chancellor's proposals for public expenditure cuts of £3.75 billion in 1976–79. Anthony Crosland, the economically erudite secretary of state for the environment, led prolonged cabinet resistance to the Treasury, arguing convincingly that there was no case on resource grounds for any cuts at all. But the "confidence" arguments finally won the day and, by the final cabinet discussion in mid-January 1976, Denis Healey had secured a cuts package of £3.5 billion for 1976–79. It was a personal triumph for the Chancellor, who had taken on his cabinet colleagues by himself and slowly ground them down by the sheer weight of his argument and determination.

For the first time since 1974 the Chancellor seemed fully in the saddle. But this reassertion of Treasury authority in early 1976 was quickly subject to external pressures and afflicted by management failures. The Treasury decided in February 1976 that it wanted a lower value for sterling to maintain the "competitiveness" of British industry. The Bank of England mishandled this policy and what started as a maneuver to edge the currency down developed quickly into a flight from sterling, which fell below the psychological level of $2 in early March. Substantial reserves had to be spent supporting the currency and Prime Minister Wilson, who was secretly intending to resign within a few weeks, gave the Chancellor a stern reprimand.

This was the serious situation which James Callaghan inherited in

April 1976. Incomes policy had already been sorted out satisfactorily, although each year required a new round of intense discussion with the TUC over the new pay norm. Reductions in future public expenditure plans had been approved, but the political consequences in terms of lost payments and jobs had still to be faced. Nor was it any way clear that enough had yet been done to restore confidence in the currency, even though the whole of the 1976–77 public expenditure contingency reserves had been allocated in the first month of the financial year and sterling remained weak.

In fact the technical management of the currency at this time was seriously open to question; and it was so questioned from No. 10. It was widely accepted that further devaluation was required to maintain competitiveness, but the approach of the banking authorities was to try to secure a "smooth" downward adjustment—a cosmetic approach which cost one-third of Britain's reserves during March and April 1976 simply trying to smooth out the fall. It seemed to us in the Policy Unit more sensible to effect a swift "step" devaluation to a desired level (e.g., $1.80) and then to use the reserves to defend that rate.

In June 1976 sterling again came under serious pressure. The Treasury and the governor of the Bank of England communicated to No. 10 that it would not be possible to hold the currency without a further package of public expenditure cuts. The Prime Minister resisted them at first, insisting that they go to the IMF for a six-month swap facility to boost Britain's reserves. But he privately told me afterwards that there was no way of avoiding further cuts. Deep down he believed that this was right, that public expenditure was still out of control, and that, if tough action had to be taken, he would prefer it to be done early in his administration.

From this point in June 1976 Callaghan progressively increased his influence on economic policy-making. He brought his own style to the conduct of government, insisting that economic questions be fully and openly discussed in the cabinet. The "Treasury bounce" was banished. Callaghan in the cabinet openly authorized the Chancellor to introduce his emergency package of cuts and said that it was most important that the cabinet choose its own priorities for cuts and not have the IMF do it for them. He held a private meeting with the Treasury and his own staff at Chequers at the end of June and personally supported the Chancellor's arguments for £1 billion of cuts, even questioning whether this was enough. When he subsequently saw the governor of the Bank of England he again questioned whether

£1 billion would be enough to restore confidence—and was assured it would be.

Prime Minister Callaghan was already edging into the lead hard-line position on sorting out the government's public expenditure problems. He also brought his cabinet colleagues actively into the economic discussions during a succession of seven cabinet meetings during July. The objective was to cut £1 billion from the already agreed total of the existing public expenditure plan (PESC). But since there had already been an overspend of £1 billion above that total, in practice cuts of some £2 billion (or an increase in taxation equivalent to that) were needed. The cabinet was broadly divided into four camps on this issue: those supporting the Treasury line from conviction (Healey, Dell, Prentice, the Prime Minister, and Chief Secretary Barnett who attended these discussions by special invitation); the "Keynesian dissenters," led by Crosland and Lever, who argued that during a recession it was wrong on resource grounds to make further deflationary cuts in expenditure; the left-wing led by Benn and Foot (here also supported by the idiosyncratic Shore), who wanted an "alternative strategy" based on import controls and increased public expenditure; and a rump, or "King's party," who gave their ultimate support to the Prime Minister, though hoping to minimize the particular cuts to their own departmental budgets along the way.

The traditional "Treasury bounce" approach would have been to try to railroad the cuts quickly through the cabinet on the back of a currency crisis, real or inspired. Ministers would have had little chance to argue the strategic and philosophical implications. James Callaghan improved radically upon this. He allowed the issues to be put openly and the arguments to develop. Crosland and Healey argued their corners with an intellectual force and clarity to which few British academics aspire. During this debate the Treasury was forced by Crosland to refine its arguments and base its case almost entirely on "confidence" in the currency. Crosland supported an immediate approach to the IMF in order to minimize the amount of cuts which would be required later if nothing were done now. The left-wing opposition were always numerically in a cabinet minority, but Callaghan allowed them every opportunity to put their case and deliberately did not bring the individual cabinet meetings to a conclusion so that every member could feel still involved in the debate. He once said to me, "They discuss the cuts so often they come to think they have agreed to them." He also frequently met Healey, Foot, and

Crosland privately between cabinet sessions to discuss economic questions in general and public expenditure in particular. He nurtured his colleagues toward the desired conclusions and, unlike Wilson, was not averse to having face to face disagreement with them. The main conclusion was reached on 21 July when at the seventh cabinet session in the series (and the second that day) the cuts figure of £1 billion was achieved with the aid of some massaging of debt interest figures—and the Chancellor immediately "doubled up" by revealing his previously hidden intention to raise another £1 billion of tax revenues through extranational insurance contributions. Callaghan then set about selling the new policies to a wider audience, meeting with all his junior ministers to explain them, and also personally telephoning President Ford, Chancellor Schmidt, and President Giscard. His only cabinet problem was inevitably with Tony Benn, who telephoned him to say that he would be taking the advice of his local party activists on whether to resign over the cuts and that anyway he would continue to campaign publicly against the measures. The Prime Minister advised Benn to make up his own mind whether to resign; and he added that, if he did campaign publicly against the cabinet of which he was a member, he would be sacked on the spot. That was the end of that.

However, a wider constituency which remained unconvinced was the international financial community, who saw a yawning balance of payments deficit ahead. By late September sterling had fallen toward $1.70 and Britain's reserves were disappearing fast. Healey revealed to the cabinet committee on economic strategy that he proposed to approach the IMF for another loan and that he had a scheme to introduce import deposits at seven-day readiness. But he still resisted pressures from within the cabinet to go the whole hog for import controls. When the Prime Minister addressed his party conference at Blackpool a week later, he made a remarkably tough and realistic speech to the uncomprehending party faithful. It included sentences about the impossibility of reflating back to full unemployment which seemed to economic cognoscenti to reflect a conversion to many of the basic tenets of the monetary faith. This actually exaggerated his stance, since he was not by temperament a theologian. But, always conservative in economic affairs, he had come to accept that certain monetary disciplines were essential to good economic management and conversely that monetary laxity would certainly undermine the foundations of sustained economic growth. Within those limited definitions, and also without the monetary theology, it was a view which I shared and reflected in my advice from the Party Unit.

For the last three months of 1976 Callaghan's Labour government was engaged in a massive economic crisis which threatened to tear it apart politically. At times there were major disagreements between the Prime Minister and his Chancellor, between No. 10 officials and the Treasury, and between ministers within the cabinet. But that was an inevitable part of the democratic process. Overall, my main impression was of the skillful leadership of Callaghan and the incredible resilience of his Chancellor. Neither could have succeeded without the other. But Callaghan emerged as the dominant figure, with unquestioned authority over his cabinet and, when henceforward he chose to exercise it, over Treasury economic policy.

The basic problems in the autumn of 1976 were that, domestically, we were running well above the (unpublished) 12 percent money growth target and, externally, we could not finance the widening trade deficit. In this situation the City would not buy more gilts without evidence of a further squeeze on public expenditure and equally the IMF was refusing to make more loans without such a squeeze. The Treasury and the Bank of England shared these views. It was therefore highly likely that sterling would again collapse.

To some extent the problem was one of timing. The government's existing policies of devaluation, plus an incomes policy, plus the expenditure cuts already initiated, were already squeezing real incomes and improving Britain's relative competitiveness. Given time, that policy might have proved sufficient; but the immediate pressures meant that time would not be given. Something had to be done in the short run. Furthermore, certain people in the Treasury, and especially at the top of the Bank of England, saw this short-term crisis as an opportunity to make a major alteration in Britain's long-term economic posture, primarily through a massive switch of resources from the public to the private sector. The strategy later expounded and partly implemented by Mrs. Thatcher was actually first prepared and launched (under the auspices of the IMF and of Mr. Ed Yoder of the U.S. Treasury and backed by the Bank of England and some of H.M. Treasury) by James Callaghan's Labour government in 1976. That set the political climate within which the great arguments took place. It was not a question of whether to implement further public expenditure cuts: except for the left-wing minority, most people in government accepted that need and the Prime Minister and his staff in No. 10 were most active in exploring the possibilities of cuts. It was mainly a question of the scale of the deflation to be imposed and the amount of resources to be transferred out of the public sector. The IMF, the Bank, and officials in the Treasury proposed cuts of an order which would have produced a major slump and would probably have destroyed the political base of the Labour cabinet. The Prime Minister's great contribution was to resist these more extreme proposals and to argue with the Treasury and the IMF in great detail for a more modest package, one sufficient to restore confidence in sterling but not so great as to destroy his government's raison d'être. In doing so he was assisted by the financial creativity of his colleague Harold Lever, who always argued that loans could be raised without spilling the last drop of Labour blood, and Tony Crosland and other Keynesian moderates, who exposed the Treasury proposals to proper scrutiny and then finally fell loyally into line behind the Prime Minister's compromise package. For all involved it was an exhilarating and exhausting three months of economic policy-making. It also demonstrated the pluralism of economic decision-making in Britain, with the Treasury, the Foreign Office, the No. 10 Policy Unit, the Bank of England, and the IMF all deeply involved as institutions (curiously the CPRS made very little contribution), as well as the central concern of the cabinet, its committees, and its ministerial members.

The Treasury's initial package in early October contained a minimum lending rate of 15 percent and special deposits on imports. But sterling continued to fall—assisted by a leak from the Treasury to the Sunday Times that the IMF would require sterling to fall to $1.50 (which in those pre-Thatcher days seemed immorally low). At the beginning of November the Treasury asked for a further £1 billion off the PSBR in 1977–78 through taxes or public expenditure cuts, but by the end of the month the IMF delegation was in London negotiating with the Treasury and was demanding much greater reductions: £3 billion off the 1977–78 PSBR, bringing it down to below £7 billion, and £2 billion off the following year. The implied cuts were so savage that the cabinet strongly resisted and the Chancellor and the Treasury (which was internally divided) retreated in defeat. At this point the Prime Minister moved in to take a more active direction of the negotiations. He had a private meeting with Witteveen and Whittom from the IMF at the beginning of December and pressed them hard on their minimum position. Afterwards he told me that we would not get away with less than £2 billion off the 1977 PSBR, and the Policy Unit began working on detailed ways of achieving that with the minimum of inevitable recessionary impact.

The Prime Minister also continued to give free rein in the cabinet to his left-wing colleagues who submitted papers on an "alternative strategy" based on import controls and effectively creating a "socialist fortress Britain." But the most worrying criticisms again came from the Crosland-Lever camp, supported by Roy Hattersley and Shirley Williams. Significantly all of these dissenting ministers employed special economic advisers, the new breed of outside advisers introduced by Harold Wilson to strengthen ministers against the conventional wisdom of the Whitehall machine. Benn and Shore were also similarly supported and the resulting debate was repeatedly commented on approvingly by the No. 10 civil servants. Nearly all the rising young Turks in the cabinet had special advisers. Only the old stagers, such as Peart, Jones, and Mason, did without and they rarely intervened in the economic discussions. There is no doubt that the introduction of the special adviser system has significantly improved the quality of economic discussion and therefore of the economic policy-making process in Britain and that it has seriously undermined the traditional hegemony of the Treasury. Denis Healey was the first Chancellor to face a cabinet composed of colleagues fully and independently briefed on his policies. Fortunately he was one of the best qualified, in brains and muscle, to confront that exhausting prospect.

After meeting Witteveen and Whittom the Prime Minister decided it was time to bring his cabinet into line. He saw Crosland and Lever privately and their rebellion then collapsed. He secured their support for cuts of £1 billion for 1977–78 and then influenced the Chancellor to go for that kind of figure instead of the IMF's targets which in early December were still to get a total of £5 billion of cuts in 1977–79. Discussion then moved to the 1978–79 PSBR where cuts of £1–2 billion were also being sought (if Britain's growth rate proved higher than expected). At two crucial cabinet sessions in the morning and evening of 7 December the detailed expenditure cuts were approved, without ministerial resignations. It was a triumph for the Prime Minister. Politically he had retained the unity of his cabinet while agreeing to some rigorous and painful measures. He had delivered the ministerial support to the Treasury. Equally he had personally conducted detailed arguments with the Treasury and the IMF and had forced them to modify their excessive proposals. He was particularly involved with the precise commitments contained in the letter of intent to the IMF, insisting that various monetary targets be loosened. He also continued to negotiate personally with Chancellor Schmidt and President Ford to arrange a "safety-net" for the sterling balances. Although many had contributed to the debate and the final policies agreed upon in 1976, there is no doubt that the biggest single influence on the final shape of the IMF economic package was that of the First Lord of the Treasury, James Callaghan.

One consequence of the IMF negotiations was to entrench monetarism, or some aspects of monetarism, publicly in the Labour government's policy-making. A range of monetary targets had been accepted and would be published. Yet, interestingly, the machinery of government was not organized for the transition from Keynes to Friedman. The Treasury was still primarily concerned with macroeconomic management; domestic monetary questions were basically left to the Bank of England; and the Treasury division which liaised with the Bank was of low seniority. Indeed, there was no cabinet committee which considered monetary matters. Questions concerning interest rates and exchange rates were not hitherto considered appropriate for ministers, and questions of money supply measurement had barely arisen anywhere at all in central government until recently. It is therefore of considerable interest and significance that following the IMF experience Prime Minister Callaghan introduced a new piece of central government machinery to reflect and process the monetarist advance. He established a small secret committee to meet regularly to consider monetary questions. It met in No. 10 under the Prime Minister's chairmanship, reflecting his preeminence in the economic policy field. Others in regular attendance were the governor and deputy governor of the Bank of England; the Chancellor of the Exchequer, his Treasury permanent secretary and sometimes his second permanent secretary responsible for external finance; the chancellor of the Duchy of Lancaster, Harold Lever; the cabinet secretary; a private secretary from Downing Street; and this author as head of the Downing Street Policy Unit. Because of the sensitivity of the issues of exchange rates and interest rates frequently under discussion, this gathering was kept secret from ministers and was not designated as a cabinet committee but was described as "the Seminar." It met regularly throughout the rest of Callaghan's premiership (and was continued, less systematically, I believe, by his successor). It was effectively a policy-making committee. It had an agenda and the Chancellor and the governor of the Bank would reveal their intentions for interest rate and exchange rate policy. The Prime Minister, who was heavily briefed by the Policy Unit, but was anyway more than competent as an ex-Chancellor to perform in these areas, would scrutinize them closely and indicate his policy preferences. It was an interesting example of the machinery of government adjusting to changes in prevailing economic theory and to the greater policy role played by the Prime Minister.

The years 1977–78 following the IMF agreement were a time of relative success for the Labour government. The incomes policy and the new monetarist regime combined to bring inflation down, finally and briefly, into single figures. The Prime Minister continued to dominate his colleagues in cabinet, though in the routine economic field, without major crises, while Denis Healey and the Treasury were able to refurbish their reputations and morale. Relations between No. 10 and the Treasury were very harmonious. With the economic strategy clearly established, the Treasury reemerged as the dominant ministry conducting the routine management of that strategy. But there was no doubt that in a crisis it would be the Prime Minister who would preeminently be in the front line. That is indeed what happened in the winter of discontent in 1978–79. Then the incomes policy so cleverly put together by Harold Wilson in 1975 collapsed under the assault of several militant trade unions, mainly from the public sector which the Labour government had done so much to protect. It was James Callaghan who took the brunt of that attack and who was again expected to deliver his government from crisis. He failed. Having built his political career in alliance with the trade union movement he was psychologically unable to break the link and lead the government and the country against his old trade union allies. He stood paralyzed while his counterinflation policies collapsed. Without him the Treasury was able to do little. The government's economic polices fell apart and it slipped inevitably toward electoral defeat in 1979.

Conclusion

The above survey of economic policy-making under the Labour governments led by Harold Wilson and James Callaghan during 1974–79 is undoubtedly selective. It represents a particular view from No. 10 Downing Street. It concentrates on two major issues: the construction of the incomes policy in 1975 and the IMF crisis in 1976. It certainly does injustice to the contributions of other ministers and departments. It especially does not do justice to H.M. Treasury, which during those five years bore the brunt of the day-to-day management of a sickly economy, under a government with ambitious electoral commitments, and as yet without the massive oil revenues which subsequently made life so much easier (for the government, if not for the unemployed) under Mrs. Thatcher. But it is a legitimate view from Downing Street, the political center of British government. It does demonstrate the considerable potential power of a British Prime Minister in economic policy-making and illustrates how that potential became reality. As was suggested at the beginning, given the will and the inclination and the advice and the opportunity of events, a British Prime Minister may operate indeed as the First Lord of the Treasury.

6

Courts of Last Resort

RICHARD HODDER-WILLIAMS

In this chapter, Richard Hodder-Williams examines the third branch of government, the judiciary. Distinguishing between three ways in which judges can be said to act politically, he notes how the courts of last resort in both Great Britain and the United States clearly do "act politically." Although the extent of their political involvement differs markedly, very similar pressures—a greater readiness by interest groups to use the courts, a greater involvement by governments in the lives of individuals, the normal duty of the courts to arbitrate between competing demands—have been at work on both sides of the Atlantic. The political importance of the United States Supreme Court, founded upon the needs of a written constitution and developed over time into a coequal branch of government, has long been recognized. What is significant in recent years has been the growth of the political role of the British courts of appeal and the judicial committee of the House of Lords. This converging trend nevertheless leaves the two judicial systems still very distinct, as the different institutional structures would lead one to expect. But Hodder-Williams concludes his chapter by addressing openly the importance of political culture and argues that the still different roles played by the courts of last resort in the two countries must be attributed in part also to the differences between British and American attitudes to the law.

Introduction

To argue that the judiciary in the United Kingdom plays a significant autonomous political role is somewhat novel. The textbooks which generations of British first-year political science students were advised to read in the 1970s hardly acknowledged the existence of the judiciary at all, let alone devoted a whole chapter or more to its activities.[1] W. J. M. McKenzie, in his extraordinary tour d'horizon (indeed a tour de force) *Politics and Social Science* wrote: "None of us can offer anything better than hunches about the role of law and judges at various levels in the operation of a technological society. . . . Without more detailed study there is little we can say profitably (for instance) about the legislative role of the courts in Britain."[2] Nor were there many courses in political science departments on the judiciary; constitutional law was very much the preserve of the departments of law (an undergraduate discipline in Britain) and sociologists tended to have colonized the study of the coercive powers, especially the police. There were, of course, some exceptions, but the essential truth was that the teaching of British politics ignored the political role of the judiciary.

It would be wrong to argue now that there has been a revolution in the last decade, but there is certainly a greater awareness of the fact that the courts do more than merely discover and announce what the law is. This awareness owes a great deal to the publication in 1977 of J. A. G. Griffith's *The Politics of the Judiciary*,[3] which, like a slightly dangerous firework, sparked off in several provoking if not altogether entirely convincing directions in rapid succession. In 1982 the first, and only, article on the British judiciary to appear in one of the two major British academic political science journals was published.[4] The judiciary may be said to have come finally of political age in 1983 when a new textbook out of the Essex University stable actually devoted a whole chapter to it.[5] Judging from panels at recent meetings of the British Political Studies Association and the failure to establish a Politics and Law group within the Association, this coming of political age has not yet given birth to much new research and writing in this area, whether by established scholars or new recruits developing a new field.

What a remarkable contrast this is to the United States! Every textbook, even those written by British scholars, devotes a lengthy chapter, sometimes more, to the Supreme Court as a political institution and the impact of the Court's decisions on the working of the constitutional system and the distribution of political power.[6] Political science departments offer several courses on aspects of the judiciary at various levels. The journals regularly publish articles on the role of the courts, on their impact on society, or on their own internal political processes. There are clearly different schools within this subfield and different fashions rise and fall;[7] in Britain, all that one can say is that nakedness has given way to the simple shift.

The reasons for this contrast are, at first sight, obvious enough. In the United States, there is a written Constitution which is the supreme law of the land and which, by convention, it is the duty of the courts to interpret; within the Constitution several individual rights are entrenched, rights which the courts have to define and preserve against governmental encroachment if they have been infringed; the United States is a federation in which the precise responsibilities of the various levels of government need to be spelled out and the courts are required to delineate the boundaries between jurisdictions. In the United Kingdom, by contrast, the prime constitutional principle is the sovereignty of Parliament and rights, although they have in certain circumstances statutory bases, can be freely abridged by the Parliament exercising its sovereign powers;[8] the unitary nature of the United Kingdom, notwithstanding the peculiarities of Scotland and Northern Ireland, does not require courts to adjudicate on disputes between governments. The sorts of issues which regularly reach the courts in the United States and which, because they are born out of political disagreement, create political responses are largely absent in the United Kingdom; the saliency of court actions has, therefore, been commensurably lower. Yet, there is little doubting that in the 1970s the courts, and particularly some of the individual judges, did become salient and appeared, more regularly and more obviously than perhaps ever before, to be involved in the political process.

The excitement of discovering the significance of the British judiciary for the political system is clearly no excuse for plowing yet again the well-tilled terrain already worked over by students of the American judiciary. Yet, there are two reasons which have emboldened me to do so. The first, perhaps, is a peculiarly British concern with its accent on the use of language. For all the work that has been done on the Supreme Court, the conceptions of its political role remain definitionally fuzzy and I think it is important to distinguish quite sharply from the outset between three distinct and separable senses in which the Justices of the Supreme Court may be said to "act politically." I use the phrase "act politically" to stress its distinctiveness from "act judicially," although, as will become clear, the precise meaning of that latter phrase is far from obvious. However, in common discussion and in the more academic literature there is a prima facie assumption that there is a qualitative difference between the two. I do not think this is an altogether helpful way of looking at the courts, either in the United States or elsewhere. My trichotomy of meaning can be applied to Britain as well. Any full understanding (and therefore proper judgment) on the judiciary of either country depends upon a clear perception of these three brands of political action.

The second reason is altogether more conjectural. Although much of the difference between the political roles of the judiciaries on either side of the Atlantic (and they are different) can be explained in the simple institutional terms to which I have already drawn attention, I do not believe that the whole explanation can be left to such contrasts. Although the notion of political culture is simpler to conceive of than to operationalize, I shall argue at the end of this chapter that the political cultures of these two essentially Anglo-Saxon democracies—especially in relation to my three brands of political action—are sufficiently different as to provide some explanation for the differences in the roles of the judiciaries (and in the study of them) in the two countries.

The Inevitability of Political Involvement

The first brand of political action I wish to discuss depends very much upon a specific definition of politics. But David Easton was surely right (in this respect at least) that the politics of the state are those activities and processes which produce "an authoritative allocation of values."[9] They are authoritative in the sense that they are legally binding upon all who inhabit that state; and they are values in the sense that they express choices between disputed alternatives rather than agreed expressions of measurable truths. Any act, therefore, which authoritatively allocates values (which affects the distribution of power, the rights of individuals or groups, the propriety and form of state policy) is by this definition political. Justice Robert Jackson was aware of this when (shortly before he died) he wrote: "Any decision which confirms, allocates or shifts power as between different branches of the Federal Government or between it and a constituent state is . . . political, no matter whether the decision be reached by a legislature or a judicial process."[10] Many decisions which courts are required to make do allocate or shift power; but one should not get too carried away by this simple understanding. Many of the

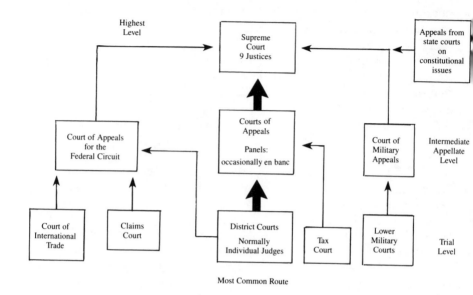

Figure 6.1   Basic Structure of the U.S. Federal Court System
Adapted from Lawrence Baum, *The Supreme Court* (Washington, D.C.:
Congressional Quarterly, 8, 1985

decisions they make are decisions on the facts of the case and have
ramifications only for the two parties concerned in the dispute; these
are not examples of this first brand of political action. Such cases may
well make up the bulk of the lower courts' caseload.

The courts of last resort, however, are different. The Supreme
Court, for instance, exercises discretionary power in deciding which
cases to hear. Nearly 5,000 cases are appealed each year, but only 150
on average are given a full hearing. This winnowing permits the
Court to set its own agenda, to decide which disputes to address,
and to exclude from consideration issues it would rather ignore.[11] As
figure 6.1 shows, the formal arrangement of the federal courts grants
to the Supreme Court a real power, or political power, which it must
exercise if it is to keep the docket down to a manageable size. Although the details of the British legal system are very different (see
figure 6.2), leave to appeal to the court of last resort, the judicial
committee of the House of Lords, is not automatic; judges in Brit-

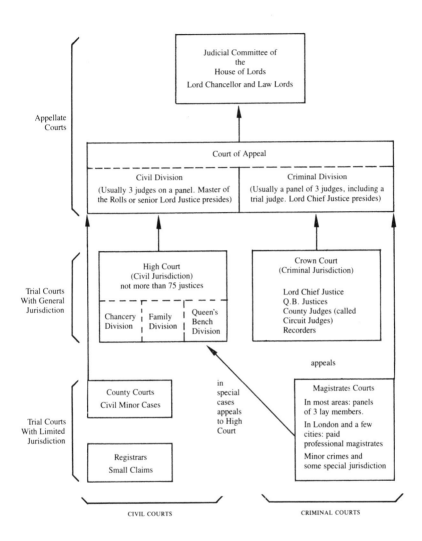

Figure 6.2   Basic Structure of the English Courts

ain, as in the United States, control their docket.[12] Most of the cases considered involve disputes whose resolution, whether through affirmation or reversal, will have wide effects. All I am saying at this juncture, however, is that in most cases the courts of last resort cannot avoid being political because, whichever way a dispute is resolved, there will have been an "authoritative allocation of values." It is a simple point, but a fundamental one.

What I take to be the inevitability of this role lies at the heart of so many studies of the Supreme Court. The enduring conflict between the advocates of "self-restraint" and the advocates of "activism" starts from the simple fact that the Court has acted politically in this definitional sense. The next stage of the argument revolves around the question whether the Founding Fathers meant the Supreme Court to be the final arbiter of constitutional meaning, reversible only by their own choice or by a constitutional amendment approved by the people themselves. The answer to this question is, I believe, undiscoverable and, indeed, largely irrelevant to students of American politics in the 1980s; the constitutional convention quite simply is that the Supreme Court may exercise judicial sovereignty. What is more interesting is to note that the questions posed by the Court are not amenable to technical solutions, discoverable by specially trained and experienced experts in the skills of adjudication. There is room for argument on both sides. I am not arguing here that all decisions are therefore equally defensible (clearly, the logic of some positions seems preferable to that of others) nor am I denying that the exercise of this power is a very proper object of examination. All I am saying is that this exercise of discretionary power, "the sovereign prerogative of choice" as Oliver Wendell Holmes described it,[13] is unavoidable.

There is, it seems to me, something a little artificial about much of the self-restraint versus activism debate.[14] These are not two single positions in political space, but broad areas along a continuum. Justices are more or less activist, more or less restraintist; they may be activist in some areas, but not in others. What they cannot properly be is so self-restrained that they do not exercise judicial power at all.[15] The courts are intended to be the forums in which disputes may be resolved and the easy cases, especially those that turn on matters of facts, never reach the highest courts of the land. These courts of last resort are called upon to make hard decisions, to balance competing principles, to meet new issues, armed primarily with the existing case law and constitutional provisions which rarely speak directly to new developments. The notion that there is a truth which good judges would discover (and this fancy surely lies behind some of the criticism of the U.S. Supreme Court in recent years) is a chimera.[16] Just as the simple idea which used to appear in the London *Times* that government would be better done by "experts" labored under the illusion that experts were agreed and united in a common understanding of a problem, so also some of the criticism of the Court labors under the implicit illusion that other men, better qualified and better trained, would see the true path. It is said that six economists in a room together would advocate seven different policies; I would be surprised if lawyers, given their training and calling, would not be equally productive.

The obvious reason for the inescapable political role played by the U.S. Supreme Court is its duty to interpret the Constitution. A constitutional system which is consciously designed to limit governmental power, which deliberately divides political authority between a national government and fifty state governments, and which attempts openly to entrench some individual rights against governmental power, must—if the principles upon which it is based have any validity—antagonize from time to time those who are the formal holders of power. As James Madison knew well, men are not angels. This power of the Court, to interpret the Constitution in such a way that Presidents and Congresses may be denied the full fruits of their electoral victories, seems all the greater because it is so difficult to amend the Constitution. One may talk of judicial supremacy, and rightly so, but it should also be remembered that the people of the United States can themselves amend that Constitution and thus negate Court decisions; indeed, this has been done.[17] The constitutions of the states are more easily and more regularly amended for the most part and the political power of judges within the state systems, although very real, appears of less significance because the political reality (in contrast to the constitutional theory) suggests that the element of finality is less.[18] That the Supreme Court must have this political power does not, of course, mean that it cannot be ill-used; but that is a different matter altogether, to be discussed later. A proper power misused does not make that power improper. For example, presidential power can potentially be abused, as surely it was by Richard Nixon, but very considerable discretionary power is necessary if the office of President is to be fulfilled satisfactorily. Once authority is delegated in any genuine way, the possibility of misuse is immediately introduced.

It is not merely the case that the Supreme Court's role is inevitably political; it has in recent years been forced to become more so. The political process, for good or ill, has expanded into the judicial field; governments who find Congress intractable will use the courts to advance their political designs; interest groups who, in a similar way, have lost out in the congressional labyrinth, turn to the Court; the pluralism that is American politics spills over into the courts and ultimately the Supreme Court must adjudicate; there is no escaping the litigious nature of the American people.[19] In short, the Supreme Court should be thought of as "another part of the whole complex web of power centres through which group demands are mediated."[20] Certainly, the expansion of the national government's activities, essentially as the consequence of President Lyndon Johnson's Great Society programs, has promoted enormous additions to the federal judiciary's caseload; the involvement of the courts in social policy may be deplored, but it appears inevitable;[21] the growth of legal aid and legal aid centers has similarly enabled citizens who in years past could never have conceived of litigation to take on the government on issues which never concerned the courts even a generation ago. Political realities, that is the actual activities of real people acting in the political arena, have forced the federal courts, and ultimately the Supreme Court, to become deeply involved in the authoritative allocation of values.[22]

The British experience at first glance has obvious contrasts. There is no written constitution or higher law limiting the sovereignty of Parliament; there is no codified Bill of Rights to which individuals can turn in defense against the overweening powers of government. There are not, therefore, the clear avenues available for litigants to draw the courts inexorably into political conflict. But that does not mean that the judges can avoid all political conflicts. Although judicial review, or judicial supremacy as it should more properly be called, is not an obvious feature of the British political system, there are still innumerable occasions (through construction of statutes, monitoring the executive branch's use of its discretionary power, and application of the common law) when the courts must act politically in my first sense. In the 1970s it seemed as though the judiciary was either being drawn unavoidably into an increasingly political role or else had actively chosen to intervene more in the political process. This impression was created essentially because the values to which some judges wished to give their authoritative blessing were not those of the government of the day. There was, indeed, a shift away from a fundamentally legitimizing role to questioning the use of the executive's discretionary power. Individual judges, like Lord Denning, began to incorporate their notions of substantive justice into their decisions; others, less exalted maybe but well reported in the press, either through obiter dicta or through their conduct of trials and sentencing practices, were visibly allocating values.

The judiciary in Britain has never been quite as isolated from the political process as is sometimes made out. The common law, after all, is judge-made law. It has developed through a process of accretion, principles being created from the controversies litigated before the judges and building upon past precedents; rather like coral, it is a slow business of tiny additions to foundations laid long ago. The common law thus depends very much on the principle of *stare decisis* (standing by decisions previously made), but not exclusively so; although the common law can be overridden by Parliament, it very rarely is.[23] It is not codified, as its equivalent in Europe is. The common law tradition in the United States outside Louisiana is, of course, important, especially in many states,[24] but the bulk of the work of the courts of last resort is the interpretation and application of statute law or the provisions of written constitutions. The extent to which the common law can lead to imaginative jurisprudence depends very much upon the judges' adherence to the philosophy of *stare decisis*. This philosophy is based upon two major principles which came under challenge in Britain only in recent years. *Stare decisis* encapsulated the virtue of certainty. Two quotations aptly summarize this view: in 1951 the Lord Chancellor, Viscount Jowitt, said:

> If a dispute does come to the House of Lords, if we examine it and discover that there is a case which is precisely in point, then whether we like the decision or whether we do not, whether we think it accords with modern requirements and conditions or whether we think it does not, we shall follow loyally the decision which has already been come to. In that way and that way only can we introduce some certainty into the law.[25]

Lord Simonds, who was so dominant a figure in the British judiciary in the 1950s, echoed this philosophy of restraint when he said in his speech in *Jacobs v. LCC:* "it would, I think, be to deny the importance, I would say the paramount importance of certainty in the law to give less than coercive effect to the unequivocal statement of the law made after argument by three members of this House."[26] The second principle was the primacy of the legislature and here again the words of Lord Simonds are appropriate: "It is . . . possible that we are not wiser than our ancestors. It is for the Legislature . . . to determine whether there should be a change of law and what that change should be."[27] Echoes of Felix Frankfurter and Learned Hand are always to be heard among senior members of the British judiciary, as they look toward the legislature as the appropriate body to make the authoritative allocation of values. This is partly a matter of legal culture, to which I will come later in this chapter, but the central point is that there has traditionally been strong pressure against creative jurisprudence in Britain and fewer chances for judges to exercise judicial power.

The process of statutory construction, or examining the exercise of discretionary power, permits judges a very real opportunity to exercise power on both sides of the Atlantic. The 1971 Race Relations Act, for instance, has been the subject of considerable judicial "legislation" in Britain as the precise meaning of its wording emerges from litigation. Race, the courts decided, refers only to color, not to national origin; hence it is lawful to discriminate against a Pole because of his being a Pole.[28] The prohibition against racial discrimination by anyone "providing services to the public or a section of the public" was deemed not to apply to private clubs.[29] These cases illustrate the way in which judges will inevitably be political; to have decided the other way would have allocated values as authoritatively and would have been equally political.

In the 1970s, the British judges, as I have said, appeared to move decisively deeper into the world of politics; and the reasons for this were not much dissimilar to those which affected the American courts. The growth of welfare legislation and the expansion of state power inevitably created more points of tension and conflict between citizen and government; even more starkly, the government itself demanded that the courts be involved in matters of great political sensitivity by establishing, for example, the National Industrial Relations Court (NIRC), which was required to adjudicate between unions and employers and use the authority of the judiciary to impose a set of values on unwilling union officials.[30] Although this was technically no more than applying the law as passed by Parliament, it in fact drew the court into the center of political discord and, by the appointment of Sir John Donaldson as President of the Court, ensured that the political nature of the court would be manifest. Finally, there has been an enormous growth of litigation by groups to advance their own political aims; just as in the United States those groups which have lost out in the legislative process take their case to the courts, so, too, in Britain, there has been an increasing tendency to employ injunctions and other judicial devices to check policies that are disliked or to reverse decisions of ministers which are disapproved. Even the Labour party itself went to the courts to object against the decisions of the Boundary Commission. Much of this litigation has been directed toward the Court of Justice of the European Communities and the more controversial Commission and Court of Human Rights, whose decisions are, through the 1972 European Communities Act, binding on the British courts and are based upon written documents setting down limitations and rights along the lines of the United States Constitution; accordingly, one recent analysis suggests, I am sure correctly, that "not only European courts but also domestic courts will become regular targets for interest group activities during the 1980s."[31]

This first brand of "political action," therefore, is inescapable. That is to say, so long as disagreements occur and the courts of last resort are given the role of adjudicating between rival claims of a political nature, the courts must be political. They exercise political power. But they do not exercise raw political power, untrammelled and illimitable. They are constrained by the simple fact that they respond to disputes rather than seek them out; that they do not innovate policies but react to policies; that they operate in a legal culture which recognizes quite clearly a qualitative difference between the judicial and the political function, even if it cannot define the difference so clearly. A few years ago I wrote as follows about the Supreme Court (sentiments which apply as much to the appellate courts of the British system):

> There is a great danger in laying too much stress on the subjective nature of judicial decision-making and in emphasizing the boundless authority of the Supreme Court. . . . it is nevertheless a court of law. It is bound by accepted procedures, by accepted conventions, by an interest in establishing a coherent and lasting system of law, and by its awareness of its status and importance as the court of last resort and the fountain of certain law.[32]

The skill in understanding the political role of the courts lies in striking the right balance between the untenable extremes of those who minimize and those who maximize that role. In striking that balance, however, we must move on to those other brands of political action which directly affect the outcome of that political involvement which the courts cannot avoid.

Calculations and Adjudication

Adversarial litigation, in which both American and British courts are exclusively concerned, by definition involves two sides to a question. Judges must employ criteria of one kind or another. They could, for example, always defer to the government's interpretation of statute or constitution. That is of itself a form of "calculated action," my second brand of political action. I use this phrase consciously as the antithesis of the two central pillars which support the notion of mechanical jurisprudence. The first pillar conceptualizes the process of judging as an individualistic intellectual enterprise applying judicial rules to the facts of the case; in short, nothing intervenes between the judge's examination of the facts and arguments presented and the judgment delivered, except the technical skill of the judge himself. The second pillar extends this idea of nonintervention to include extraneous calculations of likely impact; the law, with apologies to Gertrude Stein, is the law is the law.

It seems hardly necessary in 1984 to state that Justices of the Supreme Court do not accept this model of judging. "Calculated action" takes place in two distinguishable spheres. Within the Court itself, individual Justices do not operate in hermetically sealed chambers wrestling with cases on their own. The reality of a collegiate Court (together with its convention, wisely instituted by John Marshall, of issuing an opinion of the Court as an institution rather than the opinions of its several members) has inevitably encouraged interaction between the Justices. They argue points; they seek votes for their positions; they amend their opinions to meet others' wishes; they use intermediaries, memoranda, law clerks or other Justices, as well as—only occasionally—personal visitations or phone calls to bring pressure to bear on their Brethren. There is no simple relationship between the so-called "result-oriented" Justice (like William Douglas) and the so-called "self-restrained" Justice (like Felix Frankfurter) on this point. Frankfurter lobbied constantly and obsessively; Douglas, especially in his later years, largely disdained this practice. The Justices, frankly, do not share the view of Justice Owen Roberts that the "judicial branch has only one duty: to lay the article of the Constitution which is invoked beside the statute which is challenged and to decide whether the latter squares with the former."[33] Not only is the process of judging more complex; the need to gain votes for reversing or affirming, or support for a given opinion, necessitates the consideration of others' points of view, at the very least. Calculating what will satisfy one's Brethren is a major skill of the most successful Supreme Court Justices.

The second, and I think more interesting, sphere in which "calculated action" takes place is the concern for consequences and external repercussions. The most obvious, and well-documented, instance relates to the two *Brown* v. *Board of Education* decisions.[34] But oral argument, intracourt discussions, and the final opinion in *Gideon* v. *Wainwright* all addressed the practical consequences of establishing the right to counsel in state courts.[35] In framing relief, most Justices—particularly those with practical experience of public politics—are aware of, and take into consideration, the reality of the political world outside. In deciding *Miranda* v. *Arizona*, Warren was very conscious of the existing practices of the FBI and his own experiences as a prosecutor in California.[36] The power of the Court, after all, ultimately depends upon widespread voluntary acquiescence and respect and the Justices are largely aware that respect will be forfeited if judgments too often open up Pandora's box or seem unenforceable or stray too far from a general consensus among the political elite.

This concern for respect leads the Court to consider not merely the content but also the form of its decisions. There are many ways in which this concern for image expresses itself. It can, for instance, be seen at the very early stage of granting certiorari; both *Gideon* v. *Wainwright* and *Coker* v. *Georgia* were carefully selected to exclude extraneous issues of race or juvenility.[37] It is apparent in the determination to seek unanimity in cases of considerable saliency. It emerges during conference discussions as the precise grounds on which the decision is to be based are considered. It can be evident when opinions are assigned; the Chief Justice's retention of the most salient and important cases, the choice of Stanley Reed in *Smith* v. *Allwright* or Tom Clark in *Abington School District* v. *Schempp* are well-known instances.[38] Justices, therefore, calculate not merely in terms of the content of their decisions and the consequences; they calculate also in terms of the decision's image.

At this stage, two observations should immediately be made. First, although the literature is now replete with examples of politically calculating actions of the kinds to which I have referred, it should not be thought that every case is dealt with in so politically calculating a manner. It is essential for any understanding of the Supreme

Court to realize that within a universe of 150 or so cases each term there is a hierarchy of importance which dictates, because of a case's subject matter or saliency in the wider political world, greater consideration. Henry Hart was long ago aware of, and unhappy about, this;[39] and Felix Frankfurter's near annual complaints to conference that some cases were too hastily considered bears testimony to this point. Second, it should be remembered that the Supreme Court is in the business of dispute resolution and that successful resolution is a terminal act. Given that neither the other branches of government nor the sovereign people acting through the amending process have in fact managed to resolve many issues of profound dispute, the fact that the Supreme Court has done so—largely, but by no means entirely, convincingly—can only be viewed as one essential explanation for the United States' improbable ability to run so industrialized, technological, and ethnically diverse a state according to a constitution devised for a political environment almost unimaginably different. Adaptation requires Supreme Court suppleness; there is, indeed, a real need for a continuing Convention.

All the examples to which I have alluded so far are drawn from the United States; and they could be replicated many times over just by a cursory glance through Bernard Schwartz's very recent biography of Earl Warren or the less reliable, but not-to-be-ignored, "exposé" provided by Bob Woodward and Scott Armstrong.[40] Examples of this kind are much less readily discoverable in the United Kingdom. Judges, unlike politicians, have not committed their diaries or recollections to print; nor have their private papers been quarried for judicial biographers. The available material is thin. But the most obvious reason for this is simply that many fewer examples exist. The judicial committee of the House of Lords is not the same kind of collegiate body as the Supreme Court; usually five members, often quite randomly selected, sit on each case from a pool of about fifteen and there are only about fifty cases considered each year. The Law Lords, however, do act as something more than five independent voices; discussions, brief and informal though they are, take place throughout the hearing of a case and the ensuing conference permits those who have taken part in the case to exchange views. Speeches are circulated among the participating Law Lords and sometimes result in amendments to take account of opposing arguments. Only in exceptional cases is much time spent as a body seeking to hammer out an agreed position; unanimity is not valued that highly.[41] But in certain cases, there is no doubt that some Law Lords do attempt to persuade their colleagues, and occasionally succeed. "Everybody now knows," Wedderburn wrote in 1967, "that in *Donoghue v. Stevenson* Lord Atkin talked the majority round. It is now generally known that in *Rookes v. Barnard* in 1964 Lord Devlin did much the same."[42] In this latter case, Devlin was originally in a minority of one (or two, for accounts differ), but, after Lord Reid had reconvened the appellate committee and further argument had been heard, a unanimous decision upholding the appeal finally emerged. There is little doubt that here genuine cases of conversion took place.

The time and care taken in *Rookes v. Barnard* was a sign that the Law Lords realized full well the political significance of the case. Conferences normally last only twenty minutes or so on each case, but occasionally much more time is spent in collegiate discussion. In *Heaton's Transport Ltd v. TGWU*, for instance, a whole day was spent considering the matter, and it was agreed that the Court should take the unusual step of delivering a single speech in order to strengthen the impact of the decision. As Lord Reid later said, approving this action of his colleagues: "You see you have to take public opinion and public policy into account and that [decision] was for consumption by non-lawyers and it might have been confusing."[43] A more obvious instance of "calculated action" is hard to describe. That, however, was only part of the story, for the decision in the case was handed down with almost unprecedented speed, only a week elapsing between the end of the hearing and Lord Wilberforce's opinion. The reason for this was almost certainly a matter of political calculation, for it allowed the National Industrial Relations Court, which had committed dockers to prison for flagrant contempt of court and thus fueled a movement toward a general strike, to exercise some nifty judicial footwork and, on the strength of the *Heaton's Transport* decision, release the dockers and defuse a difficult situation.[44]

There is little doubt that the Law Lords (although not necessarily the courts of appeal) have become more politically aware in the last two decades, due almost certainly to the leadership of Lord Reid and the innovatory judgments of Lord Denning. (It is perhaps ironic that in these same decades political experience and connections have been less significant factors in deciding who are made judges.) Given the way in which the judiciary is inextricably bound up in the political process on both sides of the Atlantic, it is perhaps as well that the members of the highest courts have political acumen. The tendency of Republican appointments to be stronger on judicial than political experience might account in part for that tendency of a majority of the Burger Court to elevate case-by-case adjudication over the establishment of broader principles and thus give the impression of a Court buffeted on a sea of unprincipled ad hoc-ery.

The first brand of political action brings judges into the political process. Once in that process, they tend (not always, to be sure) to act politically in a second way, by basing their performances on calculations of intracourt dynamics and extracourt consequences. As a general proposition, this seems to me not only unexceptionable but admirable. The function of courts as dispute settlers (or tension managers) is probably best done if there are intracourt deliberations and considerations of impact. To argue that "the law is the law is the law" is to divorce the process of adjudication from the reality in which it occurs and on which it impinges. However, when I claim that my second brand of political action is functional to the judicial enterprise, I do not also claim that these functions will inevitably be well done. Once again, we revert to the problem of discretionary authority; without it, modern political systems can hardly operate; but there is no certain way of ensuring its proper exercise. This, at last, brings me to the third brand of political action.

Independence and Partisanship of Judges

The third branch of political action is the antithesis of that neutrality which is supposed to lie at the heart of the process of adjudication. In this form a judge's actions are dominated by his personal ideological preferences, so that, in the words of a recent article, the U.S. Constitution is regarded "as a kind of letter of marque authorizing [the Justices] to set sail at will among laws, striking down any they find displeasing."[45] Felix Frankfurter thought he saw such cavalier behavior on many occasions; a splendid example is this draft concurring opinion from 1942 which, unsurprisingly, was never circulated:

> I greatly sympathize with the essential purpose of my Brother (former Senator) Black's dissent. His roundabout and turgid legal phraseology is a cri de coeur. "Would I were back in the Senate," he means to say, "so that I could put on the statute book what really ought to be there. But here I am, cast by Fate into a den of judges devoid of the habits of legislators, simple fellows who feel that they must enforce the laws as Congress

wrote them and not as they really should have been written, that the task which Congress has committed to the Interstate Commerce Commission should be left to that Commission even when it decides, as it did in this case, against the poor farmers of the Middle West."[46]

Many Justices have not kept such feelings locked up in their unpublished private papers, but have expressed them in dissent, complaining that the majority has exercised raw judicial power. This rawness lies in the assumption that votes are cast merely as expressions of the individual's substantive preferences.

The essential characterization of this sort of political action is its personal, normative, and distinctly nonjudicial quality. When the man in Peoria complains that the Supreme Court is "political," he is drawing attention to what he sees as "purely partisan" action, to crude judicial legislation, to actions, in short, which are predicated upon nothing more than a Justice's private notion of good policy. Because cases are not resoluble by technical skills, an element of subjectivity is inevitably thrust upon judges; but what is significant in the caricature of the political judge I have just drawn are the words "purely," "crude," "nothing more than."

Nor is the man in Peoria alone in this perception; there are more than enough law professors, and not only from the Chicago and Harvard stables, who can be cited to buttress the argument that a majority of the Justices during the later Warren Court frequently acted in this way. Nor is this merely the perception of lawyers; one school of political scientists takes this criticism as a central assumption of their jurimetric work. They assume that votes cast in conference represent personal positions on the merits of the case and use this assumption to scale the Justices' ideologies.[47] There is something circuitous about such a methodology, because it assumes as real that very result-oriented ideology it later describes. Furthermore, it assumes that the "meaning" of votes are relatively easy to discern and that there is little "fluidity of judicial choice."[48] It assumes, in short, that Justices are wholly independent, in the sense that there are no constraints upon their translating political preferences into judicial decisions.

This notion of independence is worth worrying over a little more. First, it suggests a freedom from the sorts of outside pressures which cannot be gainsaid. Judges in most of Africa, for example, are not only often directly approached by government or publicly rebuked, they are also sometimes removed for making the "wrong" decisions. Clearly, they lack the independence to express their personal preferences. Although the process of appointment to the United States Supreme Court is very much a political process, and seen by political actors to be so, once on the Court, a Justice is independent of direct interference from other branches of government. The Court can of course be made well aware of the displeasure of the legislature or executive; salaries can be stingily enhanced (but never reduced); solicitors-general can express government's disagreement with the Court's jurisprudence. But direct intervention is very rare. Eisenhower, perhaps, came very close to pressurizing Earl Warren over Brown[49] and in the Nixon years, it is said, the Justices were made aware of the White House's preferences.

The separation of powers in the United Kingdom, to which Montesquieu so erroneously drew attention, is refuted categorically by the existence of the Lord Chancellor. He is a politician, appointed by the Prime Minister to the cabinet and to what is, in effect, a Department of Justice in the executive branch, where he is primarily responsible for law reform and for the initial selection of judges as well as their later elevation; he is also a judge, being a member of the judicial committee of the House of Lords; he is also a legislator, being the speaker of the House of Lords, a position closer to Tip O'Neill's than to Bernard Wetherill's. The Law Lords are not so inextricably linked to the other branches of government, but they do sit in the House of Lords and are entitled to participate in its activities. Generally speaking, they do not take up this entitlement. Indeed, even on those matters concerning the functioning of the legal system on which they might be expected to express an expert opinion, they frequently absent themselves and rarely discuss, as a body, the matters coming before the House.[50] In practice, therefore, the highest judges of the land operate as though they were quite independent of external political pressures. At issue is how this independence is used.

A second notion of independence carries the very opposite connotations from those held by the man from Peoria. It implies a lack of bias, an independence from party allegiance or factional loyalty, a peculiarly judicial neutrality which is dominated by the accurate search for the facts rather than the subjective expression of principle. If there is a divisive issue requiring a commission of inquiry, governments have frequently turned to senior judges to chair it. This is particularly true of Britain; judges are overwhelmingly the persons most frequently chosen to chair Royal Commissions and departmental committees. Lord Scarman, on the Brixton riots, and Lord Diplock, on court procedures in Northern Ireland, are only the latest in a long line of extremely important such instances. But it is also true of the United States, where Owen Roberts chaired the inquiry into the surprise Japanese attack on Pearl Harbor and Earl Warren chaired the commission of inquiry into the assassination of President John Kennedy. The independence of the judiciary, according to this lexicon, denies the judges any value preference of their own and sees them, in contrast to politicians and most other members of the public, as peculiarly qualified to produce apolitical analyses and proposals untainted with the brush of partisanship.

Third, and following from this, the notion of independence can imply a broader freedom, a freedom from the very process of socialization which inculcates in a person a very special set of values. I take this to be Griffith's fundamental concern when he implies that judges in Britain are not independent but are the products of their upbringing and therefore essentially conservative.

> Their view of the public interest contains three elements and derives from their socialisation, in middle class homes and at the bar: first, the interests of the state (including its moral welfare) and the preservation of law and order, broadly interpreted; secondly, the protection of property rights; and thirdly the promotion of certain political views normally associated with the Conservative Party.[51]

Stressing a class bias can be too simplistic for it is too blunt an instrument and has difficulties in explaining the very real differences which occur between members of the same class, most notably, perhaps, in the United States. Research aimed at linking social background to jurisprudence is a dry hole; party allegiance, especially in the state courts, is a better indicator of different understandings of the law.[52] There were clearly some long-term ideological differences between Lords Reid and Dilhorne, despite their similar "class origins"; Lord Reid was much less likely to convict criminals or uphold tax assessments than Lord Dilhorne and much less likely to take sympathy on the weaker side in public or civil law cases.[53]

Nevertheless, in Britain, lawyers are a small band of people whose ideals and values are constantly reinforced from the teaching of law through the Inns of Court to the clublike atmosphere of collegial discussion in the course of business. Griffith was quite right to draw attention to the internalized values of most judges, which are a combination of those espoused by their own friends and contacts (particularly on moral matters) and those espoused by the legal fraternity. It should be remembered, however, that the law itself is essentially conservative in both the United States and the United Kingdom to the extent that its historical development has refused to accept Proudhon's aphorism that property is theft and has tended to assume, as a part of its instinctive philosophy of self-restraint, that governments' judgments of the national interests are largely to be taken at face value. The antipluralist argument in the United States, that a divided elite in fact observed a basic consensus on fundamental values, has its parallel here: courts, even divided courts, state the primary concerns and assumptions of the propertied middle classes.

As I have argued, the courts of last resort on both sides of the Atlantic are faced with decisions which are not only intrinsically political (in my first sense) but also political in the sense of demanding a choice between alternative courses of action which is not already preordained (an element of independence). This discretion cannot be value-free. Wherever choice exists, the choice made will be representative of some set of values; neutrality is illusory. There is no denying that individual conceptions of justice or equity obtrude at this juncture and judges can be result-oriented on occasions. I have little doubt that on most labor cases this was true of Hugo Black and William Douglas and on capital punishment and most race issues it is true of Thurgood Marshall; Lord Denning, too, in several areas of the law sought to impose his notion of justice, an attempt which did not always find favor with the Law Lords on appeal. But these instances do not amount to a finding that judicial independence will inevitably, or has in fact, led to judges setting sail "at will among laws, striking down any they find displeasing." There are very real constraints in operation.

The legal culture of the two countries cannot be ignored. In the United Kingdom particularly, the importance of *stare decisis* remains fundamental, though not entirely determinative. In 1966, the Law Lords introduced their Practice Statement which was consciously designed to permit them greater freedom to depart from precedents and thus (although they would never have said so openly) more easily to "make law."[54] It has not, however, revolutionized the operations of the judicial committee, which still prefers to stand by its earlier decisions or subtly distinguish cases rather than reverse itself. The very high levels of unanimity to be found, especially given the lack of conferences and other procedures toward unity, reflect a general disposition to eschew creative jurisprudence. The U.S. culture is different, partly because of the process of selection to the bench and partly because the Supreme Court has a much longer history of consciously overruling its earlier decisions. Yet this can be stressed too much; the legal culture on both sides of the Atlantic values certainty and this inevitably constrains most judges from striking out in innovative directions.

Similarly, the notion of neutrality remains very much in the minds of most judges. It may be a hopeless ideal; but it clearly acts as a constraint. Whether Felix Frankfurter's public determination to avoid personal preference was real or a mask for an essentially conservative ideology may be a matter of dispute;[55] but there is no escaping that in many cases legal professionalism constrains judges. A classic example is Lord Hailsham's speech, when giving judgment in a case where a woman was being prosecuted for breaking regulations governing overcrowding in boardinghouses, although she was actually running a refuge for battered wives:

> At the beginning of this opinion, I said that my conclusion, though without doubt, was arrived at with reluctance. . . . This appellant . . . is providing a service for people in urgent and tragic need. It is a service which in fact is provided by no other organ of our much vaunted system of public welfare. . . . When people come to her door, not seldom accompanied by young children in desperate states and at all hours because, being in danger, they cannot go home . . . the appellant does not turn them away . . . but takes them in and gives them shelter and comfort. And what happens when she does? She finds herself the defendant in criminal proceedings at the suit of the local authority because she has allowed the inmates of her house to exceed the permitted maximum, and to that charge, I believe, she has no defence in law. My Lords, this is not a situation that can be regarded with complacency by any member of your Lordship's House, least of all by those who are compelled to do justice according to the law as it is, and not according to the state of affairs as they would wish it to be.[56]

He then cast his vote against the side he undoubtedly favored. But even a justice as result-oriented as William Douglas was constrained by the requirements of the law. In *Lassiter v. Northampton County Board of Education*, for example, he accepted as constitutional North

Carolina's requirement that qualified voters should be able to read and write any section of the state constitution, since there was a rational purpose behind the requirement, although he added gratuitously that he thought it bad policy.[57]

It would be an error, however, to go too far in arguing that the complex nature of judicial independence results in judges wielding only marginal power when exercising their discretion in hard cases. Much depends upon their conception of the judicial role.[58] And here there is plenty of room for dispute. Disparate conclusions rarely occur from a different perception of the facts; they follow from different interpretations of their meaning and from different conceptions of the judicial role. Distilling meaning from facts is not a technical exercise. Whether all speech or all forms of communication are protected by the First Amendment is one obvious example; when demonstrations or picket lines become inimical to law and order is another. Personal value systems are the determining force here and those values grow out of particular socialization processes. Here Griffith is surely correct when he writes:

> From all this flows that view of the public interest which is shown in judicial attitudes such as tenderness towards private property and dislike of trade unions, strong adherence to the maintenance of order, distaste for minority opinions, demonstrations and protests, indifference to the promotion of better race relations, support of governmental secrecy, concern for the preservation of the moral and social behaviour to which it is accustomed, and the rest.[59]

This tendency is well-exemplified in sentencing policy where judges have traditionally been granted considerable freedom and where exemplary punishment clearly expresses a value position as does lenient treatment. Early in 1983 the United Kingdom courts were embroiled in political dispute because the exercise of this discretionary power had been interpreted as unnecessarily chauvinist in several rape cases where the responsibility of the girl had been given great weight, and unnecessarily pro-government in the Sarah Tisdale case involving the Official Secrets Act, where the judgment explicitly stressed its deterrent intention. The Law Lords, by contrast, have in the last few years tended to redress the more clearly "political" (in its partisan sense) judgment of the lower courts, especially in trade union cases, partly in terms of Parliament's intent, partly out of their "political" (in its calculatory sense) awareness. But this must be tempered by the cultural constraints on judges. These are no more, and no less, *self*-imposed than are their assumptions about the national interest. Both grow out of a person's life experience and socialization. Hence, judges are as independent (or not) in expressing ideological preferences as they are constrained (or not) by their conception of the judicial role.

Finally, Justices of the Supreme Court and the Law Lords act politically in this "partisan" sense outside the structure of litigation. In the United States, the Justices of the Supreme Court, and especially the Chief Justice, have a role to play in organizing the federal judiciary and there have been many administrative developments recently which have a legislative quality about them. In addition, the current United States Chief Justice has taken an active lobbying role in a laudable, but perhaps too time-consuming, attempt to improve the judicial system of the United States.[60] The Law Lords have not often used their membership in the House of Lords to express their own opinions about the desirability or technical quality of legislation, but a powerful intervention by Lord Simon on the recent Housing Bill is a reminder that membership of one chamber of Parliament is no dead letter. More significantly, in 1981, the home secretary, faced with gross overcrowding in the country's prisons and public complaints from his prison governors, considered introducing regulations to give nearly all prisoners automatic parole after they had served part of their sentence. The Lord Chief Justice called a meeting of all high court judges; the home secretary was later informed that the judges would merely increase the sentences they handed down to offset such liberalization. The proposal was dropped.[61]

It is this partisan brand of political action which causes the man in Peoria, and the Fleet Street editorialists, the greatest problems; it is, after all, usually the sum of their perceptions. But it must be seen in perspective. The growing incidence of broadly drafted legislation inevitably gives rise to increasing uncertainty about a law's meaning or the executive actions it sanctions. Faced with questions about the rationality of a minister's decision or the meaning of the public interest, judges have little guidance; in the United States they may look to the *Congressional Record* (which explains some of the otherwise inexplicable speeches on Capitol Hill) but in Britain they may not look to *Hansard*, only the words of the statute itself. Many occasions arise, therefore, when a decision *must* rest upon a judge's "ideology," his set of precepts for judicial behavior, his concept of rationality or public interest, his view on the relative rights of executive and citizen. Disagreements are usually disagreements on matters of principle on which intelligent and able men may rightly disagree. In the United States, the opportunity for judicial partisanship is greater, partly because the constitutional system demands it, partly because the precedents are so many and so varied, and partly because tradition has given Justices a greater freedom at the margin to express their notions of justice. In Britain, the opportunity is less, partly because the principle of parliamentary sovereignty seems to clothe the executive in a presumption of virtue, partly because the precedents for creative jurisprudence are few, and partly because the judicial culture is deferential. Once the model of mechanistic rule-applying is rightly jettisoned, the issue is how much, or how little, partisanship takes place.

Political Culture and the Performance of the Courts

As I have looked at the higher British judiciary through the lenses of a Supreme Court watcher, I have been surprised at the number of parallels that can be drawn. The similarities, of course, flow from the very essence of dispute settlement. But one must not be deluded into believing that these similarities, perhaps even growing similarities, make the judicial branches the same. The political impact, the political power indeed, of the United States Supreme Court is incomparably greater than that of its British counterpart. I would still argue that the majority of decisions, big and small, affecting the American citizen's life are made by the legislatures and executives of the state and national governments. But there is no doubt that the Supreme Court's influence, sometimes directly, sometimes indirectly through the gradual changing of public philosophies (as with civil rights), has been far-reaching. By contrast, it is difficult to think of major principles affecting individual rights or the distribution of power which have been enunciated by the judicial committee of the House of Lords remotely comparable to those established by the United States Supreme Court. The committee has called "foul" from time to time; but it has not amended the rules of the game.

The reasons for this are obvious enough. A written constitution as the supreme law of the land, separate branches of government sharing power, a federal system, a variety of rights entrenched in the written constitution, all mark off the American environment as something distinct and different. The power of the Supreme Court grows to a large extent out of its position *between* several institutions (federal and state, executive and legislative); the weakness of the British judiciary lies partly in its location as a potentially countervailing power to all the democratically legitimated institutions of the state. The state-centered nature of the British system is of central significance. Argument over a possible British Bill of Rights bogs down in the fundamental question of the proper relationship between government and citizen. Parliamentarians of both major political persuasions see it as a potential check upon themselves to do good if in office; both share positive attitudes toward the state as the vehicle for progressive change. They differ over the definition of that progress, but they agree in their belief in the strong state. So institutions and philosophy go hand in hand to pull the countries apart.

I would not like to leave the discussion there, however. It is easy enough to argue that the objective significance of the Supreme Court as a political institution logically entails considerable political science attention; and the reverse would hold in British academia. But I would like to press the issue of legal culture a little further. Notwithstanding the manifest differences of an institutional kind, it is still useful to remind ourselves that the exercise of "partisan" power on the Supreme Court has ebbed and flowed and owes not a little to the accident that John Marshall was Chief Justice for so many of the early years of the republic;[62] nor should we forget that in the early 1970s the higher British judiciary did double guess the politicians more than ever before. Perhaps the dynamics of modern capitalism, the growth of the administrative state, and the development of a more individual-centered jurisprudence are pushing the British judiciary inexorably more in the American direction. The advent of increasing numbers of cases before the European courts might hasten this process further. Could the British judicial culture manage so fundamental a change?

Let me begin, perversely, by noting some interesting things about attitudes in the United States toward the Supreme Court and litigation. I think it is fair to say that Americans are schizophrenic about their Supreme Court. Its political saliency cannot be denied; and yet to some extent it is denied. Presidents are fully aware that one of the most politically significant nominations they can make is to the Supreme Court; yet, the virtues of the candidate are normally presented in coded form in public. Privately, the real political motives are more in evidence. Theodore Roosevelt, emphasizing the primacy of ideology even over party loyalty, expressed this view to Henry Cabot Lodge in 1912 when discussing the possible nomination of Horace

Lurton. He wrote: "The nominal politics of the man has nothing to do with his actions on the bench. His real politics are all important. . . . He is right on the negro question; he is right on the power of the federal government; he is right on the Insular business; he is right about corporations; and he is right about labor."[63] Political scientists and legal scholars are well aware of this double standard although (to my surprise) many still feel obliged to spell out this fact as though it were newly discovered. One reason is a widespread belief that the myth of a neutral judiciary should be kept as unsullied as possible.

I sympathize with such a view. What holds societies together are often insubstantial beliefs and inaccurate perceptions. The task of sociologists, it might be said, is to strip away deceptive illusions and lay bare the "real" forces which underpin societal stability. The "truth," however, is not always easy to live with. And the notion of a neutral judiciary, showing favor to neither rich nor poor, to neither radical nor conservative, is a comforting illusion which cements a certain distribution of ordered power. The publication of *The Brethren* in reality only publicized what was increasingly known by the aficionados; heroes do have feet of clay. The criticisms of that book, it seems to me, lay quite as much in its symbolic impact as in its errors of fact and balance. This explains to some extent why criticism of the Court almost always coincides with dissatisfaction with some specific judgments. The accusation of legislating or acting politically has come from both right and left; instead of asserting a personal objection to the tenor of the Court's judgment, however, critics are forced to state their complaints in the language of the myth, claiming that it has given up its proper—and presumably attainable—function of neutral adjudication. Think of the New Dealers in 1935 and 1936 and the Moral Majority today.

The schizophrenic nature of American attitudes is exemplified also in the way political disputes—disputes over the precise values to be authoritatively allocated—frequently masquerade as adversarial litigation. De Tocqueville, of course, noted this a very long time ago when he observed that scarcely an issue which divided the people of the United States did not ultimately reach the Supreme Court for resolution. His observation is perhaps even truer today. Look at the *New York Times* almost any day of the week and see how many stories concern litigation; the London *Times* carries only a summary of the law reports. So political action is not merely intimately involved in the judicial system; it is forced upon it. It fuels some of the litigation, it affects the choice of judges, and it permeates the conception of the issues being presented and of the remedies available to judges. Yet, at the same time, the myth that the judicial process and those who work in it are disinterested servants of the state seeking, through expertise and technical skill, the "right" answer is hopefully preserved.

In the United Kingdom, this myth of judicial exclusivity, as I might call it, runs deeper. Historically, of course, judges in the United Kingdom have been enmeshed unmistakably in the political process; but this is manifestly less the case now. The process of appointment to judicial office is arcane and is now apparently little affected by the executive branch's wishes. (Of course, if judging were merely a technical exercise, there would be little reason for governmental involvement.) Lord Chancellors seem to experience little role conflict in being senior members of the executive and also head of the judiciary. Even given the narrow field from which judges of the High Court can actually be chosen (Queen's Counsel of about fifty years of age willing to exchange a lucrative practice at the bar for the bench), there is room for some careful selection. I guess that there is a "black ball" system operating in the files of the Lord Chancellor's office which weeds out unacceptable judges. I also guess that in recent years the present Prime Minister's greater readiness to use her powers of patronage to favor her ideological preferences may have seeped across into the judicial world. Sir John Donaldson's spending years in the comparative wilderness after the Labour party's dismantling of the National Industrial Relations Court was not entirely accidental; nor was his appointment to be Master of the Rolls after Mrs. Thatcher became Prime Minister. The one was the Labour party's punishment for his actions as president of the NIRC, the other a Conservative leader's reward for able service stoically performed.

Nor is there in the United Kingdom a great tradition of litigating for political purposes. Interest groups are not awash with lawyers, nor are law journals full of suggestions for future arguments to advance new rights. Of course, trade unionists and individuals have sought the protection of the courts against governments and their agents, but the dominant political culture stresses resolution without confrontation. Tribunals and ombudsmen are the more usual form for defusing conflicts. That is, I would suggest, part of a traditional conservative ideology which shies away from institutionalized conflict (such as adversarial litigation or elections for party leaders) and prefers informal processes from which an acceptable compromise can emerge. It is, in a sense, the ideology of anti-ideology, for it implicitly assumes that tensions can be managed by "sensible" men arriving at "sensible" solutions.

In the United States, there is a general recognition that politics is both important and inevitable. The Revolution acknowledged that. And the Constitution was the deliberate conclusion of men who were unashamedly conscious of political realities and the need to restrict their excesses. In the United Kingdom, there has been no comparable break with the undemocratic past; rather, there has been a gradual evolution which has tended to hide the significance of political conflict. Perhaps, more accurately, the political culture has seen political conflict as an unfortunate necessity, too partisan in its roots and potentially difficult to manage. Hence, the perjorative connotations of the term politics in the United Kingdom relate not to corruption, for example, as might be the case in the United States, but to its allegedly unfortunate divisive consequences. This incidentally extends into the academic field where students of politics have a much lower status than students of political science in the United States. In the United States political science has a long pedigree (the *Political Science Quarterly* is into its 99th volume, the *American Political Science Review* into its 78th); in the United Kingdom, by contrast, politics is a johnny-come-lately discipline (*Political Studies* is only in its 32nd volume) and distinctly of lower standing than its intellectual parents, law and history. Teachers of politics in my experience often have to defend their endeavor because there is a common belief that the dangerous activity of partisan politics is being taught rather than the analysis and explanation of others' political activity. I do not get the impression that teachers of political science in the United States have to mount such defenses so often.

The legal culture in the two countries is so different that it is not surprising to find legal practice very different. In the United States, the bright young Arts and Social Science graduates go to law school before entering the wider world (their British equivalents probably become accountants). Lawyers, hence, are more broadly educated and much more widely spread. Litigation has become a normal mode for advancing policy goals and obtaining redress; the extent to which political life (and the public generally) has become judicialized is remarkable. No school board dares to be without an active lawyer. The open interconnection between law and politics is one of the most striking features of American public life, epitomized in its way by the traditionally political routes followed by Justices of the Supreme Court, especially under Democratic regimes.[64] In Britain, by contrast, the legal profession is self-policed, hierarchical, elitist, sharply divided between solicitors and barristers (that smaller elite within an elite, who plead cases in the higher courts and provide the pool from which judges are chosen), and still socially cohesive. There are changes afoot; the wider spread of educational opportunities following the Robbins expansion of university places, the existence of a few law departments concerned more with law's social relevance than its technology (still, however, of low status), and the diminished need to have private means in order to survive the early years of a barrister's career have diluted the profession somewhat. Especially at the higher levels, however, it remains remarkably homogeneous and overwhelmingly conservative in judicial philosophy (if not also in political loyalty). This is not an environment in which creative jurisprudence is likely to develop; each new generation is socialized, as undergraduates and in small law firms, into the prevalent norms and hence are temperamentally unenthusiastic about employing the law to advance their clients' political interests. The introduction of a Bill of Rights might make little change; judges would most likely favor government over the individual, respect the minister's evaluation of the public interest, and feel little empathy for those whose words and actions challenge the social order. The myth that the law is self-executing would surely have a strong hold over any judges appointed to monitor the Bill of Rights; indeed, the judicial culture might well make such appointees so self-restrained that they would fail to perceive the major function of a Bill of Rights, which is to grant individuals rights *against* the government.

There is one final aspect which merits comment. It concerns part of a broader political culture. In the United Kingdom, there is a privacy of politics. That is to say, the public expression of partisan loyalties and partisan views is limited. This is reflected in the conventional view among most middle class hosts and guests that politics, like religion and sex, is not a topic fit for social conversation. It might be divisive; it might arouse passions which have their basis in faith rather than considered thought; in short, it might not be manageable. Indeed, it *is* difficult, outside the tiny circle of professional politics watchers, to discuss contemporary politics in a disembodied way if supporters of both the Conservative party and Labour party are present. I am also surprised how many middle class people refuse to answer political questions on questionnaires because "their vote is secret." This seems an attitude peculiar to the professional classes. But the contrast with the United States, although difficult to quantify, is considerable: to support the "other" party is naturally an error, but it is not an error that implies yet further bad characteristics. Split-ticket voting, an unashamed admission that party loyalty is not all and a genuine belief that neither party nor any political grouping necessarily has a monopoly of wisdom, marks off the United States from the United Kingdom. The politics of coalition building and negotiation is very different from adversary politics; and this feeds back into attitudes about the law and how litigation is employed. Class and party are still inextricably tied in the ordinary mind and the fit between unions and Labour and the judiciary and Conservative too close to allow litigation much of a role in tension-management that would enjoy a wide legitimacy and consent.

I hope that in this chapter I have gone some way to answering the Examiners' instruction: "Compare and contrast the political nature of the courts in the United States and the United Kingdom." For one whose primary interest is the politics of the United States Supreme Court, the similarities to be found in the United Kingdom were greater than the political science literature generally would have suggested. It is wrong to exaggerate those differences. The constitutional arrangements, the format of the court structure and the legal profession, and the disparate political cultures ensure that these differences exist. But, given the political nature (in my first sense) of all courts of last resort and the greater readiness of people to use the courts to advance their political (partisan) interests, it is not surprising that in Britain, as in the United States, the higher courts are showing increasing readiness to be political in my second sense just as they cannot avoid, being human, to some extent be political in my third sense. A recent letter to the *Times* is very much to the point:[65] "Given the constant changes wrought in the law by the judiciary, and with the Trinity Bar finals approaching like a trough of low pressure, we would be obliged if you would refrain from publishing any further law reports until 1.00 pm, 3rd June 1984." Law school graduates in the United States have long appreciated this plea.

7

Sex, Money, and Power

ANTHONY KING

In this chapter, Anthony King turns his attention specifically onto one aspect of political culture—the definition and explanation of scandals—and incidentally introduces the new subdiscipline of scandology. As he examines scandals involving sex, money, and power, he draws attention at first to the broad similarities between the political cultures of the two countries, but he also points to significant differences. The cause of these, he suggests, lies not in some higher, or lower, general moral tone on one side of the Atlantic but more in the institutions and practices of the political systems. In fact, he draws attention to several central issues of earlier chapters such as the nature of the parties, the paths to leadership positions, and the career civil service to show that behavior is intimately related to the actual operation of politics in a country. What might at first sight seem a rather esoteric aspect of political culture turns out to encapsulate the central themes of nearly all the chapters in this volume; for it transpires that institutions and political culture enjoy a symbiotic relationship, each influencing the other and also altering slowly over time in response to major changes in the economic and social environment. In effect, living under a particular political system is an educative experience, teaching subjects what to expect in political life; these expectations in turn color the institutions and patterns of behavior acceptable to a people.

Introduction

The purpose of this chapter is to throw light on British and American political culture, and on the functioning of British and American political institutions, but also to make out a case—by example if not in theory—for the comparative study of political scandals. Political scandals, it is here contended, deserve to be studied for two quite different reasons.

The first is that, like all other scandals, they are tremendous fun—except, of course, for those personally affected by them. The spectacle of great men making fools of themselves, of their being caught out behaving in disgraceful or disreputable ways, appeals to the desire of most people to pull down the mighty from their seats, to be reassured that the rich, famous, and powerful are, after all, just as vulnerable as they are themselves. The details, moreover, of political scandals are often very amusing. Who is there so stony-faced that he or she does not still laugh aloud at the recollection of Wilbur Mills, portentous, upright, and unbending chairman of the House of Representatives Ways and Means Committee, cavorting on the banks of Washington's Tidal Basin at 2:00 in the morning with his favorite striptease artist, Miss Fanne Fox (known to her many admirers as "The Argentine Firecracker")? The British are not a people known for their political humor, but the Profumo affair prompted even them to compose such ditties as "Just a Thong at Twilight" and to suggest that, when Mandy Rice-Davies came to write her memoirs, she should call them "My Life Under the Tories."[1]

Second, and more solemnly, political scandals are worth studying for the light they can throw on a country's political culture and political system. Is there behavior that is regarded as scandalous in one country but not in another? If so, what is the explanation? Do different political systems and political cultures affect the probability that scandalous behavior will, or will not, as a matter of fact, be indulged in? Are behaviors that are universally acknowledged to be scandalous more likely to be exposed in one country than another? (After all, a scandal, by definition, is not a scandal until knowledge of it becomes public.) In considering all of these questions, we should never forget that political scandals can have momentous consequences. In recent years, more or less political scandals have toppled one President of the United States, one leader of a major British political party, at least two senior White House aides, three senior British cabinet ministers, two United States senators, and at least thirteen—

possibly more—members of the United States House of Representatives. Love and scandal may be, as Henry Fielding claimed, "the best sweetners of tea"; but, precisely for that reason, scandal, at least, is a great destroyer of political reputations.[2] So useful, indeed, do political scandals turn out to be as a means of exploring different countries' political values and institutions that the study of them really deserves to become a recognized academic subfield. If it should succeed in establishing itself in this way, it will clearly need to have a name. "Scandalosophy" is tempting, combining as it does the idea of a scandal ("a grossly discreditable circumstance, event, or condition of things") with the idea of sophia ("knowledge"). Scandalosophy also has the advantage of being easy to pronounce. Unfortunately, however, a word with "osophy" as its suffix inevitably carries with it the connotation that anyone interested in a subject is a practitioner as well as a student. Thus, a philosopher is someone who both loves knowledge and practices philosophy. In connection with the study of scandals, this particular connotation would be unfortunate. A more detached term is needed. "Scandalology" is better, since "ology" implies the idea of learning without implying the idea of active participation; but, since scandalology is hard to pronounce (and "scandalological" even harder), a shortened version of it, "scandology," is probably better still. Scandology and its cognates will be used in this chapter, but anyone offended by the violence thus done to Greek grammar, or for any other reason, should feel free to suggest any alternative that occurs to them.[3]

The rest of this essay constitutes a tentative, preliminary exploration of the field of scandology. It has to be tentative because theory in this new field is nonexistent. It has to be preliminary because many data are not available, for reasons that will become apparent, and also because many of the data that are available cannot be published, for reasons that will likewise become apparent. What follows is a sketch-map that, with luck, will encourage other budding scandologists to explore further.

Political Scandals in Britain and the United States

Scandalous behavior is behavior that offends against a society's ethical norms. It may be common, but it is disapproved of. Not all behavior that offends against a society's norms, however, is usually thought of as scandalous. Scandals occupy a sort of middle ground of impropriety (which is one of the reasons they are such fun). On the one side, they shade into such petty misdemeanors as speeding or drinking too much at private parties; on the other, they shade into the realm of serious crime. A British cabinet minister in the late 1960s regularly got drunk (some said he was always drunk), but his behavior only began to border on the scandalous when he turned up half seas over at ministerial meetings and international conferences. At the other extreme, it is a scandal if a British Prime Minister is known to frequent brothels or an American President uses his position to enrich members of his family; but scandal would obviously be too weak a word if Margaret Thatcher were to murder Denis or Ronald Reagan turned out to be a leading Mafia godfather.

It goes without saying that what exactly is deemed scandalous is a function of time and place, i.e., is culture-bound. In ancient Rome the Empress Messalina won a competition with a leading Roman courtesan by having sexual intercourse, in public, with no fewer than twenty-five men in a single prolonged session. At the time people were greatly impressed by Messalina's stamina, but no one was particularly scandalized. Today such behavior on the part of—well, perhaps it would be better not to name names—would be considered hugely scandalous.[4] In our own time, President Sukarno of Indonesia not only had five wives, one more than the quota established by Islamic law, but was sexually active outside even those very wide bounds of matrimony. And the scale of his sexual exploits was well known in his country, not just in governmental and diplomatic circles. In the West such activities would be considered scandalous and therefore politically damaging, but in Indonesia the stories of Sukarno's sexual potency did not diminish his political potency but, on the contrary, enhanced it. Indeed "some of those close to him in later years kept close watch on his casual amours . . . in the belief that a lessening of his sexual energies would be a sign that his power would leave him and that his political fortunes would decline."[5] To repeat: it largely depends on where you live, and when.

Partly because definitions of scandalous behavior differ from place to place, the patterns of public scandals are also likely to differ. Consider the cases of Great Britain and the United States. Most Americans would probably be surprised at the number of, and the type of, political scandals that have taken place in Great Britain just since the general election of June 1983. First, the secretary of state for trade and industry, Cecil Parkinson, a close friend and confidant of Margaret Thatcher, felt compelled to resign his post when it became known that his former secretary was expecting his child and when it became known, moreover, that Parkinson had reneged on a promise he had made to marry her. A few weeks later, the Labour member of Parliament for Carmarthen was convicted for homosexual importuning; he subsequently announced his intention to resign his seat. Meanwhile, another Labour backbencher, the MP for St. Helens South in Lancashire, got into trouble with the Labour activists in his constituency when newspaper reports revealed that he had been having, not one but two, extramarital affairs. There was talk at the same time that yet another Labour MP would shortly find himeslf in trouble with the police, also on charges of homosexual importuning. Finally, in May 1984 the parliamentary private secretary to the secretary of state for defence resigned after reports reached the government that he had been arrested in a gay strip club. (Readers alarmed by the security implications of the last case should remember that, in Britain as in the United States, the importance of a political office usually varies in inverse ratio to the length of the title attaching to it.)

To this catalog of actual scandals should perhaps be added mention of "the Mark Thatcher affair." The prime minister was alleged to have helped win a contract for a British company in Oman even though she knew that her son Mark was acting indirectly for the company as a public-relations consultant. It is not clear that Margaret Thatcher's behavior, even if the allegations were true, would have been improper since no other British company was competing for the contract; but in any case the affair never reached the proportions of a scandal because not enough people in Britain believed both that the allegations were true and that the prime minister was therefore guilty of serious misconduct. Even so, the episode is said to have caused Margaret Thatcher considerable distress, and her son Mark has since emigrated to the United States.

But, if Americans might be somewhat taken aback by the number and character of Britain's political scandals, it is probably fair to say that most British people would be absolutely flabbergasted if they were aware of the scale of politically related misconduct in the United States. No one in Britain has ever bothered to count up the number of MPs and former MPs who find themselves before the courts each year, partly because the number—perhaps four or five a year—is so small and partly because the offenses with which they are charged (speeding, obstructing the police, being drunk and disorderly, etc.) are usually so trivial. (A spectacular exception to this latter rule will be noted later.) By contrast, in the United States a standard reference work on American government and politics, the prestigious

Congressional Quarterly Almanac, publishes every year page after page of details on the wrongdoings of current and former members of the House of Representatives and Senate. In some years, it even feels the need to compile a "box score."

For example, page 853 of the 1978 *Almanac* is headed "House Members Jailed or Charged." The text under the heading begins: "The conviction of Rep. Charles C. Diggs Jr., D-Mich., on felony charges was the most serious action against a member of Congress in 1977–78 but it was only one of a number of criminal or ethical problems faced by representatives and senators." There follows a list of five members of the House and nine former members of the House who had been indicted, convicted, fined, or imprisoned during the previous year. Their combined prison sentences totaled thirteen years and two months.[6] A year later, the 1979 *CQ Almanac* likewise produced a list, under the heading "Legal Actions Against Members of Congress," of three serving House members and three former members who had already been convicted by the courts or were currently under indictment. As in the previous year, most of the crimes and alleged crimes related directly to the individual's service as a member of Congress. Typical entries read:

Rep. Charles C. Diggs Jr., D-Mich., lost an appeal of his 1978 conviction on 29 felony counts centering on charges that he illegally diverted his congressional employees' salaries to his personal use. . . .

Former Rep. Joshua Eilberg, D-Pa. (1967–79), pleaded guilty Feb. 24 to charges that he illegally accepted money for helping a Philadelphia hospital get a $14.5 million federal grant. . . .

Rep. Daniel J. Flood, D-Pa., whose trial on 11 counts of bribery, conspiracy and perjury, ended in a mistrial Feb. 3, 1979, was tentatively set to be retried early in 1980. Government prosecutors alleged that Flood received bribes totaling almost $60,000 in cash, checks and stocks between 1971 and 1976 in return for using his influence as chairman of the House Labor-HEW Appropriations Subcommittee. . . .

Former Rep. Nick Galifianakis, D-N.C. (1967–73), was indicted by a Washington, D.C., federal grand jury April 10 for perjury during 1978 testimony before the House Committee on Standards of Official Conduct in which Galifianakis denied receiving a $10,000 cash campaign contribution from South Korean businessman Tongsun Park. The charges were dismissed Aug. 3, after a U.S. district court judge ruled that the alleged perjury actually had taken place during the taking of an unauthorized deposition by Rep. Millicent Fenwick, R-N.J., and a Standards Committee attorney.[7]

While all this was going on, Senator Herman E. Talmadge of Georgia was "denounced" [sic] by the Senate for a wide variety of financial irregularities.

The evidence adduced thus far, however, is piecemeal and impressionistic and could not in good conscience be made the basis of a serious scandological study. For this reason, table 7.1 represents an attempt to set out all of the important political scandals that have taken place in Britain and the United States in the past quarter-century. The various scandals are roughly categorized according to whether they arose out of lust for sexual gratification, lust for money, or lust for power; but of course the three categories overlap: a politician may seek to conceal his sexual activities because he wants power; he may want political power because he is financially greedy; and so forth. The only category that is conspicuously missing is one relating to physical addiction. It would seem that addiction to alcohol is so common that, although it may damage a politician's career, it is no longer regarded (if it ever was) as being scandalous. In the case of drugs, it looks as though most politicians on both sides of the Atlantic have been sufficiently circumspect, or sufficiently frightened, to avoid violating their society's current norms. Whiskey has so far wrought more political havoc than heroin.

The table is almost certainly not complete; the reader is invited to add any data that he or she thinks are missing. It is also confined to national-level politics in both countries. Britain has experienced a certain number of scandals involving local councillors and local-government officials, but few have been thought worth reporting in the national press. In the case of the United States, scandals of one sort or another at the state and local levels are endemic, and it would take a much longer chapter than this to do justice to them. In an ideal world, the table would also take into account the experience of other countries, but scandology is an infant science and a multinational study would probably be too ambitious at this stage. Finally, it needs to be pointed out that to identify an individual in the table in connection with a particular scandal is not to suggest that he or she behaved in a criminal way or even necessarily a scandalous way. It

Table 7.1   Political Scandals in Britain and the United States 1959–84

BRITAIN	UNITED STATES

Sex-related

John Profumo (1962)
Army minister involved with prostitutes one of whom had Soviet connections. Lied to House of Commons. Resigned both as minister, as MP.

Lord Jellicoe (1973)
Leader of the House of Lords admitted using services of prostitutes. Resigned.

Lord Lambton (1973)
Air Force minister involved with women in a large way, drugs in a small way. Resigned both as minister, as MP.

Jeremy Thorpe (1976)
Acquitted of conspiracy to murder former homosexual lover. Resigned as leader of Liberal party, lost seat at next election.

Cecil Parkinson (1983)
Senior minister, member of Thatcher inner cabinet during Falklands war. Admitted being father of his former secretary's child, reneged on promise to marry former secretary. Resigned as minister, not as MP.

Walter Jenkins (1964)
Top aide to Lyndon Johnson. Arrested for homosexual acts in Washington YMCA. Resigned.

Chappaquiddick (1970)
Senator Edward Kennedy failed to report accident in which he was driving, woman passenger was drowned. Did not resign from Senate, but political prospects damaged.

Wilbur D. Mills (1974)
Chairman of House Ways and Means Committee consorted openly with striptease artist, not his wife. Remained for time member of House but lost chairmanship.

Wayne L. Hays (1976)
Chairman of House Administration Committee and Democratic Congressional Campaign Committee. Kept mistress on congressional payroll. Resigned from House.

Congressional pages (1983)
Two members of the House reprimanded for having sex (one homo-, one hetero-) with congressional pages (one boy, one girl). Neither resigned from House.

Money-related

**Reginald Maudling,
John Poulson (1972)**
Maudling, home secretary, former chancellor of the exchequer. Said while out of office to have accepted favors from property developer

Bobby Baker (1963)
Secretary to Senate majority. Charged with using inside information to further business interests. Subsequently convicted of fraud, tax evasion. Resigned.

Table 7.1 (*Cont.*)

BRITAIN	UNITED STATES
Poulson. Denied impropriety, was never charged with any offense, but resigned from government.	*Adam Clayton Powell* (1967) Chairman of House Education and Labor Committee. Expelled from House for using official expenses to pay for private trips. Triumphantly reelected in special election.
	Thomas J. Dodd (1967) Senator censured for financial misconduct. Defeated at next reelection attempt.
	Spiro T. Agnew (1973) Vice President of the United States. Accused of conspiracy, extortion, bribery while Maryland state official. Pleaded nolo contendere to income tax evasion charge. Resigned.
	Bert Lance (1977) Head of Office of Management and Budget. Allegations of wide-ranging malpractices chiefly involving bank he had run in Georgia. Resigned.
	Tongsun Park, "Koreagate" (1977–78) Illegal, illicit efforts by South Korean government to buy influence in Congress. Three members of House reprimanded.
	Herman E. Talmadge (1979) Chairman of Agriculture Committee, ranking Democrat on Finance Committee. "Denounced" by Senate for financial misconduct. Defeated at next reelection attempt.
	Billy Carter (1979–80) President Carter's brother accepted money from Libyan government, acted as intermediary in Libyan-U.S. dealings. President seriously embarrassed.

Table 7.1 (*Cont.*)

BRITAIN	UNITED STATES
	Daniel J. Flood (1979–80) House member charged with bribery, conspiracy, perjury. Pleaded guilty to charge of defrauding United States by seeking illegal campaign contributions from persons seeking federal contracts. Resigned.
	Charles C. Diggs (1979–80) House member convicted of diverting congressional employees' salaries to personal use. Resigned.
	"Abscam" (1980–82) FBI undercover agents posing as wealthy Arab businessmen and sheiks implicated members of Congress in bribery, corruption, other financial malpractices. One Senator, six House members convicted in courts. All seven expelled from Congress, resigned, or lost in re-election attempts.
	Richard V. Allen (1981) President Reagan's National Security Adviser. Allegedly paid for interceding with Nancy Reagan on behalf of Japanese newspapers. Resigned.

Power-related

BRITAIN	UNITED STATES
	Watergate (1972–75) Not one scandal but many, involving illegal campaign contributions, wiretapping, telephone-bugging, suborning of security agencies, attempts to obstruct justice. Countless convictions, resignations, most notably that of President of the United States.

Table 7.1 (*Cont.*)

BRITAIN	UNITED STATES
	Environmental Protection Agency (1983) EPA head Anne M. (Gorsuch) Burford accused of incompetence, conflict of interest, failure to implement environmental protection legislation, administering agency in Republicans' partisan interest. Resigned (after assistant administrator had been fired).

is merely to report that he or she, fairly or unfairly, has become widely associated in the public mind with the scandal in question.

Table 7.1 makes fascinating reading, as much for what it does not contain as for what it does. The large empty spaces leap to the eye. If the coverage in the table is reasonably complete, then there are far more political scandals in American national politics than in British national politics, and almost all of Britain's political scandals have to do with sex. The widespread perception that British scandals are peculiarly sexual scandals is true, but not because Britain has more sex scandals than the United States—it does not—but rather because Britain has almost no scandals of any other kind. That said, it should probably be added that Britain's sex scandals have almost certainly done Britain's reputation abroad a power of good. The image of the ultra-proper passionless Englishman, with his furled umbrella and boringly respectable home life, cannot have survived the steamy events of the past few decades. Englishmen who were in the United States when the Profumo story broke in 1963 report that their American friends and acquaintances looked at them with an altogether new respect.

One additional point about the table is worth making. The reader will notice that nearly everyone mentioned or alluded to in it, on whichever side of the Atlantic, either held elective office or else had been appointed on a political basis by someone who himself held elective office. The table does not contain the name of a single career civil servant or judge (though Abe Fortas's resignation from the United States Supreme Court in 1969, following accusations of financial impropriety, might possibly have been added to the list). Part of the explanation undoubtedly lies in the fact that scandals involving career civil servants and at least minor judges attract relatively little publicity and normally do not have important political consequences; but it is probably also the case that the professional norms of career civil servants and judges are such as to preclude the kind of behavior that gets other people into trouble. Civil servants and judges in effect "take vows" of good behavior; other kinds of politicians do not.

Table 7.1 provides food for thought and the raw data for the rest of this chapter, but by itself it clearly does not take us very far. We need to know more about the behavior that is, and is not, regarded as scandalous on the two sides of the Atlantic, about the proportions of scandalous behavior that are, and are not, exposed, and about the likelihood in the two countries that scandalous behavior will in fact be exposed. We also need to account for the differences in the patterns of the two countries' political scandals that the table so strikingly reveals. Let us consider these topics under the three headings already employed: sex, money, and power.

Sex

Short of the publication of some kind of Kinsey or Hite report on the sexual behavior of British and American politicians, no one will ever know either the extent of illicit sexual activity among politicians on the two sides of the Atlantic or whether the patterns of such activity are different in the two countries. It is equally hard to be sure how much illicit sexual activity among politicians is known to insiders in Westminster and Washington but never reaches the public prints. In both countries, the ratio of potential to actual sexual scandals is knowable in principle but largely unknowable in practice. Nevertheless, a few things under this heading can be said with considerable confidence.

The first is that sexual behavior that would be regarded as scandalous in one country would almost certainly be regarded as scandalous in the other. For the time being at any rate, Britain and the United States operate under very similar sexual codes. Normal heterosexual activity among married couples is, of course, all right; so, nowadays, is normal heterosexual activity among couples who are not married either to each other or to anybody else. But adultery, if it becomes public knowledge, is liable to get one into trouble, even in the 1980s; and so are indiscriminate philandering, fathering (or mothering) illegitimate children, frequenting prostitutes, and being homosexual or engaging in homosexual acts. In all of these connections, public opinion is, for better or worse, gradually becoming more permissive, but the penalties inflicted on politicians who transgress the accepted code, and are known to have transgressed it, can still be severe. The British MPS involved in the sex scandals of the past two years have all paid a price, in some cases a heavy one.

That the sexual codes operating on both sides of the Atlantic are similar is suggested by a reexamination of the first section of table 7.1. It seems clear in every case that, had the sexual transgression in question taken place in the other country, the political consequences would have been pretty much the same. An American assistant defense secretary who was found, like John Profumo, to have shared the favors of a call girl with the Soviet naval attaché would similarly have no alternative but to quit public life—and in a hurry. A Downing Street aide arrested, like Walter Jenkins, on a homosexual importuning charge would also have to go. So would an American party leader who, like Jeremy Thorpe, confessed to having had at least one homosexual affair and who had been tried, even though acquitted, on a charge of conspiracy to murder. And so on. There are one or two doubtful cases, such as that of Cecil Parkinson (would an American cabinet officer necessarily have to resign if he were publicly named as the father of an illegitimate child?); but such borderline cases are almost certainly borderline inside each country, not just between them. British and American politicians operate in pretty similar moral climates. Only the sexually explicit political culture of San Francisco, where "gays" openly campaign as gays, has no British equivalent.

Another point of substantial Anglo-American similarity concerns the likelihood that any piece of scandalous behavior will, as a matter of fact, become public knowledge. Even in the absence of a comparative Kinsey or Hite report, no one doubts that far more adultery, philandering, prostitute purchasing, illegitimate-child parenting, and sexual intercourse between consenting males takes place—and is known by journalists and other politicians to take place—than is ever reported in newspapers or on television news bulletins. The ratio of potential to actual sex scandals, while unknowable with precision, is nevertheless certainly very high. Some barrier must thus stand between private behavior and the public's knowledge of it. The explanation seems to lie in a kind of implicit journalistic code which prevents reporters, editors, and proprietors from printing information that they have in their possession (even though they can be confident in many cases that it will be of considerable interest to their readers).

It is for students of journalism to say exactly what the terms of this implicit code are, and why it operates as it does, but the general rule seems to be that, provided the behavior in question is normally thought of as "private," and provided that so long as it remains private it has no evident political implications, it ought not to be reported. The rule seems to be "live and let live."

As already indicated, moreover, this rule appears to operate in Britain and the United States in much the same way. For example, one of the two congressmen involved in the "congressional pages" affair (see the table) was well known on Capitol Hill to be a homosexual long before the sexual proclivities of congressional pages and their employers became a matter of public knowledge, but no newspaperman thought this fact an appropriate one, on its own, to reveal. Likewise, it is well known in political circles in Britain that at least two senior politicians, one Conservative, one Labour, are homosexuals, but there is a tacit treaty that this fact will be made public only if the individuals themselves make it public (neither has "come out"), or if they run foul of the law or otherwise draw attention to themselves. On balance the British press is probably fractionally more reticent than the American—the amours of one prominent Labour politician have not been publicized nearly as widely as those of Edward Kennedy—but this probably has less to do with differences in the two countries' implicit codes than with Britain's tougher libel laws and the fact that politicians in Britain are almost never thought of as "stars" in the way that Edward Kennedy and members of Britain's royal family are.

One by-product of the workings of roughly the same tacit treaty on both sides of the Atlantic is that no one in either country can really be sure what sexual behavior in the 1980s actually is regarded as scandalous, in the sense that it could damage or destroy someone's political career. Politicians try to keep their private lives private; the press generally assists them in this; the public is none the wiser. For example, not enough homosexual politicians have "come out" for it to be known whether or not declared homosexuality will now be tolerated in public life. It is of course precisely because of this uncertainty that homosexual politicians do not "come out." Likewise, when the British scandal sheet *Private Eye* revealed that Cecil Parkinson's former secretary was expecting his child, no one, including the Prime Minister, could know at first what effect this would have on Parkinson's political future. Parkinson in the end resigned, but even now it is impossible to say for sure whether this was because he was found to have had an affair with a woman not his wife, or because this woman was bearing his child, or because he had apparently reneged on his promise to marry her. What is certain is that, had all these circumstances remained private, had they been known only to, say, the Prime Minister and the Conservative chief whip, or even to Parkinson's fellow Conservative MPs, nothing would have happened. It was not Parkinson's behavior as such that destroyed his ministerial career; it was the fact that his behavior became public, i.e., a scandal. Whether politicians should in principle be forced to adhere to a stricter sexual code than people in other walks of life is an important question, but, since it is clearly one for moralists rather than scandologists, it is beyond the scope of this chapter.

Mention of this moral issue leads, however, to the final point that needs to be made about sex scandals in this context, which is that, in an importance sense, sex scandals involving politicians do not deserve to be called "political" scandals at all. They may have important political consequences—many of them have had—but they are not normally political in motivation (politicians are highly unlikely to sleep with prostitutes or have sexual relations with congressional pages with a view to furthering their political careers), nor do they normally involve an abuse of political power (British and American heads of government do not, like oriental despots, force members of the opposite sex to go to bed with them on pain of execution). Rather, sexual scandals in politics involve an eruption of the private realm into the public. In scholastic language, they are political scandals by accident, not in essence. The same cannot be said for the next two kinds of scandals to be considered—the kinds that, as it happens, are much more common in the United States than in Britain.

Money

An awful lot of national-level American political scandals, and almost no national-level British political scandals, have to do with money. The first possibility that has to be considered is that financial behavior considered improper and therefore scandalous in the United States is considered perfectly proper and therefore not at all scandalous in Great Britain. With one important and interesting exception, to be discussed below, this seems unlikely. The details of the relevant British and American laws vary widely, but the broad principles governing such matters as fraud, bribery, embezzlement, extortion, and the diverting of public funds from one purpose to another are much the same in the two countries, and it seems clear that most of the United States politicians listed in the second part of table 7.1, had they been British politicians and had they been found out in Britain, would also have come to grief. A crook in Durham, North Carolina, would easily be recognizable as a crook in Durham, England, and vice versa.

The other possibility to be considered is that, while definitions of financial crookery are broadly similar in the two countries, American crooks are much more likely to be found out than British crooks, thus accounting for the apparently greater number of financial scandals in the one country than the other. Again, this seems unlikely. The British police and British parliamentary committees may well be less efficient than their American counterparts, and it may well be the case that the United States enjoys both a more vigilant press corps than Britain and a larger corps of public-spirited whistle-blowers in government agencies; but, even if all this were true, it could hardly account for the gross discrepancy between the left- and right-hand columns of the table. Moreover, for what it is worth, political gossip in Britain does not suggest the existence of some vast underground reservoir of financial corruption just waiting to be tapped. Were Robert Caro to ply his trade in Britain, he would probably find the pickings slim.[8]

The observed differences between the two countries being almost certainly real, what is the explanation for them? A number of answers suggest themselves, some of them having more to do with practical politics than moral rectitude.

One answer probably does relate to a difference between the general cultures, not just the political cultures, of Britain and the United States. Hard data are lacking, but the general impression is probably correct that money—the desire to have it, the desire to spend it, the desire to be seen to spend it—plays a larger role in American life than in British. Money is a more frequent subject of middle class dinner-table conversation in the United States than in Britain; social status is more tightly defined by money in the United States than in Britain; far more Americans than Englishmen (or Scotsmen or Welshmen) have the making of money as their principal goal in life. The transatlantic difference is not a matter of absolutes; it is only a matter of more and less. But it is important all the same. One result, appropriately, is that the British in general are poorer than the Americans in general. Another result, probably, is that American politicians are more prone than their British equivalents to try to exploit their political positions for personal financial gain: American culture licenses, indeed positively encourages, the underlying motive.

Hard data are also lacking on another part of the explanation that is probably equally important: the view taken by politicians in the two countries of the role of politics in their personal advancement. Crudely, most British politicians see political activity as a means of acquiring power over others, or as a means of individual self-expression, or as a means of desperately trying to persuade themselves of their own importance, or as a means of serving free enterprise, social justice, the labor movement, or some other cause; but they do not see it as a means of upward social, let alone financial, mobility. Someone who wants to make money in Britain (and there are many) does not normally go into politics; he tries to find a lucrative profession, or goes into the stock exchange, or sets up a new business. In fact, some Conservative would-be politicians set out to make money precisely in order to have the financial security to enable them to undertake a political career; they perceive money as a means to politics, not politics as a means to money. To be sure, there are exceptions; every British reader can think of Tory politicians who use their membership of Parliament to further their business interests and Labour politicians who, coming from humble backgrounds, see politics as their personal way into the big time. But by and large financial ambition and political ambition do not, in Britain, go hand in hand. They are much more likely to go together in the United States where historically politics has been seen as one of a number of possible social and financial ladders. This view of politics in the United States, as a potentially financially rewarding occupation, probably helps to ensure that it goes on being financially rewarding. People who have gone into politics to make money, among other things, are unlikely to be too keen to blow the whistle on others similarly motivated.

A subsidiary but related factor concerns the material standard of living that politicians in the two countries expect to enjoy—and, more important, are expected by others to enjoy. Yet again, hard data are lacking, but observation suggests that American politicians spend considerably more than British politicians on houses, apartments, cars, clothes, food, drink, travel, and entertainment, not only because the overall American standard of living is higher than the British, and not necessarily because American politicians particularly want to have a high standard of living, but because in the United States having an upper middle class life style, in effect, comes with the job. Other powerholders in the society—lawyers, corporation executives, lobbyists, well-off local businessmen, the owners of television stations and newspapers—have to be met on equal or, ideally, more than equal terms; otherwise the member of Congress or political executive is in danger of not being taken seriously, of not being regarded as a "member of the club." These pressures are felt in Britain by many Conservative MPS—the Tory member for a country district is often called upon to be a pillar of society in his district—but they are often not felt by urban Conservatives, and they are not felt at all by most Labour, Liberal, and Social Democratic MPS. Most members of Congress would probably be mildly surprised at the humble circumstances in which many British MPS live, without their ability to function as MPS being in any way impaired. These lower social expectations in Britain have, of course, the incidental effect of making possible lower financial expectations and therefore of reducing the temptations to financial impropriety.

Whether or not the foregoing analysis is correct, it runs the risk, coming from a British academic, of sounding rather priggish, as though British politicians were somehow less greedy and more modest than American politicians, in fact altogether more decent chaps. Not only is no such imputation intended, but in fact the main reasons for the Anglo-American contrast observable in the table are almost certainly less "national" and more prosaic than the ones suggested so far.

A large proportion of the politico-financial scandals that take place in the United States relate to election campaigns, specifically to the raising of campaign funds and the disbursement of campaign expenses. Several of the scandals listed in the table—Lance, Talmadge, Flood, and, not least, Watergate—fall wholly or largely into this category. The reasons are that American politics is prodigiously expensive and that political candidates in the United States are forced by the weakness of America's political parties to raise a large proportion of their campaign funds almost entirely on their own. Recent changes in the law in America have done little to reduce candidates' dependence on large-scale sources of finance outside the organized parties. Small wonder then that some politicians, dependent for their political futures on givers of money, and now increasingly caught up in complicated reporting requirements, fall foul of the law. In Britain, by contrast, politics at the constituency level is astonishingly cheap. Candidates are forbidden by law from purchasing time on radio or television; travel costs are minimal; almost all political work is done by unpaid volunteers; and, in any case, legal limits on campaign spending are set very low and are reasonably strictly enforced. At the national level, campaigning is more expensive—though still less expensive than in the United States—but is almost entirely in the hands of the national political parties, and no laws exist in Britain specifically to regulate either how the national parties raise their funds or how they spend them (except that they cannot spend them promoting the causes of individual local candidates). In short, it is not that British politicians are better than American politicians at resisting the temptation to break campaign-finance laws; it is simply that the temptations themselves hardly exist in Britain.

But there is an even simpler reason why so many fewer British MPS than members of the United States Congress have found themselves embroiled in financial scandals. A glance back at the table will show that many of the most publicized American scandals of recent years—notably Koreagate and Abscam—have arisen out of efforts to induce members of Congress to use their influence, to vote for legislation, to press for amendments, to intercede with the executive branch or whatever. The unstated major premise of all these activities has been that the influence of congressmen and senators is worth buying. Putting the matter simply—but not oversimply—financial scandals have been much less prevalent in Great Britain because the influence of individual members of Parliament is so negligible as to be not worth buying. As Nelson Polsby and others have pointed out, the British House of Commons is not a legislature in the American sense.[9] It responds to government initiatives but takes few itself. It is not organized into effective committees. Its members, unless they are also members of the government, cannot propose measures that entail the spending of public money. Backbenchers and opposition MPS in fact have little more influence over most executive-branch decisions than many members of the general public. This state of affairs is due partly to the government's traditionally predominant role in the British political system and partly also to the strength of party discipline in Parliament; but the reasons for the individual MP's very limited power matter for our purposes less than the sheer fact of it. MPS are not offered bribes (except by the very ignorant) because they are not worth bribing. As in the case of campaign funds, British MPS do not have to go to the trouble of resisting temptation; they are, by and large, not tempted. The more difficult question of why there have been so few financial scandals in the executive branch— i.e., involving members of the government—will be dealt with in the next section.

The bald assertion just made, that backbench MPs lack real political power, is broadly true and needs to be emphasized, if only to point up the contrast between MPs and members of Congress. But, having been made, it needs immediately to be qualified. Government backbenchers do sometimes rebel. They can introduce amendments that the government will want to listen to. Members on both sides of the House have the ear of civil servants even if they lack the power to influence them directly. Members are also uniquely well placed to influence other members and to keep outsiders abreast of parliamentary developments. For all of these reasons, lobbying groups frequently think it worth their while to employ a backbench MP (or indeed several backbench MPs) to hold a watching brief for them in the House of Commons. And the appropriate word is "employ." MPs are not permitted to accept money for making a particular speech, or moving a particular amendment, or casting a particular vote; but they are permitted to accept retainers (supplements, in effect, to their salaries) for being, in effect, the lobbying group's parliamentary assistant.

For example, in the early 1970s, Brian Walden, then a Birmingham Labour MP, now a well-known television interviewer, signed a five-year £25,000 contract with the National Association of Bookmakers (NAB) to act as their parliamentary consultant. He had already taken the NAB's side in opposing a government bill that, in its original form, would have seriously damaged the bookmakers' interests. Walden made known the terms of his contract with the NAB, though not the sum of money involved, and he also indicated that he was not prepared to lobby his fellow members of Parliament on the NAB's behalf. Because Walden declared his interest in the bookmakers' affairs, he was not considered, and is not now considered, to have done anything improper.[10] The Police Federation of England and Wales likewise employs a parliamentary adviser, who was at one time James Callaghan, later to become Labour Prime Minister. Much the largest group of members with direct connections with outside lobbying organizations is the trade-union group of sponsored Labour MPs. A sponsored MP receives help with his or her election expenses and may also receive a modest retainer and help with running his or her parliamentary office.

The reasoning behind these arrangements is perfectly straightforward. Backbench MPs are not members of the government, and the House of Commons is widely perceived in Britain not as a body that somehow rides above the competition of interests but rather as one in which the competition of interests actually takes place. It follows that there is no bar to members' having outside interests, indeed outside employment, including employment by organizations that wish to exert influence over government and Parliament. The only requirement, which was met by Brian Walden, is that such outside interests be declared. You can be a parliamentary "kept man" provided everybody knows that you are. Needless to say, arrangements of this kind, considered perfectly proper in Great Britain, are not considered at all proper in the United States Congress, where members are supposed to maintain a much more arms-length relationship with bodies seeking to exert influence. Since some congressmen and senators have difficulty in keeping lobbying organizations at arms length, they become involved in politico-financial scandals. Such scandals do not occur in Britain simply because such behavior is not considered scandalous. Here is one of the few cases where the two countries' norms significantly differ. One or two other instances will be cited in the last section of this chapter.

Power

Some scandals are motivated by sex. Others are motivated by money. Still others are motivated by the hunger for power; and these can be the most sinister of all, since at their worst they can subvert a country's institutions and undermine faith in the integrity of its leaders. Sexual and financial scandals offend against the canons of the system; power-related scandals are offenses against the system itself. "Scandal" in fact seems too weak a word to describe breaches of trust of this type. "Crime" is usually thought a more appropriate description.

Only one major power-related scandal has occurred on either side of the Atlantic in recent years: the extraordinary concatenation of wiretaps, break-ins, blackmails, extortions, perjuries, burglaries, breaches of trust, and breaches of the criminal law known collectively as Watergate. Even Americans, relatively inured to scandals in high places, were more than scandalized: they were horrified. Since there can be no doubt that the actions of Nixon, Haldeman, Ehrlichman, Magruder, Mitchell, Colson, Dean, Liddy, Hunt, Strachan, McCord, and the rest of that curious galère would, had they been committed in Britain, have been regarded as just as reprehensible as they were in the United States, and since there can also be no doubt that, whatever the alleged weaknesses of the British press, a scandal on the Watergate scale would have been exposed as surely and as swiftly in Britain as in the United States, two questions arise. How likely is it that a scandal of the Watergate type could occur in Britain? If, as is the case, it seems very unlikely, why should that be so? (It should only be added that, if a Watergate-type scandal seems unlikely in Britain, it also seemed unlikely in pre-1972 America. Even a dozen years later it takes an effort of will to believe that Watergate actually happened.)

There are five reasons why a Watergate could probably not occur in Britain (though, in saying that, one crosses one's fingers). They all tap profound differences between British and American politics; they all tend to reinforce one another. Together they help to explain not only why a British Watergate is unlikely but why Britain is considerably less prone than the United States to scandals relating to money.

The first reason has already been referred to briefly: the extreme party-centeredness of British politics as compared with American. It is political parties that organize election campaigns in Britain; it is a political party that, following an election, collectively takes over the reigns of government. The Prime Minister does not walk through the door of 10 Downing Street as an individual but as the leader of his or her party; if the Prime Minister ceases for any reason to be party leader, even while in office, then he or she ceases to be Prime Minister. Party-centered politics, as contrasted with America's more individual-centered politics, reduces the likelihood of power-related scandals for both technical and psychological reasons. Technically, political parties, being complex institutions involving large numbers of persons, would find it very hard to organize Watergate-type activities and then to cover them up afterward; likewise political parties, whatever Liddy and McCord may have thought about the Democratic National Committee, are, again because of their size and complexity, much harder to infiltrate and subvert than the smaller, more ad hoc groups that come together around individual candidates. Psychologically, party-centered politics tends to induce a party-centered rather than an individual-centered cast of mind. The ambitious politician moves forward partly through his own efforts but largely through the efforts of his party; if his party does not gain office, he does not gain office. Intense competition between individuals as a result takes place more within parties than between them. In such a setting, individual-centered banditry of the Nixon type is out of place. On the one hand, inter-party battles are fought out by the parties themselves, not by individuals; on the other, intra-party battles need to be fought out within strict limits, so that the party itself will not be damaged.

The party-centeredness of the British system is, second, related to another of its essential characteristics: its highly collegial nature. The British are not notably suspicious of individual political leaders, but they behave all the time as though they were. Thus, apart from the Prime Minister's power to hire and fire government ministers, there are almost no decisions in British government that any one individual can take entirely on his or her own. At the apex of the whole system sits not the Prime Minister but the cabinet. The cabinet's work is organized through a network of cabinet committees. This network of cabinet committees in turn intersects and overlaps with a corresponding network of committees of civil servants. In Whitehall, far more than in Washington, "coordination" is the name of the game. Even the political parties (though the Conservatives less so than the other parties) are organized on this highly collegial basis. The result again is to inhibit outrageously scandalous behavior. Everyone checks everyone else. Everyone knows too well what everybody else is up to.

(In this context, the obvious point probably also needs to be made that a great deal of scandalous behavior is, of its nature, individual behavior. A committee cannot commit sodomy or father a child; a whole committee is unlikely to fiddle expenses or accept bribes; and only a very peculiar committee, like CREEP, could possibly dream up, and then implement, a Watergate.)

The third and fourth factors can be labeled simply but meaningfully "propinquity" and "longevity." A striking feature of British politics, obvious to outsiders but taken for granted by insiders, is the extent to which it takes place within a very small geographical compass. More than that, a very large proportion of those involved in it are members of a single institution: the House of Commons. Someone bent on taking a political walking tour of London would probably start at Labour party headquarters in Walworth Road south of the Thames and head north toward Conservative headquarters in Smith Square. By the time he reached Conservative headquarters, he would have covered perhaps two miles and taken about half an hour. After that, each stretch of the journey would be much shorter. The walk from Tory Central Office to the Palace of Westminster would take only ten minutes—even if our walker were to make a short detour to SDP headquarters in Cowley Street. From the Palace of Westminster to Downing Street would take only another five minutes—even with pauses to admire the Treasury, the Home Office, and the Foreign Office. It is only another couple of minutes to the Cabinet Office and to four or five other government departments. If our walker cheated and took a cab from Walworth Road to Smith Square, he could complete the entire journey in half an hour at most.

The Palace of Westminster, high point of the tour, contains the House of Commons, and in the House of Commons is congregated almost the whole of Britain's political elite, certainly of its elected elite. Its members—the Prime Minister, other cabinet ministers, junior ministers, budding statesmen, elder statesmen, leaders of the opposition parties, rank-and-file backbenchers—live politically on top of one another. Not only do they participate together in the great parliamentary occasions—the big set-piece debates and Prime Minister's question time on Tuesdays and Thursdays—but they see each other in the corridors, troop together through the division lobbies, pass each other in the corridors and bump into one another frequently in the House of Commons Library. Most of Britain's political writers also operate out of the House of Commons, and even their head offices are typically no more than a ten-minute taxi ride from the Westminster members' entrance. The same goes for the television networks. Even those government departments that are further removed from Westminster and Whitehall are seldom more than fifteen or twenty minutes away. Political London is thus, geographically, a fraction the size of political Washington—and even political Washington, the focus of American political life, does not contain the headquarters of the major broadcasting organizations or of several politically important newspapers.

The upshot of political propinquity in London is the existence of a village-like political community in which everyone knows everyone else, in which everyone keeps an eye on everyone else, and in which people spend enormous amounts of time rating one another. People are ceaselessly rated—on scales of intelligence/stupidity, industriousness/sloth, gregariousness/solitariness, honesty/dishonesty, trustworthiness/untrustworthiness, straightforwardness/deviousness, rising/falling, and so on. Everyone in the Westminster village is a village gossip, and the gossiping goes on all the time. Many dislike this hothouse atmosphere and find it claustrophobic, but it is one in which people get to know one another quite well. Those who are too greedy for money or too avid for power are identified and marked down: the House groans, or empties, when they rise to speak; they fail to win elective posts inside their parties; they fail to be appointed to ministerial office or, if they are appointed, fail to gain promotion. The process is not perfect, but it does tend to weed out, to keep at a distance from positions of power and influence, most of those who might, in a different political environment, become involved in money-related and power-related scandals. By contrast, almost all of those involved in Watergate were outsiders to political Washington (which in any case is much more loose-textured than political London); and even Nixon, who was not an outsider, would probably not have been able to survive a long period of intense peer-group scrutiny.

To political propinquity must be added, as just hinted, political longevity. The House of Commons and wider political London function effectively as people-assessors, partly because they are so proximate geographically, but also because most of those who dwell in the Westminster village have dwelt there for a very long time. The Watergate culprits were not only outsiders; in most cases, they were very recent outsiders, with the result that their peers, insofar as they had any, had been given little or no time in which to assess their capacity and their probity. British party leaders and government ministers have far longer track records. Every member of Margaret Thatcher's present cabinet has been in Parliament for at least ten years; the Prime Minister herself was first elected in 1959. The new Labour leader, Neil Kinnock, is widely thought of as a relative political neophyte, but in fact he has been an MP since 1970. His fellow MPS have had time in which to size him up.

The fifth and final reason why a Watergate—or anything like a Watergate—is unlikely to occur in Britain arises out of the central role played in the British system by the career civil service. Career civil servants in Britain work far more closely with their political masters than do their American opposite numbers. They occupy positions far higher up each department's and agency's hierarchy, and their working collaboration with politicians and political appointees is far more continuous and intimate. Civil servants man (and woman) every minister's private office. They see all of his papers. They monitor all but his most personal phone calls. They are extremely reluctant to let their minister out of their sight. As a result, a minister who wished to abuse his power, whether for political or pecuniary gain, would find it almost impossible to act entirely on his own; he would have to carry his civil servants with him. And this he would find very difficult to do. Not only are British civil servants brought up to be scrupulously honest, not only do they not normally have political axes to grind, not only are they almost always anxious to safeguard their future civil service careers, but they, like everyone else, can be held legally accountable for their actions. To take the extreme case, the permanent secretary (the most senior civil servant) in each department is that department's accounting officer and as such personally responsible to the Comptroller and Auditor-General and to the House of Commons' Public Accounts Committee for the spending of every penny that passes through the department's hands. In such a constrained working environment, even a would-be John Mitchell would find it very hard to do much damage. The central role of civil servants largely explains why powerful ministers in Britain, as well as impotent rank-and-file MPS, have been astonishingly free of the taint of scandal—apart, of course, from scandals of the sexual variety.

Mention of sex scandals not only takes us back toward the beginning of this chapter but raises a question that may already have been worrying some readers, especially British readers. If all of the foregoing is correct, what are we to make of the Jeremy Thorpe case? After all, Thorpe was a long-serving member of Parliament at the time of his fall and was also the leader of an important political party. Moreover, although the Thorpe affair has been categorized as a sex-related scandal in table 7.1, it could equally well have been listed as power-related, since Thorpe's efforts to conceal the fact that he had had a homosexual love affair arose out of his desire to remain an MP and leader of his party. The Thorpe case seems to be the exception that proves the rule—i.e., tests to destruction the theories set out above.[11]

In fact, the case does the theories very little damage. British politics is party-centered politics, and Thorpe was a party leader; but his party, at the time he led it, had only thirteen members in the House of Commons and a tiny headquarters organization, and Thorpe's go-it-alone self-centered style of leadership was one that only such a small party could tolerate (and even then only reluctantly). British politics are highly collegial; but again Thorpe was unusual among British party leaders in never having been a minister and in never having had any occasion to subject himself to the discipline of collective decision-making. The British civil service is both powerful and honorable; but Thorpe was not a minister and therefore was not subject to civil service influence. Thorpe's motive may have been power, but the political issue in his case could not be power because, as leader of the small out-of-office Liberal party, he did not have any. With regard to propinquity and longevity—that is, to the House of Commons as a mechanism of continuous assessment—it is interesting to note that his colleagues were worried about Thorpe long before the scandal involving him became public and that it was his Liberal colleagues in the House of Commons who forced him to resign as party leader well before he was brought to trial. To paraphrase the title of a recent book on the end of the Vietnam war, "the system worked." Thorpe's tragedy in the end was a personal tragedy, with few political consequences.

To Confuse the Issue

We are nearing the end of this chapter, and at this point the reader may well feel that the author has everything pretty well wrapped up: a sensible taxonomy of political scandals, some plausible data bearing on Anglo-American differences, some convincing-sounding theories to explain those differences. Scandology, however, is a young science, one that the author hopes has a bright future (in the hands, he hastens to add, of others). It would be a pity therefore if this new science were, so to speak, to reach middle age only 26 pages after being born. It would also be a pity if the foregoing led British readers to think that they have nothing to worry about and that, at least so far as Britain is concerned, everything is for the best in this best of possible worlds.

So here, to confuse the issue, are three British potential scandals that have not become actual scandals. Should they have done? And why have they not? They are listed in no particular order.

First, it was remarked earlier that no laws exist in Britain specifically to regulate how national political parties raise their funds. Yet both of the two largest parties raise substantial proportions of their funds in ways that would probably strike most Americans as bizarre and even—dare one say it?—scandalous. The Labour party receives roughly 80 percent of its national income from trade unions and in consequence is often described, with some degree of accuracy, as a wholly-owned subsidiary of the trade union movement. Such a degree of dependence of a political party on a single interest group (or at least a cluster of interest groups) raises interesting questions (what would Americans think of a political party financed entirely by the banks or the big oil companies?), and there is a good deal of evidence that most British people, including most supporters of the Labour party, object to it. But it has never become a scandal. Why?

Labour's financial dependence on the unions is at least open and above board. Anyone can find out how much each union contributes each year. Much more mysterious are the Conservative party's sources of finance; and one relationship, in particular, has all the makings of a splendid scandal but has never become one. The relationship in question is that between large companies' donations to the Tory party and a curious tendency for the chairmen of those companies to become peers of the realm—i.e., lords—in subsequent Conservative honors lists. Specifically, the five chairmen of the five companies that contributed most to the Conservative party in the early 1980s all received peerages between 1980 and 1983. In the early 1920s, there was a "sale of honors" scandal that still rates as one of the juiciest in recent British history. No one would suggest that nowadays honors are being "sold" or that the Thatcher administration is doing anything improper. Even so, it is a little surprising that this—how shall one say?—"tendency" has attracted so little public attention. Far from its having become a public scandal, only a little-known left-wing magazine called *Labour Research* has paid any attention to it.[12] Here surely is a challenge for scandologists.

A second British scandal that never was—or at least that never really took off—relates to the time in the late 1960s when Britain, along with other members of the United Nations, was seeking to impose economic sanctions, in particular oil sanctions, on the white-dominated illegal regime of Ian Smith in Rhodesia. Ministers and civil servants in Britain learned that, in defiance of the sanctions, multinational oil companies, notably Shell and Total, had organized swap arrangements whereby they sold oil legally to South Africa and then illegally exported equivalent amounts of oil from South Africa to Rhodesia. The British government might have been expected to take action against the companies in the interests of enforcing the sanctions, but ministers did not want to damage the companies, especially the British ones, and were anxious not to do anything that might undermine Britain's profitable trading relations with South Africa. Accordingly, they took care not to find out too much about what was going on, gave highly misleading answers to questions asked by MPs in the House of Commons, and at all times made it clear to the oil companies that, whatever stirring speeches were being made in public, they could be confident that no serious steps would be taken against them.

A certain amount of all this was known, or at least knowable, at the time, and more and more details were revealed in subsequent years. A journalist named Martin Bailey wrote a thoroughly researched book called, predictably, *Oilgate*. His subtitle, optimistically, was *The Sanctions Scandal*.[13] But, despite Bailey's best efforts, and although the Sunday newspapers published a good deal of careful investigative journalism, the sanctions-busting episode never really became a scandal. No heads rolled; the general public took little interest. Why? One possibility that has to be entertained is that the British public is readier than the American public to accept "reasons of state" as a legitimate excuse for illegal, or at least highly questionable, actions and that British governments, having inherited their power and authority from kings, have also inherited some part of the kingly capacity for behaving arbitrarily and for treating their subjects with contempt. Perhaps one of the reasons Americans have more scandals than the British is that, in some fields at least, America has higher standards.

The third topic that ambitious scandologists might like to explore is related to the second and concerns the extreme secretiveness of British government generally. After all, a scandal need not arise out of a specific act; as the dictionary indicates, it may arise out of a "condition of things" (as in "It is a scandal that . . ."). The secretiveness of British government would amaze most Americans—and does amaze American reporters posted to London. Britain has no Freedom of Information Act and no equivalents of the various American pieces of sunshine legislation. Government policy is made almost entirely behind closed doors. The factual basis on which government decisions are made is frequently not revealed. Ministers and civil servants are not required to appear before parliamentary committees and, when they do appear, typically give little or nothing away. The chief function of government information officers, despite their title, is to conceal information (the existence of which, in any case, they usually profess ignorance). A casual caller, phoning to request details of government plans in some wholly innocuous field of domestic policy, can count on being treated as though he or she were an agent of the KGB. The concerned civil servant leaking documents to the press is apt to find himself (or, more recently, herself) in jail.

The extent of secrecy in British government should not be exaggerated; opposition and backbench MPs can find out a lot, and Britain has an active, free, and inquisitive press. Moreover, a campaign for the passage of a Freedom of Information Act modeled on the American has been gathering momentum and has a fair chance of achieving its objective before the end of the decade. Nevertheless, British government secretiveness, although it is argued against and objected to, has in no sense achieved the status of a public scandal. People are not outraged by it. The onus is still on the inquisitive member of the public to show why government information should be made freely available rather than on the government to show why it should not. Scandologists might like to explore the origins of this disposition, which are clearly cultural as well as political. They might want to take as their jumping-off point the title of the Conservative MP whose arrest in a gay strip club was referred to earlier. Before his resignation, he was the parliamentary *private* secretary to the secretary of state for defence (who, incidentally, is a member of the Queen's Privy Council). The origins of British secrecy clearly go back a long way.

A book chapter of this sort is supposed to have conclusions. The main conclusions of this one are, first, that political scandals, their incidence, their content, and their consequences can throw important light on the political system and political culture of a nation; second, that Britain's and America's political scandals do in fact reveal a good deal about political life in those two countries; and, third, that the comparative study of political scandals should as quickly as possible be extended to other countries. Now take France, for example. . . .

Notes

Introduction

1 Dennis Kavanagh, "An American Science of British Politics," *Political Studies* 22 (1974): 251–70.
2 See, in particular, how Samuel Beer's appreciation of the British political system has shifted between the late 1960s and the late 1970s.
3 Nelson Polsby, "The British Science of American Politics," *British Journal of Political Science* 2 (1972): 491–99.

1 Executive and Legislative Roles

BIBLIOGRAPHIC NOTE John Mackintosh, *The British Cabinet* (2nd rev. ed.; London: Stevens, 1968), is the most thorough examination of the cabinet and sets forth its historical evolution in great detail before analyzing its contemporary functioning. Richard Neustadt, *Presidential Power: The Politics of Leadership from FDR to Carter* (New York: John Wiley & Sons, 1980), is generally regarded as the most insightful analysis of presidential power. It provides a guide to how Presidents manage to be effective and illustrates the constraints they must overcome. Christopher Pollit, *Manipulating the Machine: Changing the Pattern of Ministerial Departments, 1960–83* (London: Allen & Unwin, 1984), is meticulous, erudite, but deadly dull. Nonetheless, it is an essential reference work for information on structural changes within the British executive and includes discussion of the Prime Minister's role in this process. Richard Rose and Ezra Suleiman, eds., *Presidents and Prime Ministers* (Washington, D.C.: American Enterprise Institute, 1980), covers much ground. The chapters by Rose on Britain and the United States are the most relevant ones, but further comparative perspective is also provided by chapters on Canada, France, Germany, Italy,

Norway, and Spain. Theodore Sorensen, *A Different Kind of Presidency* (New York: Harper & Row, 1984), is a good example of the reforms a thoughtful, knowledgeable person feels the U.S. system requires. There was never a chance that his proposals could have been adopted, and they became rather irrelevant once the inauguration occurred in 1985. Harold Wilson, *The Governance of Britain* (New York: Harper & Row, 1976), is not nearly as informative as it should have been. Nevertheless, given its author, it cannot fail to provide some data concerning the structure and operation of the British executive. Finally, the American edition of a new book entitled *The British Prime Minister* (co-published by Duke University Press with Macmillan Publishers Ltd., 1985), includes an interesting comparative analysis of the British prime ministership with the U.S. presidency.

1 Arthur Schlesinger, Jr., *The Imperial Presidency* (Boston: Houghton Mifflin, 1973).

2 John Mackintosh, *The British Cabinet* (2nd ed.; London: Stevens, 1968 [first published 1962]), pp. 411–15, 428–531, 610–27; R. H. S. Crossman, "Introduction" to Walter Bagehot, *The English Constitution* (London: Collins, The Fontana Library, 1963), pp. 48–53; and Richard Crossman, *Inside View* (London: Jonathan Cape, 1972).

3 Bagehot, *The English Constitution*, p. 59.

4 Ibid.; James Bryce, *The American Commonwealth* (3rd ed.; New York: Macmillan, 1895 [first published 1888]); and Woodrow Wilson, *Congressional Government* (New York: Meridian Books, 1956 [first published 1885]).

5 Philip Norton, *The Commons in Perspective* (New York: Longman, 1981), p. 19.

6 A. Lawrence Lowell, "The Influence of Party upon Legislation in England and America," *Annual Report of the American Historical Association for the Year 1901* (Washington, D.C.: Government Printing Office, 1902), 1: .532.

7 *Origins and Development of Congress* (Washington, D.C.: Congressional Quarterly Press, 1976), pp. 103, 108.

8 Ibid., pp. 109–13. Charles O. Jones, "The Minority Party and Policy-Making in the House of Representatives," *American Political Science Review* 62 (June 1968): 483, 485.

9 *Origins and Development of Congress*, pp. 113–15. Jones, "The Minority Party," p. 485.

10 *Origins and Development of Congress*, pp. 115–16.

11 Ibid., pp. 153–54.

12 Ibid., pp. 155–62, 163–66.

13 Ibid., pp. 162–63.

14 Lance Lelop and Steven Shull, "Congress Versus the Executive: The 'Two Presidencies' Reconsidered," *Social Science Quarterly* 59 (March 1979): 705. But see Walter Lippmann—"The power of the executive has become enfeebled, often to the verge of impotence"—*Essays in the Public Philosophy* (New York: New American Library, Mentor Books, 1955), pp. 48, 50.

15 Bryce, *The American Commonwealth*, p. 85.

16 Wilson, *Congressional Government*, pp. 22, 23.

17 Schlesinger, *The Imperial Presidency*.

18 Richard Neustadt, *Presidential Power: The Politics of Leadership from FDR to Carter* (New York: John Wiley & Sons, 1980), p. 241. See also Thomas Franck and Edward Weisband, "Congress as a World Power," *Worldview* 22 (October 1979): 4; Charlotte Saikowski, "Does the American Presidency Work?" *The Christian Science Monitor*, 5 June 1984, pp. 20–21; and Murray Marder, "Congress' Drive for Strings on Reagan's Foreign Policies," *The Washington Post National Weekly Edition*, 17 September 1984, p. 12.

19 The figures in table 1.1 for 1953–75 are calculated from Lelop and Shull, "Congress Versus the Executive." The data for the figures for 1976–82 have been provided by courtesy of James McCormick, Iowa State University. I would like to thank him not only for this material, but also for helpful comments on various aspects of this chapter. His data were compiled from relevant *Congressional Quarterly* almanacs. For 1953–75 presidential positions are initiatives. Since *CQ* has ceased to identify such actions, it was necessary for 1976–82 to use as presidential positions those issues on which the President had taken an identifiable stand.

20 Aaron Wildavsky, "The Two Presidencies," *Transaction* 4 (4 December 1966); Donald Peppers, " 'The Two Presidencies': Eight Years Later," in Aaron Wildavsky, ed., *Perspectives on the Presidency* (Boston: Little, Brown, 1975), pp. 462–71; and Lee Sigelman, "A Reassessment of the Two Presidencies Thesis," *Journal of Politics* 41 (November 1979): 1195–1205.

21 See the comment of Richard Bolling in "Governing America: A Conversation with Richard Bolling, David Gergen, and Theodore Sorensen," *Public Opinion* 7 (February/March 1984): 6.

22 Franck and Weisband, "Congress as a World Power," p. 6.

23 Leloup and Shull, "Congress Versus the Executive," p. 716.

24 *The Guardian*, 7 August 1980, p. 8.

25 *The Economist*, 19 December 1981, p. 51.

26 Rose, *Do Parties Make a Difference?* (Chatham, N.J.: Chatham House, 1980), pp. 70–72.

27 Ibid., p. 149.

28 R. Gordon Hoxie, "The Cabinet in the American Presidency, 1789–1984," *Presidential Studies Quarterly* 14 (Spring 1984): 220.

29 Quoted in ibid., p. 227.

30 Ibid., p. 226.

31 Richard Rose, "Governments against Sub-governments: A European Perspective on Washington," in Richard Rose and Ezra Suleiman, eds., *Presidents and Prime Ministers* (Washington, D.C.: American Enterprise Institute, 1980), pp. 292, 290–312.

32 For an example of organization in recent years, see Harold Wilson, *The Governance of Britain* (New York: Harper & Row, 1976), chap. IV, esp. pp. 91–98.

33 Rose, "British Government: The Job at the Top," in Rose and Suleiman, *Presidents and Prime Ministers*, pp. 24, 34, and 35.

34 Rose, "Governments against Sub-governments," pp. 291–92.

35 "The Lady vanishes into her last ditch," *The Guardian*, 18 March 1981, p. 13; and "We think your cabinet is wonderful," *The Economist*, 30 May 1981, p. 48.

36 *The Economist*, 10 March 1984, p. 18. See also pp. 57–58. *The Economist*,

6 February 1982, p. 34, shines some light on the organization of the *terra incognita* of cabinet committees.

37 "Doing it her way?" *The Economist*, 22 September 1979, pp. 13–16; Simon Hoggart, "Call me madam, chaps," *The Guardian*, 16 April 1980, p. 9; "Britain's two prime ministers," *The Economist*, 4 October 1980, pp. 11–13; "Put up or shut up," *The Economist*, 16 October 1982, pp. 16–17; and "Britain's Foreign Office," *The Economist*, 27 November 1982, pp. 19–26.

38 *The Guardian*, 13 March 1981, p. 1.

39 Rose, "Governments against Sub-governments," pp. 290–312.

40 *The Economist*, 27 December 1980, p. 47, and 27 November 1982, p. 26.

41 Richard Norton-Taylor, "Signals Failure," *The Guardian*, 7 February 1984, p. 21; and Ian Aitken, "Oh my, Oman, is this bunker the triumph of the will?" *The Guardian*, 17 February 1984, p. 9.

42 David Butler and Anne Sloman, *British Political Facts 1900–1979* (5th ed.; London: Macmillan, 1980), pp. 82–83.

43 "The power and the glory of resignation politics," *The Guardian*, 3 February 1984, p. 10.

44 *The Economist*, 9 July 1983, p. 52.

45 Richard Norton-Taylor, "Mrs Thatcher's knight swoap," *The Guardian*, 27 September 1983, p. 17.

46 Hoxie, "The Cabinet in the American Presidency," pp. 223–24.

47 Wilson, *The Governance of Britain*, p. 198.

48 Butler and Sloman, *British Political Facts 1900–1979*; and "The Doctrine of Individual Ministerial Responsibility Is Alive and Well," *British Politics Group Newsletter*, no. 28 (Spring 1982): 5–6.

49 *The Guardian*, 27 January 1984, p. 1. See also *The Guardian*, 28 January 1984, p. 12, and 10 February 1984, p. 5.

50 Barnett Cocks, "Prop group," *The Guardian*, 19 October 1981, p. 13. See also Rose, "British Government," pp. 13, 16.

51 "Questions in the House," *The Guardian*, 3 February 1983, p. 14.

52 Rose, "British Government," p. 14.

53 Richard Neustadt, *Presidential Power*.

54 Franck and Weisband, "Congress as a World Power," p. 6.

55 For one example, see Kenneth Waltz, *Foreign Policy and Democratic Politics* (Boston: Little, Brown, 1967).

56 See Jorgen Rasmussen, "Party Responsibility in Britain and the United States," *Journal of American Studies* 1 (October 1967): 233–56; and Rasmussen, "Was Guy Fawkes Right?" in Issac Kramnick, ed., *Is Britain Dying? Perspectives on the Current Crisis* (Ithaca: Cornell University Press, 1979), pp. 97–98.

57 Rose, "Government against Sub-governments," pp. 287, 299, 311–44.

58 "Governing America," pp. 2, 5. See also Theodore Sorensen, *A Different Kind of Presidency* (New York: Harper & Row, 1984), pp. 20, 50, 53, 99–100. And note Bolling and Gergen in "Governing America," pp. 3, 5, and 7.

59 Hoxie, "The Cabinet in the American Presidency," p. 228. Although it would appear to be a minor change, even Bryce, *The American Commonwealth*, p. 290, was cautious about implementing this reform.

60 Jorgen Rasmussen, "Is Parliament Revolting?" in Donley Studlar and Jerold

Waltman, eds., *Dilemmas of Change in British Politics* (London and Jackson: Macmillan and University Press of Mississippi, 1984), p. 42.

61 Hugh Berrington, "Partisanship and Dissidence in the Nineteenth-Century House of Commons," *Parliamentary Affairs* 21 (Autumn 1968): 363, 371–72.

62 Kenneth D. Wald, *Crosses on the Ballot: Patterns of British Voter Alignment since 1885* (Princeton: Princeton University Press, 1983).

63 Bo Sarlvik and Ivor Crewe, *Decade of Dealignment: The Conservative Victory of 1979 and Electoral Trends in the 1970s* (Cambridge: Cambridge University Press, 1983).

64 Rasmussen, "Is Parliament Revolting?" pp. 33–41.

65 James Douglas, "The Conservative Party: From Pragmatism to Ideology—and Back?" in Hugh Berrington, ed., *Change in British Politics* (London: Cass, 1984), pp. 66–69.

66 Everett Ladd, Jr., "The New Lines Are Drawn: Class and Ideology in America," *Public Opinion* 1 (July/August 1978): 48–53, and (September/October 1978), 14–20. See also his "Converging Currents in British and American Politics," *Public Opinion* 6 (June/July 1983): 4–6, 55–56.

2   The Revival of Laissez-Faire

BIBLIOGRAPHIC NOTE   Although there is, as yet, no definitive comparative study of recent developments in economic policy in the United States and Britain, the student in this field can find excellent comparative analyses of state intervention in the economy and a number of up-to-date, country-specific studies of the politics of economic policy in the United States and Britain.

Of the former, Anthony King, "Ideas, Institutions and the Policies of Governments," *British Journal of Political Science* 3, nos. 3 and 4 (1973), is already a classic in the field. Perhaps the best recent treatment of comparative economic policy is Arnold J. Heidenheimer, Hugo Heclo, and Carolyn Teich Adams, *Comparative Public Policy* (New York: St. Martin's Press, 1983), chap. 5, which covers a great amount of material in an intelligent and readable way.

The most up-to-date and accessible treatment of economic policy in the United States is Herbert Stein, *Presidential Economics* (New York: Basic Books, 1984). Steven Rhoads, *The Economists' View of the World: Governments, Markets and Public Policy* (Cambridge: Cambridge University Press, 1985), cogently analyzes the reasons for economists' support of market-oriented public policy from a political scientist's perspective. James Ceasar, "Reagan Administration and the Crisis in American Liberalism," in Lester M. Salamon, ed., *Governance: The Reagan Era and Beyond* (Washington, D.C.: Urban Institute Press, 1985), explores the political implications of the practice of neo-laissez-faire in terms of the Reagan administration's conservative public philosophy.

On recent developments in politics and economic policy in Britain, Samuel H. Beer, *Britain Against Itself* (New York: W. W. Norton, 1982), offers a masterly analysis of the cultural and organizational causes of Britain's problems. Colin Crouch, *The Politics of Industrial Relations* (London: Faber, 1984), is a highly readable and informed analysis of what is probably the most crucial sphere of British public policy, and David Coates, "Britain in the 1970s: Economic Crisis and the Resurgence of Radicalism," in A. Cox, ed., *Politics, Policy and the European Recession* (New York: St. Martin's Press, 1982), presents an insightful analysis of policy stagnation from a Marxist perspective.

1 See, for example, Arthur J. Taylor, *Laissez-faire and State Intervention in Nineteenth-century Britain* (London: Macmillan, 1972).

2 To these one might add characteristics of neo-laissez-faire that relate to social and other spheres of policy. The most likely candidate is perhaps the concern to retrench state welfare expenditures. However, in the face of opinion polls that have shown strong public support for welfare spending in both the United States and Britain, this aspect of neo-laissez-faire has generally been downplayed by its proponents.

3 In terms of average total outlays of government as a percentage of Gross Domestic Product (GDP) (1960–80), the United States ranks seventeenth and the United Kingdom sixth of the twenty-five member states of the OECD (Organization of Economic Cooperation and Development) for which data is available. OECD, *Historical Statistics, 1960–1980* (Paris: OECD, 1982), p. 59.

4 Francis G. Castles, *The Social Democratic Image of Society* (London: Routledge and Kegan Paul, 1978), p. 117. In recent years the parties of the Right in Sweden have moved closer together, and the issue of state influence in the economy has become the principal source of ideological cleavage. See Olof Petersson and Henry Valen, "Political Cleavages in Sweden and Norway," *Scandinavian Political Studies* 2, no. 4 (1979): 319–20; and M. Donald Hancock, "Sweden," in Peter H. Merkl, ed., *Western European Party Systems* (New York: Macmillan, 1980), pp. 191–93.

5 See John Fitzmaurice, "Denmark," in Stanley Henig, ed., *Political Parties in the European Community* (London: Allen & Unwin, 1979), p. 42; and Harold L. Wilensky, *The "New Corporatism," Centralization, and the Welfare State* (Beverly Hills: Sage Publications, 1976).

6 For discussion of the political orientations of Christian Democratic parties, see Seymour Martin Lipset, *Revolution and Counter-Revolution* (Garden City, N.Y.: Doubleday, 1970), pp. 276 and 363; David Martin, "The Religious Condition of Europe," in Salvador Giner and Margaret Scotford Archer, eds., *Contemporary Europe* (London: Routledge and Kegan Paul, 1978), pp. 245–46; and Harold J. Wilensky, "Leftism, Catholicism, and Democratic Corporatism," in Peter Flora and Arnold J. Heidenheimer, eds., *The Development of Welfare States in Europe and America* (New Brunswick, N.J.: Transaction Books, 1981), pp. 355–63.

7 R. E. M. Irving, *The Christian Democratic Parties of Western Europe* (London: Allen & Unwin, 1979), p. 260; Gordon Smith, *Politics in Western Europe* (London: Heinemann, 1972), p. 23.

8 Seymour Martin Lipset, "The Revolt Against Modernity," in Per Torsvik, ed., *Mobilization, Center-Periphery Structures and Nation-Building* (Bergen: Universitetsforlaget, 1981), p. 454; Anthony King, "Ideas, Institutions and the Policies of Governments," *British Journal of Political Science* 3, nos. 3 and 4 (1973): p. 415.

9   Gabriel A. Almond, "Comparative Political Systems," reprinted in G. A. Almond, *Political Development* (Boston: Little, Brown, 1970), p. 37.

10 In Arend Lijphart's schema of ideological dimensions of party systems in twenty-nine countries, only the party systems of the United States, the United Kingdom, and New Zealand, among the advanced industrial democracies, are durably oriented around a single ideological dimension—the socioeconomic. See Arend Lijphart, "Political Parties: Ideologies and Programs," in David Butler, ed., *Democracy at the Polls* (Washington, D.C.: American Enterprise Institute, 1980).

11 Alan D. Robinson, "Class Voting in New Zealand," in Seymour Martin Lipset and Stein Rokkan, eds., *Party Systems and Voter Alignments* (New York: Free Press, 1967), p. 102; Gilbert Anthony Wood, "The National Party," in Howard R. Penniman, ed., *New Zealand at the Polls* (Washington, D.C.: American Enterprise Institute, 1980), p. 120.

12 See Grant Eliot and Adam Graycar, "Social Welfare," in Allan Patience and Brian Head, eds., *From Whitlam to Fraser* (Melbourne: Oxford University Press, 1979), pp. 97–98; Barry Hughes, "The Economy," in ibid., pp. 37–39; James Jupp, *Party Politics: Australia 1966–1981* (Sydney: Allan & Unwin, 1982), pp. 72–73.

13 The average vote in congressional elections for the Republican party is 40.6 percent for the period 1951–80 (weighted by month), compared to 44.8 percent for the British Conservative party, which has the next lowest average vote among the four Anglo-American societies, excluding Canada.

14 Seymour Martin Lipset, "The American Party System," in S. M. Lipset, ed., *Party Coalitions in the 1980's* (San Francisco: Institute for Contemporary Studies, 1981), p. 434.

15 See Robert Behrens, *The Conservative Party from Heath to Thatcher* (Westmead: Saxon House, 1980), pp. 69–83.

16 Dennis Kavanagh elaborates on this in "Political Culture in Great Britain: The Decline of the Civic Culture," in Gabriel A. Almond and Sidney Verba, eds., *The Civic Culture Revisited* (Boston: Little, Brown, 1980).

17 Andrew Gamble, "The Conservative Party," in H. M. Drucker, ed., *Multi-Party Britain* (London: Macmillan, 1979), p. 45.

18 See Arnold J. Heidenheimer, Hugh Heclo, and Carolyn Teich Adams, *Comparative Public Policy* (New York: St. Martin's Press, 1983), p. 148.

19 W. W. Rostow, *The Barbaric Counter-Revolution* (Austin: University of Texas Press, 1983), p. 37.

20 David Coates, "Britain in the 1970's: Economic Crisis and the Resurgence of Radicalism," in A. Cox, ed., *Politics, Policy and the European Recession* (New York: St. Martin's Press, 1982), p. 144.

21 On the requisites of interest group concentration, see Philippe C. Schmitter and Gerhard Lehmbruch, eds., *Trends Toward Corporatist Intermediation* (Beverly Hills: Sage Publications, 1979); and Gary Marks, "The Politics of Incomes Policy," paper presented at the Fourth International Conference of Europeanists (Washington, D.C., 1983).

22 Mancur Olson, *The Rise and Decline of Nations* (New Haven: Yale University Press, 1982), p. 48.

23 Among contemporary liberal democracies, key economic sectors in Switzerland

provide the closest approximation to this type, which in this context is termed "quasi-corporatism" to distinguish it from corporatism in its original usage.

24 Philippe C. Schmitter, "Interest Intermediation and Regime Governability in Contemporary Western Europe and North America," in S. Berger, ed., *Organizing Interests in Western Europe* (Cambridge: Cambridge University Press, 1981), p. 312.

25 See Frank Castles, *The Social Democratic Image of Society* (London: Routledge and Kegan Paul, 1978), pp. 129–31; Walter Korpi and Michael Shalev, "Strikes, Industrial Relations and Class Conflict in Capitalist Societies," *British Journal of Sociology* 30 (1979): 164–87; and Gary Marks, "The Politics of Incomes Policy."

26 John Zysman, *Political Strategies for Industrial Order* (Berkeley: University of California Press, 1977), p. 195; Jack Hayward, "Mobilising Private Interests in the Service of Public Ambitions: The Salient Element in the Dual French Policy Style?" in Jeremy Richardson, ed., *Policy Styles in Western Europe* (London: Allen & Unwin, 1982), p. 125.

27 Zysman, *Political Strategies for Industrial Order*, p. 197.

28 Samuel Brittan, "A Transformation of the English Sickness?" in Ralf Dahrendorf, ed., *Europe's Economy in Crisis* (London: Weidenfeld and Nicolson, 1981), p. 79.

29 See Robert J. Flanagan, David Soskice, and Lloyd Ulman, *Unionism, Economic Stabilization, and Incomes Policies: European Experience* (Washington, D.C.: The Brookings Institution, 1983), chap. 6.

30 For an insightful analysis of economic policy-making in France that emphasizes the changing role of electoral politics as a constraint on government autonomy, see Jonathan Story, "Capital in France: The Changing Pattern of Patrimony?" *Western European Politics* 6, no. 2 (April 1983).

31 This point is made by numerous observers, e.g., Graham Wilson, *Interest Groups in the United States* (Oxford: Clarendon Press, 1981), pp. 133–34.

32 See Robert H. Salisbury, "Interest Groups: Toward a New Understanding," in Allan J. Cigler and Burdett A. Loomis, eds., *Interest Group Politics* (Washington, D.C.: Congressional Quarterly Press, 1983), pp. 355–56.

33 Robert H. Salisbury, "Why No Corporatism in America?" in Schmitter and Lehmbruch, eds., *Trends Toward Corporatism Intermediation*, p. 219; W. D. Burnham, *Critical Elections and the Mainsprings of American Politics* (New York: W. W. Norton, 1970), pp. 186–87; and Andrew Martin, *The Politics of Economic Policy in the United States* (Beverly Hills: Sage Publications, 1973), pp. 30–31.

34 Charles E. Gilbert, quoted in Joel D. Aberbach, Robert D. Putnam, and Bert A. Rockman, *Bureaucrats and Politicians in Western Democracies* (Cambridge, Mass.: Harvard University Press, 1981), p. 99.

35 Aberbach, Putnam, and Rockman, *Bureaucrats and Politicians in Western Democracies*, pp. 99–100.

36 See Hugh Heclo, "Issue Networks and the Executive Establishment," and Anthony King, "The American Polity in the Late 1970s: Building Coalitions in the Sand," both in A. King, ed., *The New American Political System* (Washington, D.C.: American Enterprise Institute, 1978); and Thomas C.

Gais, Mark A. Peterson, and Jack L. Walker, "Interest Groups, Iron Triangles and Representative Institutions in American National Government," *British Journal of Political Science* 14, part 2 (April 1984).

37 This example is taken from Heclo, "Issue Networks and the Executive Establishment," pp. 104–5.

38 Heidenheimer, Heclo, and Adams, *Comparative Public Policy*, p. 142.

39 Charles L. Schultze, "Industrial Policy: A Dissent," *The Brookings Review* (Fall 1983): 9–11; Steven Rhoads, *The Economists' View of the World: Government, Markets and Public Policy* (Cambridge: Cambridge University Press, 1985).

40 Schultze, "Industrial Policy: A Dissent," pp. 10–11.

41 Lester C. Thurow, *The Zero Sum Society* (London: Penguin, 1980), pp. 212–14.

42 Daniel Bell, *The Cultural Contradictions of Capitalism* (New York: Basic Books, 1978), chap. 6.

43 James Ceaser, "Reagan Administration and the Crisis of American Liberalism," in Lester M. Salamon, ed., *Governance: The Reagan Era and Beyond* (Washington, D.C.: Urban Institute Press, 1985).

44 See, for example, Grant Jordan and Jeremy Richardson, "The British Policy Style or the Logic of Negotiation," in Jordan and Richardson, *Polity Styles in Western Europe* (London: Allen & Unwin, 1982), and literature cited there.

45 This is the brunt of Lord Shonfield's analysis of economic policy-making in Britain. See Andrew Shonfield, *Modern Capitalism* (Oxford: Oxford University Press, 1969).

46 J. E. S. Hayward, "National Aptitudes for Planning in Britain, France, and Italy," *Government and Opposition* 9, no. 4 (Autumn 1974): 398–99; Shonfield, *Modern Capitalism*, pp. 98, 110.

47 The term "corporate bias" is that of Keith Middlemas in his study of industrial relations and economic policy in Britain, *Politics in Industrial Society* (London: Andre Deutsch, 1979).

48 See Samuel H. Beer, *Britain Against Itself* (New York: W. W. Norton, 1982), pp. 48–63.

49 See Robert J. Flanagan, "The National Accord as a Social Contract," *Industrial and Labor Relations Review* 34, no. 1 (October 1980): 48; Wyn Grant and David Marsh, *The Confederation of British Industry* (London: Hodder and Stoughton, 1977), p. 146; and Les Metcalfe and Will McQuillan, "Corporatism or Industrial Democracy?" *Political Studies* 27, no. 2 (June 1979): 273.

50 See Heidenheimer, Heclo, and Adams, *Comparative Public Policy*, pp. 144–46; and Shonfield, *Modern Capitalism*, pp. 250–55.

51 Anthony King, "Overload: Problems of Governing in the 1970s," *Political Studies* 23 (1975): 288.

52 This is most true in the initial stages of total war, until the realities of sacrifice become fully apparent.

53 There are many examples of this in Britain. In the United States, the best example is the statutory incomes policy pursued during the Nixon administration.

54 Ernest Gellner, "A Social Contract in Search of an Idiom," *Political Quarterly* 46, no. 2 (1975).
55 S. E. Finer, *Adversary Politics and Electoral Reform* (London: Wigram, 1975).

3 Changes in Party Systems and Public Philosophies

BIBLIOGRAPHIC NOTE Two useful overviews of British parties are R. Rose, *The Problem of Party Government* (London: Macmillan, 1974); and S. E. Finer, *The Changing British Party System 1945–79* (Washington, D.C.: American Enterprise Institute, 1980). Also for recent developments, see R. Rose, *Do Parties Make a Difference?* (2nd ed.; London: Macmillan, 1983); and D. Butler and D. Kavanagh, *The British General Election of 1983* (London: Macmillan, 1984). The literature on American parties is vast. For recent developments see S. M. Lipset, *Emerging Coalitions in American Politics* (San Francisco: Institute for Contemporary Studies, 1978); A. Ranney, ed., *The American Elections of 1980* (Washington, D.C.: American Enterprise Institute, 1981); and N. Polsby, *The Consequences of Party Reform* (New York: Oxford University Press, 1983). I am indebted to Ivor Crewe for supplying me with tables 3.2 and 3.3.

1 The label "two-party system" is subject to many qualifications, as will become apparent. It appears to be more accurate for the United States. Only in four presidential elections since 1860 has a non-Republican or non-Democratic candidate won a state. In recent years only Senator Harry F. Byrd (Virginia) and Senator James Buckley (New York) have not been members of one or other party in either house. But eleven different parties were represented in the House of Commons after the 1983 election.
2 Lawrence James Sharpe, "American Democracy Reconsidered: Part II," *British Journal of Political Science* 3 (1973): 129–68.
3 Dennis Kavanagh, "An American Science of British Politics," *Political Studies* 23 (1975): 251–70.
4 Leon D. Epstein, "Whatever Happened to the British Party Model?" *American Political Science Review* 79 (1980): 9–22.
5 Evron Maurice Kirkpatrick, "Toward a More Responsible Two-Party System: Political Science, Policy Science, or Pseudo-science," *American Political Science Review* 70 (1971): 965–90.
6 James MacGregor Burns, *The Deadlock of Democracy* (Englewood Cliffs, N.J.: Prentice-Hall, 1963).
7 Ivor Crewe, "Electoral Participation," in David Butler, Howard R. Penniman, and Austin Ranney, eds., *Democracy at the Polls* (London: American Enterprise Institute, 1980), pp. 219–63. See also Raymond Wolfinger and Steven Rosenstone, *Who Votes?* (New Haven: Yale University Press, 1980).
8 Stefano Bartolini, "The Membership of Mass Parties," in Hans Daalder and Peter Mair, eds., *Western European Party Systems* (London: Sage Publications, 1983), pp. 139–75.
9 Norman H. Nie, Sidney Verba, and John R. Petrocik, *The Changing American Voter* (Cambridge, Mass.: Harvard University Press, 1976).
10 R. Brody, "The Puzzle of Political Participation in America," in Anthony

King, ed., *The New American Political System* (Washington, D.C.: American Enterprise Institute, 1978), p. 325.

11 Seymour Martin Lipset, "The Paradox of American Politics," *Public Interest* (Fall 1975): 142–65.

12 Sidney Verba and Norman Nie, *Participation in America* (New York: Harper & Row, 1972).

13 Everett Carll Ladd and Charles D. Hadley, *Transformations of the American Party System* (New York: W. W. Norton, 1978); Everett Carl Ladd, "The Brittle Mandate," *Political Science Quarterly* 96 (1981): 1–25.

14 Nie et al., *The Changing American Voter*.

15 Jeane Kirkpatrick, *Dismantling the Parties* (Washington, D.C.: American Enterprise Institute, 1978).

16 Otto Kirchheimer, "The Transformation of Western European Party Systems," in J. LaPalombara and M. Wiener, eds., *Political Parties and Political Development* (Princeton: Princeton University Press, 1964).

17 Austin Ranney, "The Political Parties: Reform and Decline," in King, ed., *The New American Political System*.

18 Kirchheimer, "The Transformation of Western European Party Systems," p. 200.

19 Walter Dean Burnham, "Revitalization and Decay," *Journal of Politics* 38 (1976): 146–72.

20 Kevin Phillips, *The Emerging Republican Majority* (New York: Arlington House, 1969); *Post-Conservative America: People, Politics and Ideology in a Time of Crisis* (New York: Random House, 1982).

21 James Sundquist, "Whither the American Party System?—Revisited," *Political Science Quarterly* 98 (1983): 573–93.

22 Nie et al., *The Changing American Voter*.

23 Martin P. Wattenberg, "The Decline of Political Partisanship in the United States: Negativity or Neutrality?" *American Political Science Review* 80 (1981): 941–50.

24 Ivor Crewe, "Is Britain's Two Party System Really About to Crumble?" *Electoral Studies* 3 (1982).

25 Ivor Crewe, "How to Win a Landslide Without Really Trying," in Austin Ranney, ed., *Britain at the Polls, 1983* (Washington, D.C., and Durham, N.C.: American Enterprise Institute and Duke University Press, 1985).

26 Robert McKenzie, *Modern British Political Parties* (London: Heinemann, 1963 ed.).

27 Lewis Minkin, *The Labour Party Conference* (London: Allen Lane, 1978).

28 Dennis Kavanagh, "Power in British Politics: Iron Law or Special Pleading?" *West European Politics* 8 (1985): 5–22.

29 Paul Whiteley, *The Labour Party in Crisis* (London: Methuen, 1983).

30 Nelson Polsby, *Consequences of Party Reform* (New York: Oxford University Press, 1983).

31 Jeane Kirkpatrick, *The New Presidential Elite: Men and Women in National Politics* (New York: Russell Sage, Twentieth Century Fund, 1976).

32 Denis Sullivan, Jeffrey L. Pressman, Benjamin I. Page, and John J. Lyons, *The Politics of Representation* (New York: St. Martin's Press, 1974); and Robert Nakamura, "Beyond Purism and Professionalism," *American Journal of Political Science* 24 (1980): 207–32.

33 Martin Harrop, "Labour-Voting Conservatives," in Robert Worcester and Martin Harrop, eds., *Political Communications* (London: Allen & Unwin, 1982).

34 David Robertson, *The Theory of Party Competition* (London: John Wiley & Sons, 1976).

35 S. Patterson, "The Semi-Sovereign Congress," in King, ed., *The New American Political System*.

36 Philip Norton, *Conservative Dissidents* (London: Temple Smith, 1978).

37 Samuel Finer, *Adversary Politics and Electoral Reform* (London: Wigram, 1975).

38 Richard Rose, *Do Parties Make a Difference?* (2nd ed.; London: Macmillan, 1983).

39 T. Moore, "Democratic vs. Republican Administrations: A Quizzical Note," unpublished paper, Hoover Institute, Stanford, Calif., 1982.

40 Samuel Beer, "In Search of a New Public Philosophy," in King, ed., *The New American Political System*.

41 I have discussed this in "Whatever Happened to Consensus Politics?" *Political Studies* 33 (1985).

42 Dennis Kavanagh, "Margaret Thatcher: The Mobilizing Prime Minister," in A. Clarke and Moshe Czudnowski, eds., *International Yearbook for Studies of Leaders and Leadership* (Urbana: University of Illinois Press, 1985).

43 Richard Rose, "Two and One Half Cheers for the Market," *Public Opinion* 6 (June/July 1983): 10–15.

44 David Robertson, "Adversary Politics, Public Opinion and Electoral Cleavages," in Dennis Kavanagh and Gillian Peele, eds., *Comparative Government and Politics* (London: Heinemann, 1984).

45 Peter Steinfels, *The Neo-Conservatives* (New York: Simon & Schuster, 1980).

46 Ladd, "The Brittle Mandate."

4 Washington and Whitehall Revisited

BIBLIOGRAPHIC NOTE Political life in Washington and Whitehall is touched on in a large number of works but systematically compared in very few. In addition to looking at readings cited in the endnotes to this essay, those interested in reading further might pursue the Washington side of the story by examining James Sterling Young, *The Washington Community* (New York: Columbia University Press, 1966), for a historical perspective. In a similar vein for the more modern period are Richard E. Neustadt, *Presidential Power* (New York: John Wiley & Sons, new ed., 1980); Hugh Heclo, *A Government of Strangers* (Washington, D.C.: The Brookings Institution, 1977); Nelson W. Polsby, "The Washington Community 1960–1980," in Thomas Mann and Norman Ornstein, eds., *The New Congress* (Washington, D.C.: American Enterprise Institute, 1981); and two volumes edited by Anthony King, *The New American Political System* (Washington, D.C.: American Enterprise Institute, 1978) and *Both Ends of the Avenue* (Washington, D.C.: American Enterprise Institute, 1983).

For the Whitehall side, a comparable list would include the memoirs of a former Labour cabinet minister, Richard Crossman, *The Diaries of a Cabinet*

Minister (London: Magnum, 3 vols., 1975–77); Hugh Heclo and Aaron Wildavsky, *The Private Government of Public Money* (Berkeley: University of California Press, 1974); Ian Budge, David Mackay, et al. *The New British Political System: Government and Society in the 1980s* (London: Longman, 1983); and Samuel H. Beer, *Britain Against Itself* (New York: W. W. Norton, 1982).

1 Richard E. Neustadt, "White House and Whitehall," *The Public Interest* (1965).

2 In this and other sections I have profited greatly from Keith Hope's paper, "The Political Conception of Merit," The Woodrow Wilson International Center for Scholars, Washington, D.C., 1983.

3 George O. Trevelyan, *The Life and Letters of Lord Macaulay* (London: Longman, 1877), 1: 379.

4 Dorman B. Eaton, *Civil Service in Great Britain* (New York: Harper and Brothers, 1880), p. 430.

5 Schurz's speech is quoted in Harvard Law Review Association, "Developments in the Law—Public Employment," *Harvard Law Review* 97, no. 7 (May 1984): 1629; and Eaton, *Civil Service in Great Britain.*

6 *Report on the Organisation of the Permanent Civil Service* (London: HMSO, 1854), p. 3.

7 *The Government Regulations for the Examination of Candidates for Appointments to the Civil Service of the East India Company* (London: Edward Stanford, 1855), p. 4.

8 U.S. Civil Service Commission, *First Annual Report 1884,* as quoted in Hope, "The Political Conception of Merit."

9 Compare, for example, William Plowden, "The Higher Civil Service in Britain," in Bruce L. R. Smith, ed., *The Higher Civil Service in Europe and Canada* (Washington, D.C.: Brookings Institution, 1984), with John W. Macy et al., *America's Unelected Government* (Cambridge, Mass.: Ballinger, 1983).

10 Reinhard Bendix, *Higher Civil Servants in American Society* (Boulder: University of Colorado Press, 1949).

11 Joel D. Aberbach, Robert Putnam, and Bert A. Rockman, *Bureaucrats and Politicians in Western Democracies* (Cambridge, Mass.: Harvard University Press, 1981), p. 98 and p. 269 n. 2.

12 Statement of Donald Devine to a conference of the American Society for Public Administration, April 1981; reprinted in *The Bureaucrat* (Spring 1982): 20.

13 See, for example, the popular British television series "Yes Minister."

14 Dudley Foulke, *Fighting the Spoilsmen* (New York: Putnam, 1919), p. 263.

15 This and other figures are drawn from U.S. House of Representative's Civil Service Subcommittee of the Post Office and Civil Service Committee, *Hearings* (Washington, D.C.: U.S. Government Printing Office, 1984). An update on experiences in the Reagan administration is contained in *The Bureaucrat* (Fall 1984).

16 This issue was debated but hardly resolved between Carl J. Friedrich, "Public Policy and the Nature of Administrative Responsibility," in Friedrich and Edward Mason, *Public Policy 1940* (Cambridge, Mass.: Harvard University

Press, 1940), and Herman Finer, "Administrative Responsibility in Democratic Government," *Public Administration Review* 1 (1941). For related thoughts about discretion, see Martin Landau and Russell Stout, Jr., "To Manage Is Not to Control," *Public Administration Review* 39 (1979).

17 These examples are drawn from the articles by Heclo and Wolley in Gregory Mills and John Palmer, eds., *Federal Budget Policy in the 1980s* (Washington, D.C.: The Urban Institute, 1984), and from Lester Salamon and Michael Lund, eds., *The Reagan Presidency and the Governing of America* (Washington, D.C.: The Urban Institute, 1984).

18 Like other presidencies, the Reagan administration has been vigorous in announcing bold new reforms but weak when it comes to actually institutionalizing its desired changes. This seems true in such areas as the White House programs for New Federalism, Private Sector Initiatives, and much of the deregulation effort. The major institutionalized changes would seem to be the shadow on the future cast by large structural deficits and the indexation of tax rates.

19 For enlightening reviews of the new uncertainties about the constitutional conventions of Whitehall, see Douglas Wass, *Government and the Governed* (London: Routledge and Kegan Paul, 1984), and by the same author, "The Civil Service at the Crossroads," *Political Quarterly* (1985).

20 David Thomas, "Honing Down the Civil Service," *New Society*, January 17, 1985.

21 In the most celebrated case, Clive Ponting, a senior civil servant in the Ministry of Defence, was prosecuted under the Official Secrets Act for leaking information to a Member of Parliament; the effect of this information was to show that the government had deliberately mislead Parliament in justifying its sinking of an Argentine warship during the Falklands dispute. Ponting's defense lay in claiming that civil servants' higher duty to the interests of the state included making truthful information available to Parliament, so that providing such information to an MP who had followed legitimate procedures in questioning government action did not constitute disclosure to an unauthorized person under the Secrets Act. The prosecution acknowledged that no secrets damaging national security had been passed but argued that the information would lead to demands for further facts that were security-sensitive. The presiding judge clearly agreed with the prosecution's contention that "the interests of the state" are identical with the policies laid down by the government of the day and offered to direct the jury to find Ponting guilty. The jury returned a unanimous verdict of not guilty. A discussion of the case is contained in *The Manchester Guardian Weekly*, February 24, 1985. The relevant section of the Official Secrets Act reads, in part, that it is a criminal offense for any servant of the Crown to communicate any information "which has been entrusted in confidence to him by any person holding office under Her Majesty, or which he has obtained or to which he has had access owning to his position"; the offense occurs if he communicates such information to anyone "other than a person to whom he is authorized to communicate it, or a person to whom it is in the interests of the state his duty to communicate it. . . ."

22 The Cabinet Secretary and Official Head of the Civil Service, Sir Robert

Armstrong, has recently put into print norms of civil service loyalty that heretofore have been confined to internal Whitehall guidelines, to the effect that civil servants owe undivided loyalty and obedience to their political chiefs (*House of Commons Official Report*, February 26, 1985). There is a good article or dissertation waiting to be written analyzing comparable cases exposing the norms of loyalty in Washington and Whitehall. To go along with the Ponting matter, there is the recent U.S. case of Loretta Cornelius. Cornelius was deputy director to Donald Devine, the Reagan administration's head of the Office of Personnel Management. Devine secretly attempted to delegate himself authority to continue to run the agency after his four-year term expired and sought to have Cornelius lie or mislead Congress when she was called to testify before the Senate at confirmation hearings for his second term. Cornelius instead testified accurately, Devine withdrew in disgrace, and the White House refused to consider Cornelius for promotion from deputy and acting director to director of the personnel office. *Washington Post*, June 9, 1985, p. A3.

23 Don K. Price, *America's Unwritten Constitution: Science, Religion, and Political Responsibility* (Baton Rouge: Louisiana State University Press, 1983).

24 Robert Axelrod, *The Evolution of Cooperation* (New York: Basic Books, 1984).

6   Courts of Last Resort

BIBLIOGRAPHIC NOTE   The best general book which, although naturally concentrating on the United States, does cover both countries is Henry Abraham, *The Judicial Process: An Introductory Analysis of the Courts of the United States, England, and France* (4th ed.; New York: Oxford University Press, 1980). On the United States, there is a vast literature from which I would abstract these four books: Sheldon Goldman and Thomas Jahnige, *The Federal Courts as a Political System* (2nd ed.; New York: Harper & Row, 1976), which is very much a work of political science as its title suggests; Bob Woodward and Scott Armstrong, *The Brethren* (New York: Simon & Schuster, 1979), which, although often too selective and imaginative to be entirely fair, does tell a good deal about court politics; Walter F. Murphy, *Elements of Judicial Strategy* (Chicago: University of Chicago Press, 1964), which is more scholarly and much broader in scope; and Stephen Halpern and Charles M. Lamb, eds., *Supreme Court Activism and Restraint* (Lexington, Mass.: D. C. Heath, 1982), which is the best collection of essays in my view addressing the normative problem of an unelected and unaccountable court exercising political authority in a democratic society.

Writing on the British judiciary is much, much less prolific. For all its faults, J. A. Griffith, *The Politics of the Judiciary* (2nd ed.; London: Fontana, 1981), is a must, as is Alan Paterson, *The Law Lords* (London: Macmillan, 1982), although it is too much a lawyer's book for a political scientist's liking. Finally, a useful little book is Gavin Drewry, *Law, Justice and Politics* (2nd ed.; London: Longman, 1981).

1   None of these has more than a passing mention of the political role of the courts: R. M. Punnett, *British Government and Politics* (4th ed.; London: Heinemann, 1980); John P. Mackintosh, *The Government and Politics of Britain* (5th ed.; London: Hutchinson, 1982); Anthony Birch, *The British System of Government* (4th ed.; London: Allen & Unwin, 1980); or even Henry Drucker et al., *Developments in British Politics* (London: Macmillan, 1983), or the avowedly radical C. T. Leys, *Politics in Britain* (London: Heinemann, 1983).

2   W. J. M. McKenzie, *Politics and Social Science* (Harmondsworth: Penguin, 1967), p. 286.

3   J. A. Griffith, *The Politics of the Judiciary* (2nd ed.; London and Manchester: Fontana/Collins and Manchester University Press, 1981).

4   David Robertson, "Judicial Ideology in the House of Lords: A Jurimetric Analysis," *British Journal of Political Science* 12 (1982): 1–25.

5   Ian Budge, David Mackay et al., *The New British Political System: Government and Society in the 1980s* (London: Longman, 1983). Another who might claim this accolade, although the treatment of the judiciary is less explicitly political, is Philip Norton, *The Constitution in Flux* (Oxford: Martin Robertson, 1982).

6   An appreciable amount of the literature is concerned with individual rights and the Court's interpretation of the so-called Bill of Rights; there is a literature on rights in Britain, but it is very much a lawyer's literature.

7   See Richard Hodder-Williams, "The Recent Politics of the United States Supreme Court: A Bibliographic Essay," *Politics* 5 (1985).

8   The House of Lords' decision in *Burmah Oil Company v. Lord Advocate* was simply overruled by the passage of the 1965 War Damage Act, provisions of the legislation being applied retrospectively.

9   David Easton, "An Approach to the Analysis of Political Systems," *World Politics* 9 (1967): 383–400. See, for a conscious application of the system's approach to the Court, Sheldon Goldman and Thomas J. Jahnige, *The Federal Courts as a Political System* (2nd ed.; New York: Harper & Row, 1976).

10 Robert H. Jackson, *The Supreme Court in the American System of Government* (Cambridge, Mass.: Harvard University Press, 1955), p. 55.

11 For example, G. J. Rathjan and H. J. Spaeth, "Access to Federal Courts: An Analysis of Burger Court Policy Making," *American Journal of Political Science* 23 (1979): 360–82; and several articles by S. S. Ulmer, especially "Selecting Cases for Supreme Court Review: An Underdog Model," *American Political Science Review* 72 (1978): 902–10.

12 Louis Blom-Cooper and Gavin Drewry, *Final Appeal* (Oxford: Oxford University Press, 1972).

13 Oliver Wendell Holmes, *Collected Legal Papers* (New York: Harcourt, Brace and Howe, 1920).

14 Quite the best consideration of this debate in a political context is Stephen C. Halpern and Charles M. Lamb, *Supreme Court Activism and Restraint* (Lexington, Mass.: D. C. Heath, 1982).

15 Judge Frank Coffin has noted that the alternative to exercising this "political" power is virtually to refuse to exercise judicial power at all. *The Ways of a Judge: Reflections from the Federal Appellate Bench* (Boston: Houghton Mifflin, 1980), pp. 235–36.

16 But for a contrary view from an American in British academia, see Ronald Dworkin, "Is Law a System of Rules?" in R. Summers, ed., *Essays in Legal Philosophy* (Oxford: Blackwell, 1970).

17 *Chisholm v. Georgia*, 2 Dall. 419 (1793), was overruled by the Eleventh Amendment, *Dred Scot v. Stanford*, 19 How, 393 (1857), by the Fourteenth Amendment, *Pollock v. Farmers' Loan & Trust Co.*, 158 US 601 (1895), by the Sixteenth Amendment, and *Oregon v. Mitchell*, 400 US 112 (1970), by the Twenty-Sixth Amendment.

18 See generally R. Glick, *Supreme Courts in State Politics* (New York: Basic Books, 1971).

19 J. K. Lieberman, *The Litigious Society* (New York: Basic Books, 1981).

20 Richard Hodder-Williams, *The Politics of the U.S. Supreme Court* (London: Allen & Unwin, 1980), p. 179.

21 Donald Horowitz, *The Courts and Social Policy* (Washington, D.C.: The Brookings Institution, 1977).

22 Goldman and Jahnige, *The Federal Courts as a Political System*.

23 The 1968 Criminal Justice Act was one such instance.

24 Randall Bridwell and Ralph U. Whitten, *The Constitution and the Common Law* (Lexington, Mass.: D. C. Heath, 1977).

25 Quoted in Alan Paterson, *The Law Lords* (London: Macmillan, 1982), p. 133.

26 *Jacobs v. LCC* (1950), AC 361, at p. 373. Since the highest court in Britain is technically only a committee of the House of Lords, opinions are "speeches" (and really were once) to their fellow Lordships.

27 *Chapman v. Chapman* (1954), AC 429, at p. 444.

28 *Ealing London Borough Council v. Race Relations Board* (1972), AC 342.

29 *Charter v. Race Relations Board* (1973), AC 868. See also *Dockers' Labour Club v. Race Relations Board* (1974), 3 WLR 533.

30 See particularly Griffith, *The Politics of the Judiciary*, pp. 74–80.

31 Budge, Mackay et al., *The New British Political System*, p. 156.

32 Hodder-Williams, *The Politics of the U.S. Supreme Court*, p. 11.

33 *United States v. Butler*, 297 US 1 (1936), at 62.

34 Four sources address themselves to this seminal case; that they do not all agree on some of the crucial facts of the case in no way detracts from the point being made here. See S. S. Ulmer, "Earl Warren and the Brown Decision," *Journal of Politics* 33 (1971): 689–702; Richard Kluger, *Simple Justice* (New York: Alfred A. Knopf, 1976), pp. 657–747; Mary Frances Berry, *Stability, Security and Continuity: Mr. Justice Burton and Decision-Making in the Supreme Court 1945–1958* (Westport, Conn.: Greenwood Press, 1978), pp. 154–61; Bernard Schwartz, *Super Chief: Earl Warren and His Supreme Court* (New York: New York University Press, 1983), pp. 72–127.

35 Anthony Lewis, *Gideon's Trumpet* (New York: Random House, 1964); Schwartz, *Super Chief*, pp. 457–60, passim.

36 *Miranda v. Arizona*, 384 US 436 (1966); Schwartz, *Super Chief*, pp. 588–95.

37 *Gideon v. Wainwright*, 372 US 335 (1963); *Coker v. Georgia*, 433 US 584 (1977).

38 *Smith v. Allwright*, 321 US 649 (1944); *Abington School District v. Schempp*, 374 US 203 (1963).

39 Henry Hart, "The Time Chart of the Justices," *Harvard Law Review* 73 (1959–60): 84–125.

40 Bob Woodward and Scott Armstrong, *The Brethren: Inside the Supreme Court* (New York: Simon & Schuster, 1979). See also Walter H. Murphy, *Elements of Judicial Strategy* (Chicago: University of Chicago Press, 1964).

41 See generally Paterson, *The Law Lords*, pp. 84–121.

42 Lord Wedderburn, "Law as a Social Science," *Journal of the Society of Teachers of Public Law* 9 (1967): 341; see also Paterson, *The Law Lords*, pp. 118–19 for other cases.

43 Quoted in Paterson, *The Law Lords*, p. 98.

44 Griffith, *The Politics of the Judiciary*, pp. 74–76.

45 Walter Berns, "The Least Dangerous Branch, but only if . . . ," in Leonard J. Theberge, ed., *The Judiciary in a Democratic Society* (Lexington, Mass.: D. C. Heath, 1979), p. 15.

46 Cited in Schwartz, *Super Chief*, pp. 39–40.

47 Glendon Schubert, *The Judicial Mind* (Evanston: Northwestern University Press, 1965); Glendon Schubert, *The Judicial Mind Revisited* (New York: Oxford University Press, 1974).

48 For some criticisms along these lines, see Karl Becker, *Political Behavioralism and Modern Jurisprudence* (Chicago: Rand McNally, 1965); and J. Woodford Howard, "On the Fluidity of Judicial Choice," *American Political Science Review* 62 (1968): 43–56.

49 Earl Warren, *The Memoirs of Earl Warren* (Garden City, N.Y.: Doubleday, 1977), p. 291; Schwartz, *Super Chief*, pp. 112–13.

50 I am much indebted for material on the Law Lords to Donald Shell, whose forthcoming book should be the definitive study of the modern House of Lords.

51 Griffith, *The Politics of the Judiciary*, p. 217.

52 Philipp L. Dubois, *From Ballot to Bench: Judicial Elections and the Quest for Accountability* (Austin: University of Texas Press, 1980).

53 David Robertson, unpublished paper presented to the Political Studies Association conference.

54 See generally Paterson, *The Law Lords*, esp. pp. 146–53.

55 Harold J. Spaeth, "The Judicial Restraint of Mr. Justice Frankfurter—Myth or Reality?" *Midwest Journal of Political Science* 8 (1964): 22–38; Harold J. Spaeth, "Activism and Restraint: A Cloak for the Justices' Policy Preferences," and Anthony Champagne and Stuart S. Nagel, "The Advocates of Restraint: Holmes, Brandeis, Stone and Frankfurter," in Halpern and Lamb, eds., *Supreme Court Activism and Restraint*, pp. 277–318.

56 Quoted in Paterson, *The Law Lords*.

57 *Lassiter v. Northampton County Board of Elections*, 360 US 45 (1959).

58 Paterson, *The Law Lords*; Joel B. Grossman, "Role-Playing and the Analysis of Judicial Behavior: The Case of Mr. Justice Frankfurter," *Journal of Public Law* 11 (1962): 285–309; Dorothy B. James, "Role Theory and the Supreme Court," *Journal of Politics* 30 (1968): 160–86.

59 Griffith, *The Politics of the Judiciary*, p. 230.

60 R. Hodder-Williams, "Is There a Burger Court?" *British Journal of Political Science* 10 (1979): 192–99.

61 Budge, McKay et al., *The New British Political System*, p. 166.

62 John Marshall was not President Adams's first choice, and his elevation to the chief justiceship was very much a matter of chance. See J. P. McKenzie, *The Appearance of Justice* (New York: Charles Scribner's Sons, 1974), pp. 5–6.

63 Cited in Robert Scigliano, *The Supreme Court and the Presidency* (Glencoe, Ill.: The Free Press, 1971), p. 116.

64 See generally Lawrence M. Friedman, *American Law* (New York: W. W. Norton, 1984).

65 *The Times*, 3 April 1984.

7 Sex, Money, and Power

BIBLIOGRAPHIC NOTE Since scandology is yet in its infancy, the relevant literature is still in short supply. Useful preliminary data, however, may be gleaned from Alan Doig, *Corruption and Misconduct in Contemporary British Politics* (Harmondsworth: Penguin, 1984), for Great Britain and John T. Noonan, *Bribes* (New York: Macmillan, 1984), for the United States. Scandology is closely related to the study of corruption, but is concerned with the supplementary problem of defining the characteristics which transform potentially "scandalous" action into perceived "scandalous" action and hence the object of public censure. On corruption, there is a substantial literature of which Arnold Heidenheimer, ed., *Political Corruption: Readings in Comparative Analysis* (New York: Holt, Rinehart & Winston, 1970), provides a good overview; the supplementary question, however, still lacks scholarly explication.

1 *She actually called them Mandy* (London: Michael Joseph, 1980); the book was written in collaboration with Shirley Flack.

2 The custom on these occasions is to make oneself appear learned by looking up and then citing the original source. In fact, the Fielding quotation comes from *The Oxford Dictionary of Quotations* (3rd ed.; Oxford: Oxford University Press, 1979), p. 211.

3 The term "scandology" may be new, but of course political scientists and others have taken an interest in political scandals for many years. See, in particular, a book by the man to whom this volume is dedicated: Philip M. Williams, *Wars, Plots and Scandals in Post-War France* (Cambridge: Cambridge University Press, 1970).

4 The Empress Messalina's exploits were described in a paper delivered to the annual meeting of the Classical Association in 1984 and reported in *The Times* (London) on 9 April 1984, p. 4, under the headline "Tracing the origins of sexual guilt."

5 On President Sukarno, see Ruth Ann Willner, *The Spellbinders: Charismatic Political Leadership* (New Haven: Yale University Press, 1984), pp. 131–33. The quotation in the text is from p. 133.

6 *Congressional Quarterly Almanac, 1978* (Washington, D.C.: Congressional Quarterly Press, 1979), p. 853.

7 *Congressional Quarterly Almanac, 1979* (Washington, D.C.: Congressional Quarterly Press, 1980), p. 562.

8   The allusion is to Robert A. Caro, *The Years of Lyndon Johnson: The Path to Power* (New York: Alfred A. Knopf, 1982).

9   Nelson W. Polsby, "Legislatures," in Fred I. Greenstein and Nelson W. Polsby, eds., *Handbook of Political Science*, Vol. 5, *Governmental Institutions and Processes* (Reading, Mass.: Addison-Wesley, 1975).

10 For an account of Walden's association with the bookmakers, see Alan Doig, *Corruption and Misconduct in Contemporary British Politics* (Harmondsworth: Penguin, 1984), pp. 213–14. In keeping with the thesis of this chapter, Doig in fact reports very little corruption in modern British politics, at least at the national level. His book is nevertheless one that all scandologists will obviously need to consult.

11 The best book on the Thorpe affair, and much the most thorough, is Lewis Chester, Magnus Linklater, and David May, *Jeremy Thorpe: A Secret Life* (London: Fontana Books in association with Andre Deutsch, 1979).

12 See especially the numbers of *Labour Research* for June and July 1983. The results of *Labour Research*'s inquiries were widely publicized in British newspapers, including *The Times*—but *Labour Research* did the work.

13 Martin Bailey, *Oilgate: The Sanctions Scandal* (London: Coronet Books, 1979).

Notes on Authors

JAMES W. CEASER is Assistant Professor in the Department of Government and Foreign Affairs at the University of Virginia, Charlottesville. He is the author of *Presidential Selection: Theory and Development* and *Reforming the Reforms.*

BERNARD DONOUGHUE is Head of Investment Policy, Grievson Grant & Co., London. He taught at the London School of Economics and Political Science 1963–74 before becoming senior policy adviser to the Prime Minister until 1979. He is the author of *British Politics and the American Revolution* and (with George Jones) *Herbert Morrison: Portrait of a Politician.*

HUGH HECLO is Professor of Government at Harvard University. He was formerly a senior fellow at The Brookings Institution and has taught at the University of Essex. He is the author of *A Government of Strangers* and (with Aaron Wildavsky) *The Private Government of Public Money.*

RICHARD HODDER-WILLIAMS is Reader in Politics at the University of Bristol and was Visiting Professor at the University of California, Berkeley 1984–85. He was chairman of the American Politics Group 1981–84 and is the author of *Public Opinion Polls and British Politics* and *The Politics of the United States Supreme Court* as well as several articles on the Court.

DENNIS KAVANAGH is Professor of Politics at the University of Nottingham and was a visiting scholar at the Hoover Institute, Stanford 1984–85. He has coauthored with David Butler *The British General Election of 1979* and *The British General Election of 1983* and has edited *The Politics of the Labour Party.*

ANTHONY KING is Professor of Government at the University of Essex and was Visiting Professor at Princeton University in 1984. Formerly editor of the *British Journal of Political Science,* he has recently edited *The New American Political System* and *Both Ends of the Avenue.*

GARY MARKS is Assistant Professor in the Department of Government and Foreign Affairs at the University of Virginia, Charlottesville. An Englishman, he is the author of *Unions and Politics* (University of North Carolina Press, 1985).

JORGEN RASMUSSEN is Professor of Political Science at Iowa State University and executive secretary of the British Politics Group. He has published widely on British politics in American and British journals.

CONFERENCE PARTICIPANTS

James Ceaser, R. Taylor Cole, Carolyn Conley, Bernard Donoughue, Hugh Heclo, Richard Hodder-Williams, George Holt, Dennis Kavanagh, Anthony King, Allan Kornberg, Peter Lange, Gary Marks, Nelson Polsby, Jorgen Rasmussen, Richard C. Rowson, Donald Searing, and Robert Thompson.

Index